T0019025

Southeast Asia: A Very Short Introduction

VERY SHORT INTRODUCTIONS are for anyone wanting a stimulating and accessible way into a new subject. They are written by experts, and have been translated into more than 45 different languages.

The series began in 1995, and now covers a wide variety of topics in every discipline. The VSI library now contains over 500 volumes—a Very Short Introduction to everything from Psychology and Philosophy of Science to American History and Relativity—and continues to grow in every subject area.

Very Short Introductions available now:

For more information visit our website

www.oup.com/vsi/

James R. Rush

SOUTHEAST ASIA

A Very Short Introduction

OXFORD
UNIVERSITY PRESS

OXFORD
UNIVERSITY PRESS

Oxford University Press is a department of the University of Oxford.
It furthers the University's objective of excellence in research, scholarship,
and education by publishing worldwide. Oxford is a registered trademark of
Oxford University Press in the UK and certain other countries.

Published in the United States of America by Oxford University Press
198 Madison Avenue, New York, NY 10016, United States of America.

Library of Congress Cataloging-in-Publication Data
Names: Rush, James R. (James Robert), 1944- author.
Title: Southeast Asia : a very short introduction / James R. Rush.
Description: Oxford : Oxford University Press, [2018] |
Includes bibliographical references and index. |
Identifiers: LCCN 2017043737 (print) | LCCN 2017044526 (ebook) |
ISBN 9780190248772 (updf) | ISBN 9780190248789 (epub) |
ISBN 9780190248796 (online component) |
ISBN 9780190248765 | ISBN 9780190248765q (pbk. ;qalk. paper)
Subjects: LCSH: Southeast Asia.
Classification: LCC DS521 (ebook) | LCC DS521 .R87 2018 (print) |
DDC 959—dc23
LC record available at https://lccn.loc.gov/2017043737

Printed by Integrated Books International, United States of America
on acid-free paper

Contents

List of illustrations

Introduction

Southeast Asia is a region of vast complexity, and scholarship about it is equally vast and complex. This slender book draws upon a broad body of scholarship. Barely a sentence fails to reflect the ideas and scholarly writing of my mentors and colleagues and others from whom I have learned. Readers familiar with the literature will discern the footprints of Harry Benda, John Smail, O. W. Wolters, Benedict Anderson, Anthony Reid, James Scott, J. S. Furnivall, Thongchai Winichakul, and a host of others whose work has shaped the field.

This volume is a "very short introduction," and so it does not attempt to capture fully the deep research and nuanced arguments of this scholarship. Instead, its purpose is to tell a complicated story simply and legibly. Its historical arc focusing on kingdoms, colonies, and nations is deliberately formulaic, designed to provide a structured narrative around which otherwise random events and anecdotal information about Southeast Asia (or the day's news, for that matter) can be understood in the context of larger patterns of history, politics, and society. This narrative can be—indeed, it is meant to be—explored, elaborated, and critiqued through further study. The "Suggestions for Further Reading" at the back will get you started.

Southeast Asia: A Very Short Introduction is also intentionally colloquial. Terms are used such as trade hubs, traffic patterns, and mini-kings, for example, the latter to describe an array of persons who ruled over small territories (mini-kingdoms) throughout Southeast Asia under many different titles. Likewise, certain terms are employed that are often applied more narrowly in scholarship—mandala, for example—to describe general patterns applying to the region at large. Thongchai Winichakul's use of the term *geo-body*, to mean a modern border-bounded nation-state, is another example. The word *Native*, capitalized, is used here to convey the colonial-era practice of categorizing indigenous Southeast Asians officially (and subordinately) in the law.

Southeast Asia also prioritizes the familiar. East Timor will be East Timor, although it is officially known as Timor-Leste and also as Timor Lorosa'e. Burma will be Burma, except when referring to the contemporary state of Myanmar. Burmans will be Burmans, not Bama. And so on. The spellings of Southeast Asian names can vary considerably when rendered in English. I have followed familiar scholarly conventions.

One cannot possibly acknowledge everyone who has contributed to a general book like this one. But I am grateful to my undergraduate students at Arizona State University (ASU), in dialogue with whom the narrative of this book has evolved, and also to several former graduate students whose work has informed my work. These include Maria Ortuoste, Christopher Lundry, Duan Zhidan, Zhipei Chi, Sze Chieh Ng, and Alex Arifianto. Particular thanks go to William McDonald, an ASU student at Barrett, the Honors College, who worked diligently collecting data about the contemporary region. I am also indebted to my faculty colleagues in Southeast Asia studies at ASU from whom I am constantly learning. They include Sheldon Simon, Juliane Schober, Ted Solis, Karen Adams, Christopher Duncan (now at Rutgers), Leif Jonsson, James Eder, Mark Woodward, Pauline Cheong, Sarah Shair-Rosenfield, Peter Suwarno, Sina Machander, Le-Pham Thuy-Kim, and Ralph Gabbard. Finally, I want to express my gratitude and love to my wife, Sunny Benitez-Rush, who enriches everything I do, including this book.

Chapter 1
What is Southeast Asia?

Southeast Asia is a sprawling neighborhood of hot countries that straddles the equator. Its eleven nations lie between India and China and form the great tropical cusp of Asia. Here societies drawing from Buddhism, Hinduism, Islam, Christianity, and Confucianism (alongside myriad other traditions) have rubbed shoulders over centuries and created a vast profusion of distinctive yet ever-shifting cultures. It is among the most dynamic regions on earth.

Mainland Southeast Asia, the southern apron of the continent of East Asia, is home to hundreds of ethnic groups that are today the citizens of Myanmar, Thailand, Laos, Cambodia, and Vietnam. Island (or maritime) Southeast Asia includes the Malay Peninsula and two huge archipelagos whose even more diverse populations are now citizens of Indonesia, Malaysia, Singapore, Brunei, East Timor, and the Philippines. The entire region stretches some 3,000 miles from end to end and 2,500 miles north to south, an area larger than Europe. It contains 625 million people, around 9 percent of the world's population.

For the most part, Southeast Asia is verdant and wet, with rainfalls averaging 60 inches a year and, in many places, monsoon rains that arrive reliably each year to water the rice fields, vegetable gardens, and fruit trees that for centuries have sustained its rural villages. But here and there drier patches are found where rain is scarce. In eastern Indonesia people say that their arid islands are the dirt flicked from the fingernails of the Creator after he finished making the rest of the world.

Although Southeast Asia's complex wind, water, and elevation patterns have created multiple human habitats, scholars have found it useful to begin with two archetypal ones: hills and plains. Large expanses of the region rise above 1,000 feet. Until very recently, these hills and mountains have been a world apart, an alternative human habitat dominated by dense old-growth forests interlaced by free-flowing rivers and streams. In these vast and inaccessible uplands, farmers developed strategies for living sustainably by creating temporary hill farms amid the forest—by cutting down a patch of trees, burning the debris, and planting rice and other crops amid the charred remains. A hillside "swidden" like this could be bountiful for a year or two, after which the farmers moved on to another patch as the old one wooded over again and restored the forest.

Hill farms of this kind existed everywhere in Southeast Asia, enabling highly diverse customs and characterized by distinctive textiles, jewelry, tattoos, handcrafts, and spiritual practices. From Myanmar to the Philippines hundreds of such groups could be found. One may have heard of the Lisu, Mien, and Hmong of the Burma-Thai-Lao uplands, the Rhade and other Montagnards of Vietnam, the Iban of Malaysia and Indonesia, and the Ifugao and Mangyan of the Philippines. Hill peoples like these maintained a variety of contacts with their lowland neighbors, most especially an up-river and down-river exchange of forest products (rattan, damar, bird's nests) for lowland valuables such as heirloom porcelains and outboard motors. Otherwise, they remained aloof, clinging to the sanctuary provided by their inaccessible habitat.

These small populations of resilient, adaptable, and often-shifting hill folk built their longhouses and villages along the free-flowing mountain rivers that eventually flowed downward, aggregated with other branches, and formed the great tidal rivers of Southeast Asia's lowland plains.

Just as slash-and-burn farming became the dominant agricultural pattern of the hills, wet-rice farming dominated the plains. Instead of temporary swiddens, in the lowlands farmers created permanent, bunded fields designed to capture water and manage its depth as green rice plants sprouted, rose through the shallow waters of the artificial pond, and finally matured and yellowed as farmers drained the paddies to make dry fields at harvest time. For centuries past and until today, paddy fields have dominated the cultivated landscape of lowland Southeast Asia and supported its large sedentary populations, even as vast tracts of lowlands also remained forested until recent times.

Interspersed with vegetable gardens, fruit orchards, and lush groves of trees, this verdant lowland habitat has supported large populations of farmers as well as the region's major societies and states throughout history. It is the plains that host Southeast Asia's larger ethnic groups—the Burmans, Thai, Khmer, Vietnamese, Malay, Javanese, Filipino—as well as the greater concentrations of people adhering to major world religions. Most of Southeast Asia's Buddhists, Muslims, Christians, and Hindus are people of the plains. In short, almost always when we speak of Southeast Asia, we are speaking of the lowland societies of the plains.

Today, the old dichotomy of hills and plains is breaking down. Once a lightly populated region, Southeast Asia is now bursting with people. And they are changing its old landscapes— penetrating the hills to open giant mines and to harvest logs and palm oil; overtaking forests, vacant wetlands, and vast acres of village rice paddies to create a modern landscape of exploding megacities, sprawling suburbs, and burgeoning industrial zones; and blanketing great swaths of countryside with agribusiness

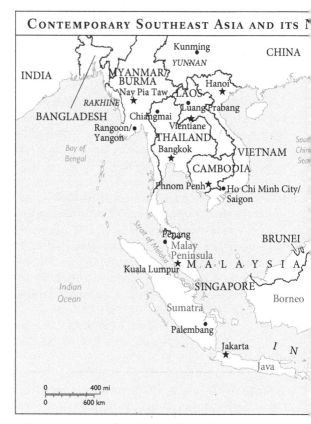

CONTEMPORARY SOUTHEAST ASIA AND ITS N

1. Contemporary Southeast Asia and its nation-states

Southeast Asia

STATES

Philippine
Sea

Luzon

PHILIPPINES

Pacific
Ocean

Mindanao

Jolo

Halmahera

Maluku

wesi

NEW GUINEA

N E S I A

Dili

EAST TIMOR

AUSTRALIA

plantations that produce bananas, coconuts, sugar, and rubber. Shrimp and fish farms now cover the region's coasts, which once were lined with mangroves.

In Southeast Asia today, no one is wholly off the grid. Even the most remote mountain sanctuaries and islands are within reach of the capital, technology, and machinery of government that are pulling every group and place into the matrix of globalization. For the Iban of the hills of central Borneo, it is logging and oil-palm plantations. For the Ifugao of upland Luzon, it is hydroelectric dams. For the Montagnards of Vietnam, it is robusta coffee farms. For the forest Tiboli of Indonesia's remote Halmahera island, it is nickel mines. Everywhere it is the same. Meanwhile, as the long arms of the global marketplace reach deep into Southeast Asia, so do the tax collectors, engineers, and schoolteachers of the region's national governments, asserting their claims of sovereignty over far-flung and disparate citizens and their valuable resources. Armies also play a role, keeping restive minorities in check and disciplining, often by use of violence, the state's claim to power.

In this climate of tectonic change, millions of people are on the move, shifting from forests into timber and mining camps, from villages into towns, and from towns into cities and megacities. Great numbers are migrating across national borders to seek work in neighboring countries. Tens of thousands every year are being trafficked as sex workers, domestic servants, and fishing-fleet boatmen. Others are fleeing violence and harassment into refugee camps and to new homes abroad. Southeast Asia is static only on the map.

Complicating these large forces is a mind-boggling heterogeneity of languages, dialects, ethnicities, religions, and customs. In Southeast Asia, multiple complex societies exist side by side. These societies have been shaped by centuries of interaction not only with each other but also with India and China and, in recent centuries, with newcomers from the West—the Portuguese,

Spanish, Dutch, English, French, and Americans, whose colonies in the region prefigured today's nation-states. The region's complex roots and its contemporary character are belied by the simplicity of the map and of popular perceptions. We talk glibly of Burmese, Filipinos, Indonesians, and Thais as though they were essential human types. Likewise, we speak of Thailand, Cambodia, Vietnam, and Singapore as entities fixed in time. These are convenient constructions, it is true, but, as in all such constructions, they mask complex realities.

Snapshots from the neighborhood

Today, all of Southeast Asia's countries conform to the model of the nation-state. Yet as nation-states they are remarkably different. Some are democratic federations and republics, others are "people's democratic republics," still others are kingdoms. They are led by prime ministers, presidents, party secretaries, sultans, and kings. As national societies, writ large, they are Muslim, Buddhist, and Christian. Two are officially Marxist. But they contain within them adherents of almost every other religion on earth as well as legions of spirit and ancestor cults—since even in these most modern of times, the spirits must be attended to. Each country in its unique way is typically Southeast Asian.

Among the predominantly Buddhist countries of the mainland, Thailand stands out as the largest by territory and second largest by population (*c.* 69 million in 2017). It is significantly more prosperous than its neighbors. A sometime democracy and oftentimes a military-led state, it coalesces around the memory of its famous nineteenth-century kings and its still-revered royal family. Cunning political actors, Thai elites avoided overt colonialism (the only Southeast Asian kingdom to do so), dodged the ravages of World War II by collaborating with Japan, and maneuvered astutely through the dangerous years of the Cold War by aligning themselves with the United States. Thailand's gross domestic product (GDP) per capita is on the rise, its strong economy is drawing migrants from neighboring countries, and its middle class is blossoming. Its capital, Bangkok, shines as a leading Southeast Asian mega city with a vibrant arts scene, business sector, and an alluring cosmopolitan face, including its smiling generals.

Meanwhile, Thailand's neighbor to the west, Myanmar (Burma), a Buddhist society much like Thailand with a population almost as large, paints a different picture. By the numbers, it is one of Southeast Asia's poorest. (Thailand's GDP per capita is seven times higher.) Once a proud kingdom like Thailand, its nineteenth-century kings were defeated by British armies and then banished as Burma was subsumed within the British Empire. It was a heavily contested theater of war in World War II, when its emergent national leaders both collaborated with and resisted the Japanese. With independence in 1948 came a dysfunctional democracy, then decade upon decade of military rule under Ne Win and his development program that wedded Buddhism and socialism. By the 1980s, Burma was backward, isolated, and riven by armed rebellions. A democracy movement led by Aung San Suu Kyi and subsequent political and economic reforms in recent years have weakened the grip of the army, ended the country's isolation, and brought elected governments to power, alongside a flood of new investments. Yet the house of Myanmar remains bitterly divided. As the world is rushing in, hundreds of thousands of Myanmar's beleaguered minority subjects are taking desperate measures to rush out.

Cambodia, to the east of Thailand, is the site of one of Southeast Asia's monstrous modern atrocities. The dark clouds of the Khmer Rouge and their "Killing Fields" (1975–1978) still hang over the nation today. Heirs of the once-monumental kingdom of Angkor (800s–1400s), Cambodia's kings of the nineteenth century attempted to steer their much-diminished kingdom to safety under French protection. Cambodia thus entered the twentieth century and the travails of World War II as part of French

Indochina with its residual monarchy neutered but intact. Hence it was a king, Norodom Sihanouk, who, repackaged as a president, took over when France departed in 1953 and who attempted to steer his small Buddhist kingdom to safety through the treacherous shoals of the Cold War, including the hot war in neighboring Vietnam. His failure and intensive U.S. bombing in Cambodia led directly to the triumph of the Khmer Rouge and the murder and manslaughter of more than two million people and, after 1979, to a long recuperation involving occupation by both Vietnam and the United Nations. Cambodia survives today as a small Buddhist kingdom of 16 million people with a constitutional monarch— Sihanouk's son—and a quasi-elected strongman prime minister who is also a former Khmer Rouge commander.

In Thailand, Burma, and Cambodia today, national leaders invoke the language of democracy and representative government even though in practice this remains largely an aspiration. Thailand is ruled, off and on, by an army junta; in Myanmar and Cambodia elections are held, but one might say that democracy as it is practiced remains highly compromised by authoritarian power structures. Southeast Asia's two other mainland states are unapologetically one-party states.

Modern Laos, a traditionally Buddhist society much like its neighbors, was formed from an amalgamation of princely domains into another French protectorate in the 1890s. The colony's affiliation with French Indochina drew it into Vietnam's long war for independence, which ended after years of confusion and turmoil in 1975 with a government led by the Communist Party in both countries. One of the quieter corners of Southeast Asia, the Lao People's Democratic Republic remains a highly agrarian and still largely Buddhist society where the largest city, Vientiane, hosts fewer than 1 million people. The former royal capital at Luang Prabang, upriver from Vientiane and much smaller, is renowned for its grace. The lowland Lao majority populates the country's narrow river valleys, yet a full 90 percent of the country's territory rises above 600 feet and is populated by non-Lao, swidden-farming hill peoples. Today, the long arm of globalization is reaching deep into Laos from every side, including from China, the country with which it shares a porous 263-mile-long border.

Vietnam's independence movement led by the Communists under Ho Chi Minh and its eventual triumph over both France and the United States is a legendary epic in modern Southeast Asian history. This is how the once domineering Confucian kingdom of Vietnam, humiliated and colonized by France in the nineteenth century, abandoned its feudal trappings to rise as Southeast Asia's strongest and, today with more than 95 million people, largest Communist state. Vietnam's victorious revolutionary struggle gave its Communist Party great authority, and the party rules up until now, despite having long since abandoned many tenets of communist ideology. In today's fast-changing Vietnam, the market is in full play and old enemies are becoming new allies.

In island Southeast Asia, Indonesia dominates. With a population of more than 263 million people, it is not only the largest country in Southeast Asia but the fourth-largest country in the world. This far-flung archipelago once hosted literally hundreds of kingdoms before being patched together into a massive tropical colony by the Dutch—a project that took three hundred years. In the early twentieth century young nationalists reimagined the Dutch East Indies as Indonesia. Through the violent interruption of World War II and after four years of revolution, in 1949 it came to be. Islam is the dominant religious culture here. And among the country's hundreds of ethnicities, the Javanese rule the roost.

Like Cambodia, Indonesia also became the site of mass killings during the region's wrenching left-right power struggles of the Cold War era. In Cambodia, Communists were the perpetrators. In Indonesia, in 1965, Communists were the victims, with some 500,000 party members and affiliates dead in army-led executions and massacres that lasted months. The military regime that followed continued for more than thirty years but it has been followed by a substantial new experiment in democracy. This includes, these days, suspenseful, hotly contested multiparty elections.

Two of Indonesia's near neighbors in the same great archipelago, Malaysia and Singapore, also owe their modern configurations to European empire-building. These territories—including the Malay Peninsula and adjacent islands as well as a large swath of northern Borneo—were cobbled together piecemeal by generations of builders of the British Empire. The territories included several Malay sultanates or mini-kingdoms, two privately held colonial domains in Borneo under British protection (Sarawak and Sabah), and two offshore island trade emporiums populated largely by Chinese migrants and other newcomers that were created by the British (Singapore and Penang). As Britain retreated from empire following World War II, it fashioned this odd collection of colonial remnants into a nation-state called Malaysia. In 1965, Singapore, the larger, richer, and most conspicuously Chinese of the trade hubs, subsequently withdrew to strike out on its own. The others have become today's Federation of Malaysia, another of Southeast Asia's authoritarian democracies in which a single political party dominates in collaboration with multisectarian coalition partners. A constitutional monarch is the symbolic face of the nation: Malaysia's king is a Malay sultan. One of Southeast Asia's smaller states, at 31 million, Malaysia is also one of its more prosperous ones, with a GDP per capita twice that of Thailand.

But Singapore is far richer. Indeed, Singapore's GDP per capita tops that of the United States. An anomaly in Southeast Asia as a predominantly ethnic Chinese city-state, Singapore is also one of the region's smallest countries, with six million people. Politically, it is a parliamentary democracy in which a single party wholly dominates. The People's Action Party (PAP) has no coalition

What is Southeast Asia?

partners. This has been true since Singapore's founding days under Lee Kuan Yew, the island nation's extraordinary prime minister, founder of the PAP, architect of the country's remarkable rise, and author of its unique way of doing things in which Confucianism, capitalism, socialism, and state-sponsored social engineering all play a part.

The final major nation of island Southeast Asia is anomalous in another way. Spain aggregated the islands of Southeast Asia's other large archipelago more than four hundred years ago and called the new entity *Las Philipinas* (the Philippines), after King Philip II. Under Spanish sway, the archipelago's lowland people adapted Christianity and evolved as a Southeast Asian society with considerable Spanish influence until being seized by the United States at the turn of the twentieth century. The Philippines today, with more than 103 million people, reflects this dual heritage. It is flamboyantly democratic and election-loving and at the same time strikingly oligarchic, with a governing class whose members compete aggressively with each other for public office and seldom yield power to the masses below. In the Philippines, elite-led democracy has proved stronger than dictatorship, an option famously tested by Ferdinand Marcos beginning in 1972 and rejected in a popular nonviolent mass movement led by Corazon Aquino in 1986. Subsequent elected presidents have included a retired general, a movie star, and the daughter of one former president and the son of another (Aquino's son, Benigno Aquino III) as well as the strong-arm populist Rodrigo Duterte, yet another scion of the governing class.

Two countries remain. The sultanate of Brunei, which rests in a tiny molar-shaped pocket of territory surrounded by Malaysian Borneo, is all that remains of a kingdom that once was much larger. But that which remains rests on one of the richest oil and gas deposits in Asia, making tiny Brunei, population 500,000, a source of stupendous wealth both for its sultan and the royal family and for Brunei Shell Petroleum. Once a British protectorate like its immediate neighbors, the sultanate declined Britain's offer to join Malaysia and carries on today as Southeast Asia's only remaining absolute monarchy.

East Timor, or Timor-Leste, is not so lucky. Occupying the eastern half of the island of Timor in the eastern Indonesian archipelago and with a per capital income of less than U.S. $4,000, it has few resources and little wealth. Evolving for centuries as a remote outpost of Portugal's increasingly impoverished empire, East Timor was jolted into the contemporary world in 1975 when Portugal moved out and Indonesia moved in, claiming the territory as a province. Its current generation of leadership emerged under the turmoil and brutality of the unwelcome Indonesian occupation and the small country's eventual liberation in 1999 and full sovereignty in 2002.

Even this poor, remote, and small Southeast Asian country illustrates the region's underlying pluralism and complex entanglements with the wider world. The 1.2 million people of East Timor comprise ten and more distinct Malayo-Polynesian and Papuan ethnic groups spread across a hilly, hardscrabble terrain. Sixteen indigenous languages are spoken in addition to the vernacular lingua franca, Tetum. During the recent twenty-nine-year Indonesian occupation, many people also learned to speak Indonesian. Today, they are learning English. Even so, the country's small elite chose Portuguese as the official national language. The Roman Catholic Church claims 90 percent of the population, yet everywhere local spirits vie with the saints for people's devotion. Aside from some coffee, cinnamon, and cocoa, East Timor's modern economy produces little for the world's hungry markets, and its hopes for prosperity lie offshore in oil and gas deposits that are also claimed by Australia. With global markets in mind, the country's leaders have adopted as its national currency the U.S. dollar.

Southeast Asia and the world

These quick portraits of today's Southeast Asian countries reveal the degree to which they have been shaped by engagements with the wider world. In modern times, the expansive powers of the West have played the dominant role. But geography is destiny. Over the long haul nearby states and civilizations in Asia have played a greater role. The archipelagos, waterways, and riverine lowlands of Southeast Asia lie adjacent to, and exposed to, two of the world's great radiating civilizations. Traffic from India and China began early in history and has remained constant through the centuries. The Straits of Melaka have been a heavily traveled maritime passageway for two thousand years. Southeast Asians established harbor-town entrepôts to capture this trade. Through them the luxury goods of India and China penetrated the region's inland kingdoms, along with new gods and goddesses, art forms, languages, and words.

Southeast Asians were especially attracted to India's civilizations and borrowed heavily over many centuries, shaping innumerable aspects of Southeast Asia today. During the same centuries, China's merchants penetrated from the north bearing porcelains, silks, useful tools, and everyday objects to Southeast Asian harbor towns large and small. In these entrepôts, the goods of India and China changed hands alongside the spices, aromatic oils and woods, birds' nests, sea slugs, and pearls that Southeast Asians themselves brought to the market. No Indian kingdom ruled territories in Southeast Asia, but several Chinese dynasties occupied the Vietnamese homeland of Dai Viet for a thousand years before the Vietnamese broke away in 939 CE, placing an indelible Chinese stamp on the independent kingdom that emerged. China also pressed into the small kingdoms along Southeast Asia's northernmost tier and accepted tribute from others farther south on the mainland and in the islands, including the tiny gold-rich kingdom of Butuan in the south Philippine Archipelago, which sent five missions to China in the early 1000s.

The wave of Western imperialism in the modern era hemmed in the power of China for more than one hundred years and brought India wholly within the British Empire. Even so, during these same years migration from China to Southeast Asia greatly expanded, profoundly altering the region's demography and economy. Today, a resurgent China is reprising its historical role in Southeast Asian commerce and also in asserting its regional preeminence. It is a primary trading partner of virtually every Southeast Asian country and the source of billions in investment annually. It looms large. More than India, it also figures centrally in Southeast Asia's security calculations.

Aside from Thailand, none of today's Southeast Asian nations existed as independent states seventy years ago. In 1945, each one was reeling in the wake of the dramatic rise and fall of imperial Japan, whose empire during World War II embraced all of Southeast Asia. After the war, some of Southeast Asia's newly independent nations formed security alliances with their former colonizers. This was true of the Philippines, which in 1954 joined the United States–led Cold War pact called the Southeast Asia Treaty Organization (SEATO), alongside Thailand, which also placed itself within the anticommunist camp. Malaysia and Singapore did the same in alliance with Britain through the Five Power Defence Arrangements (FPDA).

In Vietnam, after being rebuffed by the United States, Ho Chi Minh aligned his eventually successful revolutionary movement and the post-1954 Democratic Republic of (North) Vietnam with the Soviet Union and China, even as the post-1954 state of South Vietnam was supported and defended by the United States and its regional allies. Meanwhile, others took a neutral path and declared themselves nonaligned. Alongside Burma, these countries included Cambodia and Indonesia, whose famously mercurial leaders Sihanouk and Sukarno, respectively played to both sides in the great global rift.

The 1965 massacres of Communists in Indonesia and the onset of military rule under Suharto, following Sukarno's fall, led to a significant shift. Suharto quickly brought his country into the U.S.-led anti-communist orbit. This set the stage for the region's first successful regional organization. In 1967, Indonesia, together with Thailand, Malaysia, Singapore, and the Philippines, formed the Association of Southeast Asian Nations (ASEAN). The association was emphatically not a security alliance; rather, it was formed as a platform for mutual cooperation. Through its early meetings and nascent committee structure, the five disparate countries began working out many of the practical aspects of living in one neighborhood, such as aligning their postal services, air traffic control, and telecommunications.

ASEAN's founding members signed the Treaty of Amity and Cooperation in 1976 that struck at the heart of their security fears: they pledged to respect each other's sovereignty and to renounce the use of force in their relations with each other. This became the basis for the "ASEAN Way," an approach to resolving differences that avoided confrontation and favored patience over haste. What happens inside your borders is your business, not your neighbor's business. What cannot be agreed upon will be postponed. Although following the ASEAN Way meant that problem-solving could be glacial, it also meant that on the existential matter of state sovereignty member states could feel safe with one another. This proved to be a great boon.

At first and for many years, ASEAN represented Southeast Asia's anticommunist club; the sultanate of Brunei joined in 1984 upon its independence from Britain. But as the fate of Vietnam was resolved after 1975 and the fires of the Cold War eventually abated, the usefulness of the organization and the value of its philosophy became apparent to other members of the neighborhood. The communist states and other outliers all applied to join. Vietnam was first in 1995 followed by Laos and Myanmar in 1997 and Cambodia in 1999. East Timor awaits membership.

In the intervening years, ASEAN has served as the scaffolding for an elaborate structure of diplomatic relations both among the member states and between the collective members and the rest of the world. ASEAN coordinates officially with China, Japan, and South Korea in ASEAN+3, and its dialogue partners in the annual ASEAN Regional Forum include the major powers of Europe, Asia, and the Americas. ASEAN enjoys observer status at the United Nations General Assembly, and in 2001 it became officially a nuclear-weapons-free zone. Although ASEAN's honor-thy-neighbor policy has thwarted some much-needed reforms, its tolerant philosophy has allowed the association to endure and remain relevant. Today it is the format through which the region is exploring more advanced levels of cooperation in areas such as free trade, labor exchanges, and a monetary union.

ASEAN is only one mechanism through which Southeast Asian countries seek security today. With an eye to China and to new security threats represented by terrorism, unruly population flows, and environmental alarms, many of the nations maintain close ties with the West and also cultivate good relations with China, Japan, and South Korea, which are important trading partners, aid givers, and potential diplomatic allies. Militarily, no Southeast Asian country is in a position to secure itself independently. Only Vietnam has raised a large standing army in recent history, and despite rising military budgets and larger fleets of (mostly aging, secondhand) warplanes and warships, none of them today possesses the wherewithal to stand alone. Instead, each one engages in a variety of balancing tactics designed both to engage with the large powers of the world, on the one hand, and to keep them at a distance, on the other.

In this process today, China is all important. All of Southeast Asia's countries welcome Chinese investments to a degree. Chinese goods pour across the porous borders of the mainland states and fill the provincial markets and city stores and malls. It is hardly different in the islands. Chinese private and state-connected companies are aggressively expanding in Southeast Asia in the mining, agribusiness, and tourism sectors as well as in transportation and hydroelectricity. (In Laos, where China accounts for 40 percent of foreign investment, Chinese companies are building casinos, five-star hotels, banana and rubber plantations, and dozens of hydroelectric dams.) Meanwhile, China is expanding its strategic presence into Southeast Asia in the South China Sea. Diplomacy can contain these mounting pressures to a degree, but momentum on the Chinese side and weak leverage on the Southeast Asian side make this penetration more or less unstoppable. China cannot be contained. It must be engaged.

These days, Southeast Asian officials meet with Chinese officials at every level, both bilaterally and through ASEAN's consultative structures. More significantly, Thailand, Indonesia, Singapore, Myanmar, Cambodia, Malaysia, and the Philippines have established military-to-military links with China to facilitate aid and loans, joint training exercises, and joint production of military equipment, as well as a forum for discussing security issues. China has claimed ASEAN as a strategic partner. In 2003 it signed ASEAN's foundational Treaty of Amity and Cooperation, pledging to eschew armed conflict and to respect the sovereignty and internal integrity of its neighbors.

At the same time, most of the ASEAN countries also have security ties with the United States and welcome the presence of the American Seventh Fleet, which patrols the all-important Melaka Straits and posts some twenty thousand military personnel in the region at any given time. Singapore serves as the logistics center of the American fleet and provides both its naval base and its airfields. Thailand, Indonesia, and Malaysia have signed military access agreements, and both Thailand and the Philippines have been granted special access to U.S. intelligence as major non-NATO allies. Under a visiting forces agreement signed in 1999, the Philippines has invited thousands of U.S. soldiers to assist in its war against Muslim separatists and to engage in war games. Indonesia is happy to buy advanced weapons from the United States under special agreement and sends its officers for training in the United States. Even Vietnam is slowly opening its ports to the American navy and receives a modest U.S. military aid package. (Vietnam continues to acquire most of its arms from Russia, however—another balancing strategy.) Meanwhile, Britain and other members of the Five Power Defence Arrangements continue to support Malaysia.

Writ large, these complex arrangements balancing China and the United States (and other powers such as Great Britain, Japan, and Russia) are not designed with specific quid pro quos in mind, although much fine print is involved. Their real purpose is to create a web of interlocking and overlapping alliances and relationships that mitigates against predatory behavior and the resort to force. This is a familiar Southeast Asian approach to things. When trouble looms, rally your friends. Indonesian president Joko Widodo was not being glib when he described his country's foreign policy as "a thousand friends and no enemies."

Elites and national economies

The governing classes in Southeast Asia today have their roots in the deep past and also in more recent history. Lineage matters in Southeast Asia. In Thailand, Malaysia, and Cambodia constitutional monarchies reveal the contemporary appeal of aristocracy. Princes and princesses and hierarchies of titled people continue to exist. In Thailand, virtually all of the country's elected and nonelected leaders (conspicuously its power-seizing generals) pledge their loyalty to the king. In Malaysia, a parliamentary democracy, all but one of the country's prime ministers since independence has hailed from a royal lineage. In places where these feudal trappings have been officially abandoned, such as Indonesia, politicians and even military dictators routinely claim aristocratic roots. Sukarno did so, as did Suharto, through his wife. The Philippines lacks such an aristocracy but most of its leading politicians descend from wealthy provincial clans whose preeminence dates from Spanish times. Indeed, virtually everywhere in the region, many of today's elites are descendants of families that have enjoyed privileged status for generations, if not for centuries.

The colonial states that dominated Southeast Asia until World War II did not supplant indigenous elites; they subordinated them. Everywhere members of upper-class families continued to serve as officials in the colonial states. More importantly, colonial regimes generally limited education in Western languages and advanced subjects to members of high-status families. (This is how Sukarno became a Dutch-speaking engineer and how Tunku Abdul Rahman became an English-speaking lawyer.) This status enabled them to come forward as modern leaders in the twentieth century—to lead reformist and nationalist movements and, at independence, to become the governing classes of the region's new nations. (Sukarno as Indonesia's founding president, Tunku Abdul Rahman as the founding prime minister of Malaysia.) Independence and the advent of military rule opened new paths to political leadership; as armies became institutionalized and matured, officer corps merged into the governing classes in Burma, Thailand, and Indonesia. In Vietnam and also in Laos, it was the Communist Party that offered new avenues to power, as senior cadres and their families formed the country's new elite.

These people of high status emerged as governing classes in societies with largely agrarian economies and only rudimentary processing and manufacturing sectors. For the most part, they themselves and their families were not people of business. They tended to draw their wealth and incomes from landed properties, rent-seeking, and the perquisites of officialdom. For the most part, business and industry and the realm of money were the domains of Southeast Asians of Chinese descent. The roots of this phenomenon also lay in the colonial period when a combination of new opportunities in the Western colonies and catastrophes in China led hundreds of thousands of migrants to the region. Colonial laws and policies steered them away from rural landowning and into towns and cities, where they flourished as laborers, artisans, shopkeepers, and capitalists large and small. This occurred everywhere in Southeast Asia but was complemented in British domains by the arrival of Indians, who played similar roles but on a smaller scale. Chinese migrants became modern Southeast Asia's essential urbanites—Kuala Lumpur was founded by the mining camp boss Yap Ah Loy—and formed a distinctive commercial class.

The majority of these migrants were men, and their marriages to local women created mixed Chinese-Southeast Asian families everywhere. In the Philippines and Thailand, this mestizo class blended with high-status indigenous families and became an integral part of the nascent national elite. Corazon Cojuangco Aquino, former president of the Philippines, is exemplary of this important trend: her great-grandfather was a certain Co Yu Hwan, who migrated to the Spanish Philippines from China in the nineteenth century. Her family and many others like it are quintessentially Filipino by culture. Elsewhere, the evolving Chinese and Chinese-mestizo communities remained distinctively apart. This is true in today's Malaysia, Indonesia, and Singapore. New migrations in the twentieth century and the arrival of ever larger numbers of Chinese women also created distinctively Chinese communities even in societies with a high level of assimilation, so that we may speak of Chinese Filipinos, Sino-Thai, and Sino-Vietnamese.

The pride of place of the Chinese in the region's economy and the community's conspicuous well-being compared with the region's indigenous majorities have long been sore points. A common feature of policies following World War II in many Southeast Asian countries has been an attempt to use the powers of government to place more of the nation's wealth and potential wealth in the hands of its indigenous elites—and to enrich its indigenous populations as well. To a degree, they have succeeded.

Southeast Asians have long profited by participating in trade, introducing their own valuable products into the vital stream of commerce that connected India to China and to the wider world. (Cloves, which once grew only on a cluster of remote Southeast Asian islands, were mentioned in Pliny's *Natural History* [first century CE] and have been identified in the archaeological remains of an ancient Mesopotamian pantry.) Under European rule in recent centuries, commodities from Southeast Asia, such as coffee, sugar, tea, tobacco, and rubber, reached global markets alongside timber, minerals, and petroleum. Up until independence, the immense profits of this economy accrued mainly to the European and American capitalists, and their employees and shareholders, and to the local Chinese merchants, shippers, contractors, agents, and suppliers who made it logistically possible. For the most part, indigenous Southeast Asians participated in this economy as laborers, clerical workers, and small-time cash croppers and traders.

Following independence, Southeast Asian governing classes strove to redirect many of these profits to Southeast Asians themselves and, at the same time, to diversify their national economies by advancing manufacturing and other sectors. In this project, government has itself played a key role everywhere. By intervening directly in key sectors (such as rice, petroleum, and energy), licensing lucrative subsectors (importing automobiles, machinery, food additives, medicines), granting monopoly concessions to, say, harvest timber on government land or to establish telecommunication grids, and controlling access to loans from government banks and serving as brokers between foreign aid givers and local aid recipients, Southeast Asian governments and their regime elites have enriched themselves. They have also nourished their supporters through vast patronage networks connecting politicians, army generals, and dictators at the top to tiers of bureaucrats, officials, supplicant businesspeople, and party members on down to the lowest tiers, which, in some places, actually include voters.

Patron-client pyramids like this vary from society to society and regime to regime and take on new shapes and functions as rural people become city people, but in Southeast Asia today they underpin social structures everywhere. Built upon *personal* obligations and connections—who do you know?—they privilege loyalty over the law. They are vulnerable to nepotism, bribery, and other corruptions, but they are also highly resilient and flexible and make it possible for societies to cohere even as economies flounder and governments change. In democratic systems, patron-client pyramids realign after elections as new members of the governing class achieve top positions. They undergo major realignments with major regime changes. This occurred when Ferdinand Marcos seized power in the Philippines, for example, and when Suharto's dictatorship collapsed in Indonesia.

These underlying social constructs help to explain why Southeast Asia, despite many disruptions, is a relatively stable global region in which governing elites of various kinds seek prosperity and security by both co-opting and resisting the entreaties of greater powers—balancing this one against that one—and opportunistically manipulating access to the national economies.

Although in the early years of independence several Southeast Asian governments attempted to protect nascent home industries behind tariff walls in a strategy called import substitution, most of them eventually concluded that opening their economies to foreign investors paid higher dividends, as did prioritizing their historical strengths exporting commodities, minerals, and petroleum. Today commodities from Southeast Asia are pouring into China as well as into the rising economies of South Korea and Japan and the industrial West. This development is enriching many people in Southeast Asia, and it also accounts for the transformation of the region's environment.

Meanwhile, in most countries of the region, governments have also promoted industrialization and the growth of high-tech manufacturing that complements the resource sector and protects national economies against the vagaries of shifting global commodity prices. In Thailand, the Philippines, Malaysia, and Indonesia—Southeast Asia's newly industrialized countries (NICs)—these sectors are advanced. In Singapore they are so advanced, alongside cutting-edge banking and financial services, that the country is one of the richest in the world as measured by GDP per capita and other measures. (The Sultanate of Brunei is rich for another reason.) A huge gap separates Singapore from Malaysia, the second most prosperous country in the region, and a large gap again separates Malaysia from the other NICs. Burma, Cambodia, Laos, and East Timor remain poor by any standard, with a large majority of their populations still bound to the land and only nascent modern sectors. Even so, in each one, resource extraction in the form of logging, hydroelectricity, raw materials, and, in Burma's case, petroleum, is generating wealth for rulers and their clients as new investments from China are drawing even these slow-growing states into the needy matrix of globalization.

The rich complexities of modern Southeast Asia—its radical heterogeneity; its hills and plains; its great cities and agricultural hinterlands; its dynamic engagement with the outside world; its presidents, prime ministers, domineering military men, and kings; and its asymmetrical prosperity—all have roots deep in history. Southeast Asia is unquestionably of the moment. It is modern, but it is modern in distinctively Southeast Asian ways.

Chapter 2
Kingdoms

Rice is the foundation of Southeast Asian life. The discovery of rice cultivation appears to have occurred in southern China. People living in Southeast Asia were its early adapters. By the second or third millennium BCE, they were growing rice, domesticating pigs, chickens, and cattle, and forming the region's earliest settled communities in several mainland areas congruent with present-day northern Vietnam, Thailand, and Malaya. By the 5th century BCE, they had become iron and bronze workers. Their large and elaborate funnel-shaped bronze drums decorated with frogs, birds, and warriors in long boats—often called Dong Son drums from a key archaeological site in northern Vietnam— became one of the region's first items of luxury trade and dispersed throughout much of Southeast Asia.

In these early centuries, people occupied particularly favorable niches of the region's habitat, taking advantage of abundant fish, fruits, and animal life as they formed settled rice-growing (and in places millet-, sago-, taro-, and yam-growing) communities. These people, alongside later arrivals, were the ancestors of today's Southeast Asians, whose small communities barely altered the landscape as they formed amid Southeast Asia's vast tropical forests.

We know little about the organization of these early societies or about how these early farmers and fisherfolk at some point first

2. Wet-rice farmers work in the paddy fields of Vietnam. For centuries past and until today, paddy fields have dominated the cultivated landscape of lowland Southeast Asia and supported its large sedentary populations.

morphed into nascent polities or mini-states under the leadership of local strongmen and their kin and allies. In these times when land was plentiful and people were few, the key to amassing power lay in controlling people, not in amassing territory. By *c.* 250–540 CE, a large early state had emerged in a coastal area adjacent to the lower Mekong River: Funan, Southeast Asia's first "recorded" kingdom, that is, recorded by Chinese observers, who may have been exaggerating. For practical purposes, Funan marks the beginning of Southeast Asia's political history.

From Funan and for many centuries afterward, evidence is strong that the vast majority of Southeast Asian polities were small and local, consisting of local lords and strongmen, petty kings, perhaps, ruling over pockets of population amid the domineering forest. Many of these early polities lay nested along the fertile plains of the Mekong, Chao Phraya, Irrawaddy, and Red Rivers, and along similar but shorter rivers that formed fertile plains in Java, Luzon,

26

and other island sites. Other favored sites were river mouths and coastlines where abundant fish and opportunities to trade led to the establishment of early harbor towns augmented by nearby villages of farmers. Here and there, fertile upland valleys also hosted small states based on wet-rice farming and the presence of gold or gem mines and other resources. This occurred, for example, in West Sumatra and in the Shan and Thai highlands.

These early pockets of settled people may have been no larger than a few hundred or a few thousand people, although some grew larger; the permanence and fecundity of wet-rice farming made this possible. At any given time in these early centuries there may have been hundreds of such mini-states spread across the mainland and islands, each with a king or raja or, later, when Islam took hold in the islands, a sultan of its own. This pattern of extreme disaggregation reflected the radical heterogeneity of the people themselves, with their hundreds of languages and dialects and emerging ethnicities. Such small polities were the norm.

But occasionally, one such king or strong man succeeded in establishing domination over a larger area by conquering or otherwise subordinating his neighbors, thus making a larger kingdom from several smaller ones, that is, by subordinating more people to himself. And thus, amid a vast realm of small states, some larger ones rose that came to dominate entire river valleys and their plains, or a network of affiliated harbor towns or coastal communities. And a few of these grew to become truly large states or empires. For the most part, it is only these that we know much about.

Funan appears to have been the first of these and dominated the lower Mekong River basin in the first centuries of the Common Era. By the 700s and 800s CE, kings of the Sailendra dynasty had created a great densely populated kingdom in central Java and built immense and beautiful monuments in stone. (Borobudur and Prambanan are their legacy.) Between the 700s and 1200s, powerful rulers based at Palembang in southern Sumatra ruled a vast sea-based thalassocracy known as Srivijaya that controlled the Straits of Melaka by dominating the surrounding coastal and harbor-town polities. And by 900 or so, the Khmer kings of Angkor had achieved domination over the rice plains of the Tonle Sap and lower Mekong basin in the great kingdom of classical Cambodia that prevailed in varying degrees of strength from the late 800s to the 1400s; their architectural legacy is the monumental temple complex of Angkor. By the time of Angkor, Vietnam (Dai Viet), which controlled the Red River delta of northern Vietnam, had already evolved as a frontier territory of China for nearly a thousand years. It broke free to stand on its own in 939.

In subsequent centuries, other large states emerged in ecologically predictable sites—along the Irrawaddy River basin and delta (kingdoms of Mons, Burmans, and Pyus); along the Chao Phraya River (the Thai); along the central Vietnam coast (Chams); and again in Java (the great Javanese kingdom of Majapahit [1300-1500]) and the Melaka Straits (Malay Melaka). Although the physical and literary remains of these big kingdoms dominate the historical record, we should understand them as only part of a wider pattern in which a few big states like these nested amid hundreds of smaller ones—with the autonomy of the smaller, peripheral ones either losing or gaining in relation to the constant waxing and waning of the larger ones, and with hill peoples always on the periphery.

A world of mandalas

The concept of the mandala helps us to explain this dynamic political world. Indians of the classical age adopted this image to visualize the world and the cosmos; Kautilya used it in his famous Arthashastra (*c.* 300 BCE) to discuss diplomacy and war. Southeast Asians borrowed the concept and the Sanskrit term from them. Think of a small circle that is encircled by increasingly larger and potentially infinite concentric circles. The circles represent a kingdom. Power rests in the center, the site of the capital and the locale of the king and his core officials and also of the kingdom's core population of farmers, urbanites, and slaves over which the ruler exercises power directly and whose labor and food production—through compulsion, taxation, and religious donations—forms the economic basis of the state. Here also, in the center, dwell the holy men and scholars of the king's religious cult and the artisans, musicians, and scribes who embellish the capital with monuments, music, and (a veneer of) literacy.

In what we shall call a mandala kingdom, the king's power radiated out from the capital and, as it passed by degree through each successive concentric circle, attenuated and eventually died out altogether or overlapped with the outer circles of another mandala—all without crossing any clear border. In the outer circles of his mandala, a king may not have controlled or drawn resources from people directly but, rather, indirectly through local lords and strong men. These vassals professed loyalty and rendered tribute, taxes, soldiers, and slaves to the center as long as the ruler was strong enough to coerce them. But they may have stinted on their obligations or broken free altogether when the king was weak and ruled as independent mini-kings over their own domains of followers and resources. Or, perhaps, they may have been sucked into the orbit of a competing mandala whose gravity pulled from another direction. Keep in mind that in Southeast Asia, adjacent mandalas may well have involved different ethnicities; the underlying tensions of mandala politics was more than a raw power struggle.

One can think of premodern Southeast Asia as a world of mandala kingdoms, large and small, with the larger mandalas expanding and contracting by absorbing their smaller neighbors into their orbits and contracting when outlying domains subsequently wrested free, and with the large mandalas competing with other

3. Premodern Southeast Asia through c. 1800.

PREMODERN SOUTHEAST ASIA

CHINA

Pacific
Ocean

Luzon

South
China
Sea

SIEM RIEP AND
BATTAMBANG

Manila

CHAMPA

Butuan/Agusan

NAN

Mindanao

Brunei

Ternate and
Tidore

Halmahera

Borneo

New
Guinea

Sulawesi

Ambon

Banda
Islands

ta

Demak

Java

Surakarta

Yogyakarta

Bali

large mandalas for domination of their large domains and populations. This occurred, for example, in great wars between the Burmans and the Thais in the 18th century.

We think of Southeast Asia's mandala chiefs as "men of prowess." Their skills included not only prowess in war but also prowess in mobilizing followers to develop and sustain agricultural resources (in complex wet-rice regimes, for example), to engage in trade, and to execute essential religious rites. They were what we might today call entrepreneurs, and also politicians in the sense that their prowess involved superior rhetorical skills and diplomatic acumen. In the turbulent world of competing mandalas, high royal birth placed one in competition for power but did not guarantee it. Kings had many sons, not to mention brothers and legions of royal cousins. Queens and their progeny formed factions at court and intrigued for position; occasionally, they ruled. Succession disputes were routine and often violent. It was men of prowess (and on occasion women) who prevailed.

The power of a Southeast Asian mandala's king was measured in part by the size and splendor of his capital with its monuments and royal trappings and public pageantry designed to glorify the king and his cult. All this was embellished with tiers of officials and priests and scribes, soldiers, artisans, and other urbanites and the sea of the capital's immediate supporting population of farmers and slaves. Smaller kings ruling smaller mandalas attempted to mimic this display of power with similar elements of grandeur on a lesser scale. Underlying such displays of power were the relationships of deference and loyalty that linked the lords of outlying circles of the mandala, or the lords of smaller mandalas that were satellites of a greater one, to the center.

Coercion was a factor. Small states were conquered and seized by neighboring larger ones. But diplomacy also played a part. A mandala lord might simply acknowledge his deference to the center by sending gifts and tribute—Malay sultans sent gold flowers (*bunga mas*) to the Siamese king. He might contribute men to the king's armies. Or he might send one of his daughters or sisters to become one of the king's royal wives, thus cementing a power relationship with a family one. Such relationships, we assume, varied case by case, each one in a more or less constant process of negotiation as the screws tightened when the dominant ruler was strong and loosened when he was weak.

In smaller mandala kingdoms, Southeast Asian rulers presided over populations of farmers, slaves, and urban folk in a single niche habitat along a river, at a river mouth or favorable coastal site, or a

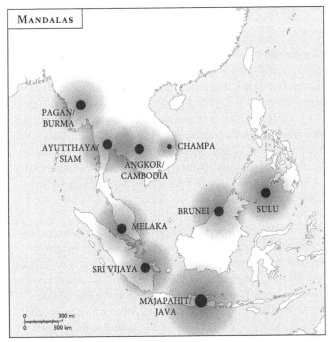

4. In Southeast Asia's mandala kingdoms—conceptualized abstractly in this map—the king's power radiated out from the capital, diminished with distance, and eventually died out without crossing any clear border.

fertile upland valley (as in the Yunnan–Southeast Asia cusp of northern Burma, Laos, and Vietnam). Here management of the realm could be more or less direct and executed by loyal kin and officials who answered directly to the king. But as the mandala expanded, taking in the territories of neighboring leaders and rival ethnicities, controlling the realm involved indirect arrangements in which local lords and their families and other elites (and their ways of doing things) were incorporated into the power structure of the large mandala, where they might remain only briefly or for several generations. Aside from establishing family ties between rulers and vassals through marriage, patron-client calculations applied in which the advantages of loyalty to the center were weighed against the costs of lost resources and the sting of deference.

One can imagine the immense complexity of large mandala states in which multiple satellite societies were linked to the center through multifarious ties of—almost always—reluctant vassalage. Larger states that dominated their regions for long periods gradually developed relatively sophisticated systems of kingdom-wide administration. Such was the case in Burma during the age of Pagan, in Ayutthaya in Siam, and, of course, in Vietnam, where China provided an advanced model. But always beneath the surface lurked the underlying dynamics of mandala contestation. When the larger kingdoms fragmented, they fragmented into familiar smaller ones.

The mandala world was therefore inherently unstable, as neighboring kingdoms small and large invariably sought to expand at the expense of each other. Violence was a constant in the form of raiding and slaving on land and sea. Power struggles among a ruler's large coterie of brothers and sons and other pretenders led to crises and civil wars when a king died. And occasionally, powerful mandala kings launched major wars against their neighbors that involved great armies of foot soldiers and war elephants (such as those rendered in stone on the walls of Angkor Wat).

In all of these encounters, the object was the same: to bring larger numbers of people into the domain of the winner. Followers equaled power. War captives were literally taken to the victor's capital. Perhaps for this reason, mandala kings preferred war strategies that mitigated against slaughter—overpowering the enemy with shock and awe, for example, or determining the outcome by way of elephant-mounted dueling princes. Even so, we can be certain there was plenty of slaughter and other destruction and insecurity when great armies took to the field and as the routine power struggles and predatory raiding of the mandala world swept over the region's settled communities. Southeast Asians adapted to these threats by moving, literally by abandoning a dangerous site for a safe one farther away. Others fled the dangers and oppressions of the mandala-dominated lowlands for safety in the region's inaccessible hills and mountains.

As a way of thinking about the myriad kingdoms and mini-kingdoms of Southeast Asia's long early history, the mandala concept applies both to the mainland and to the islands, where a ruler's mandala domain might extend no farther than a single island or two, or the lower reaches of a river (on, say, Borneo or Malaya or Sumatra) and a raja's capital at the mouth of the river. Or it might encompass several islands or harbor-town capitals and their lowland interiors, as in the great Melaka Straits mandala thalassocracy of Srivijaya or those of the sultans of Brunei or Sulu that aggregated mini-states linked by bodies of water instead of land. The mandala concept also applies to Vietnam (Dai Viet) in the early centuries, although as rulers who followed China's model, Vietnam's kings did embrace the existence of explicit borders (especially its border with China) in a way that other Southeast Asian rulers did not.

The lure of Indian civilization

These early Southeast Asian societies and states did not evolve in isolation; rather, they did so in communication with adjacent Asian civilizations in India and China. The idea of the mandala itself came from India and, for the most part, the emerging societies of the mandala world of Southeast Asia world sought to base their own rising civilizations on the older, deeper one of nearby India.

By the time of Funan, the awe-inspiring cosmos and complex spiritual culture of myriad gods and goddesses and profound philosophical ideas of the Hindu world were a thousand years old. Buddhism, an offshoot of the Hindu world, had also been evolving for hundreds of years, and between 268 and 232 BCE a great Buddhist king, Ashoka, had united virtually the entire continent and created the greatest Indian mandala yet in history. Traffic between Indian states and harbor towns and early Southeast Asian polities was already well established by the time of Funan, whose kings claimed descent from an Indian Brahmin and organized their farming communities around tanks or reservoirs, India-style. A great wave of Indianization had begun. In the following centuries, key elements of Indian religious life, arts, and language as well as law and statecraft and countless stories of heroes and villains, gods and men, and fantastical beings drifted into the region borne by merchants and holy men and travelers of all kinds, including legions of itinerant experts known as brahmins. They were embraced by Burmans and Javanese, Khmers and Chams, Thais and Malays, and countless other Southeast Asian peoples who aspired to be a part of the great civilization of India and the vast Hindu-Buddhist world.

Proof for this is to be found in a proliferation of archaeological evidence, from the great stone monuments of Borobudur in Java and Angkor Wat in Cambodia to the thousands of smaller monuments and statues, text-bearing stiles, and stone, bronze, silver, and gold figures that have been found scattered across the region as far as the remotest islands of the Philippine archipelago. But there is abundant historical and living evidence as well—religious and literary texts and law codes, genealogies, and court documents plus India-derived alphabets, words, and stories, not to mention place-names, personal names, and legions of decorative patterns, sacred symbols, and common rituals in play up until today.

In the Indianized states of Southeast Asia, kings became *devaraja*, or god-kings, and represented themselves as incarnations of Hindu deities such as Siva and Vishnu or as Buddhist monarchs in the manner of Ashoka, or as revered bodhisattvas such as Avalokitesvara (e.g., at the Bayon temple of Angkor). Their mandala kingdoms mirrored the India-conceived cosmos itself, with great temple "mountains" dominating the mandala center— depictions of Mount Meru, the mythical home of the gods around which the world revolves. The stupendous Buddhist stupa at Borobudur is an eighth-century legacy of the Sailendra kingdom of Mataram, a multitiered monument that honored Buddha and also displayed the piety and power of its king. Its architectural plan in which tiers of concentric square and round terraces (adorned with exquisite Buddha images) rise like a pyramid to a single bell-shaped stupa at the top is a precise depiction of a mandala. Nearby, about thirty miles (fifty kilometers) away, is Prambanan, another monumental temple complex and mandala center of subsequent kings in which the main temple honors Siva alongside somewhat smaller ones honoring Vishnu and Brahma, the other two gods of the Hindu Trimurti, or trinity; here, too, are representations in stone of a wide pantheon of Hindu gods and mythical beings, including Ganesha, Nandi, and Rama.

These two temple complexes, one Buddhist and one Hindu, were built only one hundred years apart. This fact illustrates how Southeast Asians partook of Hinduism and Buddhism more or less simultaneously and why we commonly refer to this long period of Indianization as a Hindu-Buddhist era. The temple complex of Angkor in Cambodia contains both the Hindu temple honoring Siva and Vishnu known as Angkor Wat and, just a few miles away, the great Bayon temple complex in which Bodhisattva Avalokitesvara (and King Jayavarman VII) looks out in all directions from the king's mandala center. The great plain of

Buddhist temples and stupas at Pagan in present-day Myanmar is another monumental mandala center.

Drawing upon the great traditions of India, Southeast Asians had many options to choose from. We can imagine that persuasive Hindu brahmins and Buddhist monks led them to one cult or sect or another, with the result that a great profusion of practices occurred within the larger Hindu-Buddhist discourse, including tantric and occult practices (in Java, for example) and original fusions of India's great traditions with local ones in which ancestral and strictly local spirits were carefully honored and appeased.

Belief in such spirits—the anima or life in all things—forms the original, primal form of spirituality in Southeast Asia. Even as Southeast Asians adapted Hindu and Buddhist (and later Muslim and Christian) beliefs and practices, they never wholly abandoned the deep belief that, for example, rice is alive and that the songs of

5. Angkor Wat is part of a monumental temple complex marking the center of the great Khmer mandala of Southeast Asia's age of kingdoms.

birds, the sudden chills of a breeze, and the stirring of volcanoes bear messages. In the twelfth-century Thai kingdom of Sukhothai, King Ram Khamhaeng devoted his realm to Buddha, whose statues adorned the cardinal points of his mandala capital (we are told this in a famous inscription), but he did not neglect to honor the powerful local spirit of Phra Khaphung, "superior to all the spirits of the country." In Java, Brahma, Siva, and Vishnu and their retinues did not erase or replace local gods such as Roro Kidul, Javanese goddess of the Southern Seas. Wise rulers honored one and all.

As elements of Indian civilization penetrated Southeast Asia, they did so unevenly and serendipitously, creating hybridities of endless variation as attractive elements of the "new" from India fused with deeply rooted elements of the "old," i.e., hallowed local traditions. Southeast Asians borrowed heavily but not indiscriminately. And they never did so wholly. The Javanese and the Khmer and the Burman did not become Indians. They became new versions of themselves. This is a process that continues today.

In Indianized Southeast Asia, the great epics and story cycles of India became Southeast Asian stories: the Ramayana and the tale of Rama and his consort Sita and Hanuman the Monkey King (whose exploits were carved onto the bas-relief walls of both Prambanan and Angkor Wat) became the basis for countless retellings in drama and dance and stone. The Mahabharata brought the deep teachings of the Bhagavad Gita to Southeast Asia and became the basis for enduring popular arts, such as the Javanese shadow-puppet theater and its fantastical nightlong renderings of the epic war-of-cousins (Bharata Yudha) in which gods and men and demons play out their fated roles. The Jataka tales retell the lives of the Buddha in countless reincarnations leading up to enlightenment. They were carved in stone on the terraced walls of Borobudur in c. 800 and are recounted popularly throughout Burma, Thailand, Cambodia, and Laos today. Alongside the Ramayana and the Mahabharata, they became part of Southeast Asia's deep pool of stories and characters that formed the basis for its pervasive Hindu-Buddhist sense of the world.

These stories and their lessons and legions of characters provided the basis for every form of popular art and theater and also provided names of untold millions of Southeast Asians up to the present. King Ram Khamhaeng of Sukhothai (d. 1298), for example, was a fervent Buddhist king who bore a Hindu name: Rama. The same is true of all the kings of Thailand's reigning Chakri dynasty, each of whom, from the founder in 1782, has reigned as Rama. For centuries in Southeast Asia, people explained the highs and lows and many nuances of human nature and the vagaries of chance and history by retelling these stories and recounting the heroism, wisdom, and loyalty of the one and the villainy, cunning, and treachery of the other. Characters became archetypes: Ananda, the kind and selfless attendant of Buddha; Bima, the bold, action-seeking leader of the Mahabharata (and, in the twentieth century, Sukarno's own self-model as a young man.) And so on.

Along with stories and names came words. Very few Southeast Asians ever learned Sanskrit or Pali, the classical languages of Hinduism and Mahayana and Theravada Buddhism (Pali); this set of knowledge was limited to priestly classes. But Southeast Asians grafted thousands of Indian-origin words into their vernacular vocabularies. Indian words became Southeast Asian words in Malay, Javanese, Thai, Burmese, and other regional languages and even penetrated the Philippines. Early Spanish missionaries there discovered that lowland Filipinos used the word "Bhatala" for god, a direct cognate from Sanskrit (*bhattara*, lord). Today the common words for horse (*kuda*), learn (*ajar*), and wise (*bijaksana*) in modern Indonesian all derive from Sanskrit— alongside thousands of others. And up until now, the Burmese, Mon, Thai, Khmer, and Lao languages, as well as Javanese, are all written in an India-derived (Brahmic) script.

This great wave of Indianization encompassed almost all of Southeast Asia, as far east as the central coast of Vietnam, where the Chams lived, and into the islands of the Philippine archipelago, where the impact was weakest. Here there were no great monuments or, as far as we know, great mandala kingdoms of the kind that waxed and waned on the mainland and on Java. Even so, in pre-Spanish times, Filipino vernacular languages were written in an India-derived script called *baybayin*, and archaeologists continue to find Hindu- and Buddhist-inspired figures in Philippine digs. (These include a *c*. eleventh-century statuette of the bodhisattva Tara in brilliant gold found in Agusan, Mindanao.)

New waves of Islam and Theravada Buddhism

The Hindu-Buddhist layer of Southeast Asian civilizations was pervasive and has been tenacious. But beginning around 1300, new waves of cultural influence again swept through the region bringing Islam and its message. Islam also came by way of India, where a Muslim dynasty gained dominance after the 1100s, although some of its earliest emissaries to Southeast Asia appear to have traveled directly from the Muslim heartland in Arabia and the Middle East. As with the older Indian influences, no army of foreign invaders carried Islam to Southeast Asia. Instead, Islam was brought peacefully by devout merchants plying the waters between India and Southeast Asia and the traveling scholars and Sufi mystics who arrived in their vessels and rooted themselves in the region's harbor towns and maritime mini-states. Again, the process took many centuries, but by the mid-1400s the ruler of the Straits-controlling mandala at Melaka had converted to Islam and become Sultan Muhammad Shah. Islam's position in the islands accelerated after that as Islam-centered mandalas defeated and incorporated others. By 1500 a Muslim sultan had seized power at Demak on Java.

Islam was soon the hegemonic religious culture in much of the island world, with its influence strongest in coastal maritime kingdoms such as Aceh, Melaka, and Makassar and with is impact attenuating among inland populations, where Hindu-Buddhist legacies were most deeply rooted. Here and there, more or less pure Hindu societies survived amid the widespread adoption of Islam. This was most remarkably true in Bali, which hosted several mini-kingdoms under its own kings, royalty, and priestly castes.

With Islam came the powerful appeal of monotheism and a body of teachings and laws whose sway stretched from Southeast Asia west to the great empires of the Mughals in India, the Safavids in Persia, and others all the way to Africa and Spain. In embracing Islam, its rules and rituals, fasting, almsgiving, and pilgrimage and habits of modesty, Southeast Asians joined a body of believers, or *umma*, that linked them to great centers of knowledge, power, wealth, and piety that spanned the globe, or seemed to.

With Islam also came Arabic, the language of the Qur'an and of Islamic scholarship. As was the case with Sanskrit and Pali, only a handful of religious scholars in Southeast Asia knew the language well. Ordinary Muslims memorized prayers and passages from the Qur'an in Arabic and adopted Arabic words into their vernacular languages, so that today, for example, in Malay and Indonesian, the words for Friday (*jumaat*), news (*kabar*), sincerity (*ikhlas*) and thousands of others are Arabic. (Persian words also arrived with Islam.)

With Islam came the sacred teachings of the Qur'an and the hallowed traditions of the Prophet (Hadith) as well as the popular tales of Sinbad and *A Thousand and One Nights* that also moved effortlessly along Muslim-dominated trade routes. Also, new names arrived. As Muslims, many Southeast Asians began drawing from the huge repository of names in the Qur'an and Hadith and other Muslim societies to become Mahmud, Umar, Abu Bakar, and Ahmad as well as Zubaidah, Chadijah, Laila, and so on.

But not everyone did so, just as not everyone adhered to the new Muslim teachings with the same degree of discipline and devotion. As in earlier borrowings, Southeast Asians adapted Islam selectively and found ways to nest it within older bodies of beliefs and practices. Old calendars, wedding rituals, habits of dress, and naming systems remained alongside the new ones. And despite the strict monotheism of Islam, many Southeast Asian Muslims continued to make offerings to venerated ancient spirits, and they remained wary of, and in awe of, certain spirit-laden sites.

A particularly complex fusion formed in Java, where Islam as commonly practiced clung to certain elements of older Hindu-Buddhist-animist ways in a sort of mystic synthesis. Just as Indianization brought not one monolithic civilization but a dazzling mosaic of Indianized adaptations, so did the spread of Islam. Southeast Asians did not become Arabs any more than Persians, Indians, or North African Muslims did. They became new Muslim versions of themselves.

The deep-to-shallow sway of Islam took in virtually all of the lowland populations of the Indonesian archipelago and Malaya and penetrated the Sulu Sea and islands of the southern Philippine archipelago—a penetration that was arrested by the arrival of the Spanish and Christianity. On the mainland, Muslim enclaves formed along the coasts of the Bay of Bengal and in Champa on the Vietnam coast.

During roughly the same period that Islam overtook the islands, a new school of Buddhism swept through most of the mainland. Theravada Buddhism was a reform movement that sought to purify Buddhist beliefs and practices of superstitions, myths, and embellishments that had occurred over centuries as the religion passed from generation to generation and into cultural landscapes far from its place of origin in India. It sought to return followers to the pure teachings of the Buddha and to a body of austere practices that stood in contrast to the veneration of bodhisattvas, tantric cults, and worship of god-like Buddhas that had proliferated in the expansive Mahayana Buddhist world of East and Southeast Asia. Beginning around the 1000s, Theravada monks bearing Pali-language sutras brought the new teachings to the lowland kingdoms of the Mons and Burmans, the Thai, Khmer, and Lao. To be sure, Burmese *nat*s and Thai *phi* and other local spirits remained and were folded into the new religious regimen.

In this way, Southeast Asia bifurcated into a Buddhist mainland and a Muslim archipelago with a Buddhist-Muslim cusp in the mid-to-lower Malay Peninsula, where the mandalas of the Buddhist Thai overlapped with the mandalas of the Muslim Malays. Thus, whereas the iconic religious architecture of the mainland became the Buddhist monastery, or *wat*, with monks in saffron or red robes, in the islands it became the mosque. Monarchs now presented themselves as patrons of Buddhism on the mainland and, in much of the island world, as righteous defenders of Islam.

China's sway

The centuries-long practice of borrowing from India and the Middle East prevailed everywhere except Vietnam. Here a different Southeast Asian society emerged under the sway of Asia's other great radiating civilization, China. Indeed, the territorial homeland of the Vietnamese along the lower reaches of the Red River and the Red River delta constituted a colony of the Chinese empire for nearly one thousand years under the Han, Sui, Tang, and intervening dynasties. Under a variety of governing arrangements and patterns of ethnic Chinese in-migration and intermarriage, the society that evolved there embraced many features of Chinese civilization and became, one might say, Chinese-like or Sinicized. So deeply embedded were these influences that even after the kingdom of Vietnam (Dai Viet) wrested its independence from the Tang in 939, the Vietnamese elites who assumed power adopted Chinese institutions of government and continued to revere the religious and philosophical systems that they had made their own.

These systems included Mahayana Buddhism, Daoism, and Confucianism—the three elements of Vietnamese (and Chinese) religion. The Confucian values of social hierarchy, in which children defer to parents, wives to husbands, and so on became deeply embedded and underpinned loyalty to the Vietnamese emperor, who ruled Chinese-style as the Son of Heaven and who performed rituals that mimicked those of the emperor of China. Scholar officials modeled on those of China governed the realm in a pattern quite in contrast with officials and regional powers in the Indianized mandala states. And the affluent and literate classes learned the Chinese language and studied the Chinese classics of statecraft, philosophy, and poetry—indeed, as in China, prospective scholar officials were examined competitively on these subjects to qualify for officialdom.

The Vietnamese possessed a language of their own, but it became one filled with Chinese words; in addition, for many centuries until the modern era it was rendered in Chinese characters. (Just as, for example, Malay was rendered in Arabic letters.) In a process of cultural radiation similar to Southeast Asian Indianized societies, Chinese stories became Vietnamese stories, with a familiar cast of characters. Alongside everyday Buddhist practices, including the veneration of Bodhisattva Kuanyin and Daoist lore, the popular culture of China penetrated the popular culture of the Vietnamese—mingling there with stories and arts and spirits of purely local origins. Indeed, local Vietnamese guardian spirits were among those honored with titles and imperial appointments under the emperor.

Despite the apparent coherence of the Chinese model, the Vietnamese Confucian state was in many ways aspirational and subject to the same forces that underlay the political instability of the mandala world. Periods of fragmentation alternated with periods of consolidation. Regional lords and their clans tested the authority of the Son of Heaven and sometimes usurped central power altogether. There were succession disputes, rebellions, and restive non-Vietnamese hill peoples to be appeased and quieted, not to mention aggressive neighbors such as the Chams. As the Vietnamese expanded southward in the 1400s and subsequent centuries, gradually marginalizing the Chams and penetrating the outer rings of the Khmer mandala in the Mekong Delta, they brought new populations under the sway of their strong culture. This created new fusions of a very Southeast Asian kind.

Even after 939, the Vietnamese had China to contend with. On two major occasions, in 1075–1076 under the new Song dynasty and later under the Mongols (1250 and again in 1278), armies from China invaded Vietnam with the intent of bringing this outlying "province" back into the fold. Vietnam's successful resistance created heroes to be long remembered.

Aside from its legacy in Vietnam, China also intervened periodically in the small non-Chinese border states on the southern tier of their empire—locales that today straddle the Yunnan–Southeast Asia border—that were also linked, mandala fashion, to larger Southeast Asian polities of the Burmans, Thai, and Lao on the mainland. Trade networks, language, and shared customs reinforced their inclinations toward Southeast Asia. In Muong Mau, Muong Laem, Muong Lau, and Sipsongpanna (Xishuangbanna), Chinese dynasties occasionally imposed frontier military administrations but usually ruled the region through elite intermediaries or local lords whose power flowed from their status and followings in their immediate domains. Like cunning mandala operators elsewhere, these men of prowess appear to have bent to China at some times and to neighboring Southeast Asian powers at others, all the while keeping advantageous channels of trade open on both sides.

Aside from these cusp societies, and the anomalous invasion attempts by the Mongols (Yuan dynasty), China did not intervene directly in the mandala world of Southeast Asia. Instead, it managed its relationships with the region's multitude of non-Chinese states through the tributary system. Under the tributary system, rulers of barbarian states—from the vantage point of the civilized Middle Kingdom—were invited to pay their respects to the Chinese emperor by sending embassies bearing gifts. These deferential acts would be reciprocated with more valuable gifts in return. This was, in fact, a form of trade that benefited both parties. Yet as a ritual, the tributary system allowed Southeast Asia's beleaguered mandala kings to claim China as a patron. At one time or another, many did so, including Vietnam, Srivijaya, Melaka, Ayutthaya, Majapahit, Champa, Brunei, and Luzon and even small states such as the tiny gold-rich kingdom of Butuan in Mindanao.

It might have been otherwise. In the early 1400s, as the new Ming dynasty (1368-1644) was flexing its muscles, Emperor Yongle (r. 1402-1424) repeatedly sent huge fleets of massive Chinese ships to Southeast Asia (and well beyond) under the command of Zheng He. In Java, Sumatra, Siam, and Melaka the message was electrifying. Nothing remotely as impressive existed in the region. Zheng He and his retinue collected tribute and established local communities of Chinese merchants and shipbuilders, traded in local products, suppressed pirates, and projected Chinese power. China's support helped establish Melaka as a new commerce-driven mandala center on the Straits.

A new era of engagement was at hand, or so it seemed. But in 1433, a new Chinese emperor canceled the project and placed the Chinese Empire behind a barrier of official isolation that lasted for the next several hundred years (during which, significantly, Chinese merchants based along the empire's southern coast continued to trade privately in Southeast Asia).

Southeast Asia on the verge

China's official withdrawal paved the way for Europe, whose first emissaries began arriving in Southeast Asia in the early 1500s. The mandala world they entered hosted hundreds of small kingdoms and a few large ones. Major states waxed and waned in the predictable verdant spots where fertile river plains facilitated large populations of settled rice growers. Along the Irrawaddy, the post-Pagan mandala center at Ava was rapidly waning in the face of competition from rival mandalas to the south (the Mons) and west (in Rakhine) and of restless vassals among the Shans and others along the Yunnan frontier to the north; by 1527 its capital had fallen. In contrast, in Siam along the Chao Phraya, Ayutthaya was waxing strong as its mandala expanded at the expense of weaker neighbors and engaging dynamically in international trade from its cosmopolitan capital. On Ayutthaya's periphery existed smaller mandala kingdoms based at Chiangmai (La Na) and Luang Prabang (Lan Sang). Khmer kings in the lower Mekong held sway over a much-reduced mandala, a remnant of the former Angkor Empire and one that found itself beleaguered by aggressive neighbors. One of these was Vietnam, also waxing strong and recently victorious over its adversarial neighbors to the south, the Chams, whose capital the Vietnamese seized in 1471.

In the island world, aside from Java, the great maritime mandala of Melaka dominated the zone of the Melaka Straits, including the small riverine kingdoms of Malaya as well as coastal Sumatra and Borneo. Aceh, Makassar, Brunei, Patani, and Bantam hosted powerful small states with mandala-like satellites of their own, outside of which smaller harbor-town, riverine, and island polities prevailed; indeed, they proliferated by the hundreds throughout the Indonesian and Philippine archipelagos. In eastern Indonesia, Ternate and Tidore dominated, and in the Philippine archipelago, small mandala-like thalassocracies orchestrated trade linking Chinese merchants to Southeast Asian maritime networks from bases in Manila and Sulu.

Southeast Asia

Although the core mainland states exhibited a certain level of coherence and permanence, despite more or less constant turbulence in the outer rings of their mandalas, as a whole, the system was inherently unstable. For the Europeans who began arriving in the region in the 1500s, this made establishing a foothold a relatively easy matter.

The arrival of Europeans speaks to yet another aspect of the times: economically, Southeast Asia was dynamic. Beginning around 1400, the region benefited from a confluence of global forces that brought new prosperity to China, India, Europe, and Japan and, in turn, higher levels of trade and prosperity to Southeast Asia. Pepper, cloves, and nutmeg as well as pearls, sandalwood, gems, resins, and delicacies such as birds' nests drove merchants to Southeast Asian ports in ever greater numbers, where they exchanged regional specialties for silks, ceramics, guns, and silver. Silver especially drove the boom as greater and greater quantities arrived in the 1500s from the Spanish Americas and from silver mines in Japan. The new money strengthened mandala centers in both the islands and on the mainland, where states such as Ayutthaya hosted communities of foreign traders at their capitals. Indeed, the region was dotted with emporiums, the richest by far of which was the sultanate of Melaka, whose fame reached far and wide. And so it was that Melaka became the first obvious target when Portuguese conquistadores sailed into the region in 1511 on a mission for gold, God, and glory.

Chapter 3
Colonies

The mandala world of Southeast Asia was fragile, but it was also rich. Merchants from near and far flocked to its markets to gather the region's unique spices such as nutmeg, mace, and cloves as well as black peppercorns, precious woods, resins, and oils. At the major entrepôts such as Melaka, these valuable items were available alongside all the select and commonplace merchandise of Asia, from fine porcelains and silks to everyday tools and pottery. Malay, Bugis, Thai, Filipino, Javanese, and other Southeast Asian merchants managed this trade with great acumen in collaboration and competition with the Indians, Chinese, and Arabs who frequented and often dwelled in the region.

Arab merchants carried Southeast Asian goods to Europe, introducing them into the Mediterranean world, including Venice, through routes that passed through the Persian Gulf and Istanbul. Europeans were drawn to Southeast Asia to gain access to the region's precious goods directly, and in doing so to cut out the Muslims, their great rivals in religion and civilization. The first to do so were the two great Iberian kingdoms of Portugal and Spain, crusading Christian kingdoms that in the 1400s and 1500s roamed the world in their agile sailing ships in search of wealth and glory, both for themselves and for Christendom.

The Portuguese arrived first. Having rounded Africa in 1488, they made quickly for India and Southeast Asia. By 1510 they had established an enclave on the west coast of India at Goa. The following year they captured Melaka, the richest commercial city in Southeast Asia and the center of a powerful Muslim mandala that controlled the Straits. They built a walled city there, with churches and convents, and began acquiring the valuable spices directly at the source in Ambon, Ternate, and Banda.

Spain came from the other side of the world, reaching the Philippine islands from across the Pacific Ocean in Mexico, which they seized from the Aztecs in 1521. In that same year Magellan, a Portuguese explorer sponsored by Spain, reached the islands and claimed them for Spain. (He was subsequently killed there.) After a few further probes, Spain established a permanent beachhead at Manila in 1571 by displacing a local Muslim sultan and building a huge walled city called Intramuros.

For a time Portugal grew rich at home on the basis of its Asia trade far away, which also penetrated China and Japan. Both Portugal and Spain sought to spread the "one true religion" among their subjects and other Asians, namely Roman Catholicism. But whereas Portugal contented itself with a string of commercial outposts and towns—of which Melaka was one of many, including Goa, Ceylon, East Timor, Macao, and Nagasaki—Spanish conquistadores claimed the entire archipelago for their king and named it after him: Las Philipinas. Subsequently, they subjugated all but the southernmost lowland peoples of the Philippines and, in not so long a time, converted them to Christianity, or at least to its outward forms.

The agents of this great cultural transformation were members of religious brotherhoods (Jesuits, Augustinians, Dominicans, Franciscans, and others), missionary monks, or friars, who fanned throughout the islands bearing the Christian doctrine in vernacular languages, building magnificent churches, and also acting as the eyes and ears of Spain's imperial officialdom. In the ensuing centuries, Spain strove to resettle lowland Filipinos within the sound of the church bells and to build church-centered urban communities throughout the islands, complete with plazas, civic buildings, and the homes of local notables—in most cases the descendants of former datus and their families, leading clans of pre-Spanish days who remained elite and influential under the Spanish as Catholic Indios, or Natives.

The friars and other Spaniards grabbed much of the best land for themselves but they also brought to the islands the civilization of Europe. They established schools and universities. (The college that became the University of Santo Tomas was founded in 1611, twenty-five years before Harvard.) And they introduced their language. Only an elite few among Spain's subjects learned Spanish properly, but untold numbers of Spanish words shifted into the vernacular languages of the islands and remain there today. It was also aboard Spanish boats that plied annually between Acapulco and Manila, the famous Manila galleons, that a great many new plants reached Asia from the Americas. These included maize, tobacco, pineapples, potatoes, tomatoes, and chili peppers. (Bananas, papaya, and mangoes sailed the other way.)

Spain's influence was profound but not total. Aside from the friars, very few Spanish people actually lived in the far-flung colony. Most who did tended to cluster in Intramuros at Manila, the center of government and Spanish life with a host of churches, convents, schools, and business houses and the homes of Spanish colonists. A scattering of Spanish officials were posted around the islands—as provincial governors, for example—but most day-to-day administration below the provincial level was carried out by elite Indios who occupied tiers of public offices in districts and towns, where they were chosen by their male peers and vetted by the Spanish priest.

In a pattern already familiar to the region, Filipinos became Christians and celebrated Christmas and Easter and the feast days of their adopted patron saints without wholly abandoning their belief in spirits; ancient spiritual anxieties and practices remained. Spain's reach was also geographically limited. It ended where the hills began and in the southern islands where Islam and a clutch of small mandala-style sultanates were rooted. Hill peoples and Muslims thus remained largely outside the colony's Hispanicizing pull. Still, Las Philipinas was an entirely new entity in Southeast Asia, one with a remarkable legacy.

Portugal's legacy is small by comparison. Although it permanently disrupted Melaka's mandala, it did not establish a landed empire in its place. Instead, it contained its political presence within the enclave itself, which became an essential hub in its operations throughout Asia. Under Portugal, Melaka became a learning and propagation center for Christianity, too. The great Jesuit missionary Francis Xavier was active there. Eventually, however, it was overtaken by aggressive newcomers; the Dutch seized it in 1641. The Portuguese left behind a tiny, neglected outpost in East Timor (until 1975!) and a legacy of cultural artifacts such as Portuguese words (the Malay words for table and shoes, for example), musical instruments, and melodic tunes. Otherwise, they changed Southeast Asia very little.

Arrival of the companies

The Netherlands, however, reshaped the region fundamentally. Its early agents in Southeast Asia were not servants of a crown, as the Portuguese and Spanish had been, but servants of a company, the Dutch East India Company, or VOC as its soon-to-be-global brand identified it. Capitalized in the Low Countries and chartered by the Republic of the United Provinces in 1602, the VOC carried forward Dutch probes into Southeast Asia that had begun in the late 1500s. Like the Iberians before them, the Dutch sought direct access to the region's profitable and unique spices.

The VOC's charter gave it a monopoly of trade in Asia and the authority to wage war, enter into treaties, collect taxes, and occupy

6. The configuration of islands comprising *"las yslas Philipinas"* was new and created wholly by Spain.

and govern territories. The small mandala kingdoms that dotted Southeast Asia's shallow seas became stepping stones for the Dutch as they penetrated the region, port by port. By 1619 they had established a walled-in enclave and hub city on the northwest coast of Java at Jakarta (which they called Batavia). In Maluku, they muscled aside the Portuguese, Spanish, and English to monopolize the nutmeg, mace, and clove trade. The process was savage. In the 1600s, agents of the company expelled or murdered indigenous local producers and confined the production of the spices to certain islands, destroying trees they could not control. In Amsterdam, the value of cloves and other spices soared.

The VOC's hub at Batavia lay on the outer fringes of a great mandala ruled by Sultan Agung, the king of Mataram on Java. Sultan Agung's armies attacked the Dutch entrepôt in 1628 and 1629 but failed to remove it. Instead, in the years and decades to come, the company expanded its presence on the island as the kingdom fell into disorder, peeling off key territories in the outer mandala such as the island's mercantile coastal cities and intervening in succession disputes and other power struggles, often in alliance with local actors. Java's kings were irreparably weakened as their mandalas grew smaller and smaller. By the 1750s the company was utterly dominant. Java's kings and princes had been subordinated to a new Dutch colonial state. The tiny kingdoms of central Java that remained with their royal capitals in Yogyakarta and Surakarta now existed wholly at Dutch discretion.

The Dutch East India Company ruled a vast population of Natives, or Inlanders (as indigenous people were now officially designated). Being parsimonious, it employed only a skeleton staff of white Dutch administrators to manage its colony. Instead, like the Spanish in the nearby Philippines, it incorporated elite local families into its system as administrators. For centuries, Javanese aristocrats, the *priyayi*, had served the island's kings as local lords of the realm, rendering their services and loyalty to kings as determined by the shifting variables of the island's mandalas.

Now, by and large, they served the Dutch; even so, they remained locally prominent and even revered as bearers of Java's high culture and reminders of its rich history.

Unlike elite Filipinos under Spain, the Javanese priyayi did not assimilate to the Dutch religion, nor did Java's common people. The VOC had little interest in promoting Christianity and permitted only a modicum of missionary activity. Nor was it interested in advancing Dutch civilization to Natives. There were no universities in Dutch Java (and no schools of law or engineering until the 1920s). As a result, the dominant culture of Java and its subcultures across the island continued to advance in the deep riverbed already established, in which Islam was the hegemonic religious culture and in which the civilization's Hindu-Buddhist and animist roots endured and evolved.

On the last day of 1799, the Dutch East India Company collapsed under the weight of its accumulated corruption and debts. Its assets and territories were assumed by the Dutch state. By this time, the Netherlands controlled multiple territories in Southeast Asia, including, aside from Java, the spice islands of Maluku and the once-great port city of Melaka. Moreover, its dominant role in maritime trade had subordinated once far-reaching indigenous seafaring traders to the lower tiers of its regional supply chain.

By this time, England had also acquired an entrepôt along the Melaka Straits at Penang, where the sultan of Kedah, a small Malay kingdom, sought protection from the expanding Thai mandala of the nascent Chakri kings to his north by entering into a deal with the English East India Company (EIC) in 1786. The Thais swallowed him up anyway, in 1821, but Penang remained British. Britain also acquired a sleepy outpost at Bengkulu along Sumatra's southwest coast.

In the unstable mandala world of Southeast Asia, Europeans had clear advantages. Europeans had surpassed Asians in matters of shipbuilding, navigation, and mapping. They were propelled by Europe's surging commercial and proto-industrial economy. And their firearms were consistently superior to those of Southeast Asia's many kings (who purchased guns avidly on the emerging global arms market.) More importantly, global empires such as those of Spain and Portugal and the era's huge chartered companies had developed the capacity to mobilize resources and to project power across great distances—a huge advantage even though much could be lost in transmission between Europe and Asia.

To Southeast Asian actors who encountered them on the spot, the links between the officials of the VOC and the English East India Company and the vast matrixes that supported them were invisible, if not incomprehensible. Southeast Asian rulers, large and small, appear to have viewed the Europeans as powerful players acting within the well-understood dynamics of their own mandala world. Depending on the circumstances, they could be either allies or enemies—as in fact, they clearly were with each other.

The establishment of many Western footholds at Melaka, on Java, and in the Philippines opened doors for European newcomers of all nationalities to make their fortunes privately in the region. Southeast Asian rulers engaged with them opportunistically, buying guns and opium from them and enlisting their services as mercenaries and as advisers and intermediaries just as, in earlier centuries, they had welcomed sojourning brahmins and wandering Sufis to their courts. (In seventeenth-century Ayutthaya— to cite a famous example—an enterprising Greek adventurer named Constantine Phaulkon rose to be a titled counselor under King Narai.)

By 1800, the European presence in Southeast Asia was large but far from dominating. Up to this point, Europeans had not yet breached the mainland. Here the kings of the Konbaung and Chakri dynasties were vigorously expanding their mandalas in Burma and Siam. Vietnam was reaching the end of a long civil war and on the brink of a strong new dynasty, the Nguyen, which was proclaimed by Emperor Gia Long in 1802. Smaller mandala kingdoms proliferated on the fringes of these large states (in Cambodia, Laos, and elsewhere along the Yunnan cusp).

In the islands, despite the maritime supremacy of the Netherlands and its domination of Java and the long-evolving hold of Spain over the northern and central islands of the Philippine archipelago, hundreds of small autonomous kingdoms and mini-states dotted the region's sprawling array of land and water. In this complex mosaic, legions of Southeast Asians still lived under the authority of their own indigenous kings while legions of others were evolving in new directions as subjects of European colonies.

Momentum favored the Europeans. Britain had long harbored ambitions in Southeast Asia but had been bested by the VOC in the early 1600s and retreated to India. By the late 1700s, through the agency of the EIC (English East India Company), a chartered company much like the VOC, it had utterly subverted the huge crumbling mandala of India's Mughal dynasty and established hegemonic control over the subcontinent. Its new probes into Southeast Asia led to the temporary occupation of Spanish Manila between 1762 and 1764 and soon yielded the Melaka Straits colony of Penang in 1789, cunningly wrested from the sultan of Kedah. In the following decades the EIC moved aggressively to expand its presence, seizing upon the opportunity of the Napoleonic Wars to grab Java from the Netherlands for four years (1812 to 1816)— returning it after the Congress of Vienna—and subsequently establishing a second Straits entrepôt at Singapore in 1819.

By design, Penang and Singapore attracted large numbers of Chinese migrants, who became the majority populations of these British-run trade hubs. In an 1824 treaty, Britain secured its supremacy over the Melaka Straits by acquiring Melaka itself from the Netherlands, swapping it for its slumbering outpost at

Bengkulu in Sumatra. The Straits now demarcated British and Dutch spheres of influence, that is, territories in which each power would be free to expand without interference from the other. This was a harbinger of things to come.

The nineteenth-century onslaught

By the early twentieth century, the colonial spheres of the Netherlands and Great Britain had expanded dramatically and both France and the United States had also seized colonial territories in Southeast Asia. Indeed, by this time, only one of the region's hundreds of mandala kingdoms had survived. The rest, large and small, had all been subsumed within the vast empires of the world's Western powers. This onslaught unfolded rapidly in the nineteenth century in a process that revealed both the competitive ambitions and the strengths of the West's rising industrial states and the inherent weaknesses of Southeast Asia's mandala kingdoms.

Britain's huge colony in India included Bengal, which lay adjacent to territories that figured in the outer circles of Burma's large mandala—territories into which the armies of the Konbaung kings were expanding violently in the late 1700s and early 1800s. The resulting rebellions and flows of refugees into British territory led to conflicts between the kingdom and the EIC. Burma's kings, flush from recent victories against China, badly underestimated their new foe. Britain's successful invasion by steamship up the Irrawaddy River led to a treaty in 1826 in which King Bagyidaw (r. 1819–1837) lost large portions of his outer mandala (in Tenasserim, Arakan, Manipur, and Assam) and also forced open the kingdom to Western trade and other influences through the Irrawaddy port city of Rangoon.

These events set the stage for further conflicts that resulted again in British invasions, in the 1850s and 1880s. The first resulted in the loss of "lower Burma," the southern half of the kingdom's mandala, and the second in the conquest of the mandala center at Mandalay. By 1886 Britain had abolished the Burmese monarchy, exiled the king and queen, and annexed the territories of the entire kingdom to British India, including many non-Burman territories of groups such as the Shan, Kachin, and Karen.

These episodes of conquest paralleled the penetration of Burma by floods of new capital and enterprises, especially in the Burma delta after Britain seized it in the 1850s; opened it to migrants from northern Burma, India, and China; and introduced its rice to world markets. By 1910, Burma was the largest exporter of rice in the world.

Similar economic forces were in play elsewhere in Britain's "sphere." Its Melaka Straits enclaves at Penang, Melaka, and Singapore—collectively, the Straits Settlements—lay alongside a collection of small Malay Muslim kingdoms on the Malay Peninsula. Before the Portuguese conquest, these river-based sultanates had been part of Melaka's great mandala. Now four of them, including Kedah, formed the lower tier of Siam's huge mandala under the Chakri dynasty. The rest were autonomous under their sultans and many titled nobles and chiefs.

Like most small kingdoms of the mandala world, the Malay states had long engaged in external trade, yielding valuable upriver products such as rattan and resins to markets beyond. And a few, Perak and Selangor in particular, hosted tin mines. Britain's new commerce-driven settlements along the coast became conduits for British investments and migrating Chinese merchants and workers into the kingdoms. As the global demand for tin rose, new capital and technologies were introduced. Mining camps with large numbers of Chinese men mushroomed into frontier boomtowns, where institutions such as secret societies arose to meet pressing social needs and to compete for the profits of labor recruiting, gambling, prostitution, and opium.

These dynamic new forces disrupted the stability of the small Malay kingdoms, several of which fell into disorder as secret society gang wars conflated with succession disputes and other mandala-like power struggles. Eventually, the mayhem spread into the Straits Settlements themselves. In 1874, Britain took action. (The English East India Company had been nationalized in 1858.) Beginning in Perak and subsequently in the other states, Britain seized control of the sultanates (in places, militarily) by placing British "residents" in charge of the territories' worldly management and allocating "religion and customs of the Malays" to the sultans, who now became British clients living in vastly improved palaces.

Although the particulars varied, this was the guiding concept of British Malaya, which by 1909 encompassed all nine of the sultanates, including Kedah and the others that King Chulalongkorn of Siam ceded to Britain in that year. Builders of the British Empire at the time spoke of a civilizing mission. One of them, Frank Swettenham, wrote, "Time means progress and expansion for all that part of Malaya which comes under British influence." Even so, he said, "the Malays are the people of the country." We have made their interests "our first consideration."

As these events transpired in the Malay Peninsula, other British actors carved out colonial territories in northern Borneo. These included the swashbuckling James Brooke, who, beginning in 1841, peeled off one outlying territory after another of the sultan of Brunei's mandala until his own private kingdom, Sarawak, controlled all but a tiny remnant at the capital. In 1888, the much-diminished sultan applied for British "protection." Secure within the sway of the British imperial navy, Brooke and his successors ruled Sarawak as white rajas until World War II.

Meanwhile, in 1881 an agribusiness company chartered in England with interests in timber, copra, and other tropical commodities acquired a vast territory in the northeast of Borneo from both the sultan of Brunei and the sultan of Sulu, each of whom claimed it as part of their overlapping mandalas. The

British North Borneo Company held the territory, now the Malaysian state of Sabah, for fifty-nine years. Thus, Sarawak, North Borneo, and the sultanate of Brunei all came under European sway by the early twentieth century.

During the same years in which Britain advanced upon Burma, Malaya, and nearby territories, the Netherlands moved forth from its stronghold on Java into the rest of the Indonesian archipelago. This staggering undertaking of the nineteenth century involved untold acts of diplomacy, threat, marauding, and outright war during which literally hundreds of small kingdoms were first subordinated to the hegemonic power of the Dutch and finally subjugated altogether. From the Dutch perspective, the autonomous mini-kingdoms of the archipelago—as well as larger and stronger ones in Aceh, Bali, and Makassar—represented territorial loose ends and openings for other European interlopers (such as privateers like James Brooke). As enclaves where contraband guns and opium were traded and where rebels and pirates could find sanctuary, they threatened Dutch *rust en orde* (calm and order).

The Dutch astutely took advantage of the big fish–small fish nature of the mandala world by guaranteeing the territories of this particular raja or that in return for deference and trade monopolies—often specified in long treaties. Mini-kings found this advantageous. Joseph Conrad remarks of one Malay chief of the 1880s (in *Outcast of the Islands*) that he sought to "apply to the Orang Blanda [the Dutch] for a flag, for that protection which would make them safe forever!"

But where sultans and rajas refused to be pliant and where local civil wars and other disruptions threatened, the Dutch were more than willing to go to war. They did so brutally against independent communities of Chinese gold miners in Borneo, against Wahabist Islamic reformers in Sumatra, against the powerful sultanate of Aceh, and, finally, against the two remaining independent kingdoms of Bali, whose kings and noble families, acknowledging defeat, committed ritual suicide as colonial soldiers closed in firing. Eventually, the Dutch replaced all the long treaties with short ones in which once-deferential allies became subjects. By the early twentieth century, the Dutch East Indies was complete, the most massive colony in all Southeast Asia.

As for France, its imperial ambitions had long been in play in the Americas and in India. French missionaries had also been among the first in Asia. One of them, Alexandre de Rhodes, a Jesuit, made early inroads in Vietnam, where in the 1600s he invented a roman letter–based system for writing Vietnamese to replace or complement the use of Chinese characters. In 1658, Rhodes initiated a French missionary society dedicated to proselytizing in Asia. Two centuries later, another French Jesuit, Pigneau de Béhaine, actively aided Nguyen Anh in the civil war that resulted in his elevation to become Emperor Gia Long and founder of the new Nguyen dynasty in 1802. By this time there were some three hundred thousand Vietnamese Catholics.

The growth of Catholicism in the years that followed led to harsh repression by the kingdom's Confucian mandarins and kings, and the action served as the official provocation for French intervention. Gunboat attacks began in 1858, and by 1867 France had established a full-fledged colony in southern Vietnam. Subsequent events revealed the degree to which French imperialists were also motivated by the desire to open Vietnam's commercial ports and to use Vietnam as a gateway to rich markets in China. In a sequence of defeats, Vietnam's kings relinquished the kingdom's sovereignty step by step until, in 1885, following a war in which Chinese armies failed to defend the kingdom, France claimed the entire state. The colony was divided into three parts: Tonkin, Annam, and Cochinchina—all governed somewhat differently. In Annam, a Nguyen puppet monarch remained. But there was no question: Vietnam was a French colony.

Meanwhile, in 1863, King Norodom of Cambodia, witnessing French victories in nearby Vietnam (his mandala enemy to the east) and facing encroachments by Siam (his mandala enemy to the west), placed his beleaguered kingdom under French protection. Likewise, in 1893, the princes of a cluster of tiny Lao polities caught in the mandala cusp between Siam and Vietnam were also persuaded to join Cambodia and Vietnam as constituent members of French Indochina.

By the 1890s, the Philippines had evolved under Spanish rule for three centuries. A mature Hispanicized society had formed, and within it a passionate anti-Spanish anger among some members of the colony's elite intelligentsia and urban dwellers. The revolution they launched in 1896 was the first of its kind anywhere in Southeast Asia. After it foundered, an improbable sequence of events involving Cuba drew the United States to the islands. In an imperial conflict with Spain, the United States at first embraced and then betrayed the Filipino republican revolutionaries and seized the Philippines for itself. When Filipinos resisted, another brutal colonial conquest followed and the United States became the final Western power to claim a vast body of Southeast Asian subjects.

The colonies of Southeast Asia were complete. Of the region's indigenous kingdoms, only Siam survived. This remarkable feat was the consequence of astute leadership. In many ways, the Chakri kings were classical mandala monarchs. They rose to power following the defeat by Burma of the former Thai dynasty at Ayutthaya. Having established a new capital at Bangkok, the Chakris advanced aggressively upon the outer fringes of the kingdom, claiming large numbers of subjects under their sway. These included Lao princes to the northeast, hill peoples in the uplands of the north, Khmer territories in Siem Reap and Battambang, and the four Malay kingdoms of Kedah, Perlis, Kelantan, and Trengannu in the far south. They differed, however, in their response to the European threat.

Rama IV, or Mongkut (1851–1868), was a well-educated polymath who studied Latin and English. He befriended Westerners who arrived in Bangkok and learned from them. He read newspapers from the British Straits Settlements. He knew what was happening in Burma and other parts of the region. By the time he became king in 1851 he was better prepared than any other Southeast Asian king to grasp the nature of the dangers his kingdom faced. Instead of resisting the demands of the West, he made deft concessions to Westerners, beginning with the British in 1855. When they asked to trade freely in the kingdom, he granted it. When they insisted on importing opium, he agreed. An ambassador in the capital? Extraterritorial rights for British subjects? Agreed and agreed. And so on. Mongkut granted the same rights to a queue of other powers, too.

Meanwhile, Mongkut and his son and successor Rama V, Chulalongkorn (1868–1910), made sure that Siam did not descend into the kind of disorder that encouraged foreigners to intervene, discerning astutely that Britain and France, the European powers advancing on the mainland, might find it useful to maintain a stable buffer between their zones of expansion in Burma and Indochina. Father and son embarked on an all-out project of self-strengthening, bringing in a slew of Western advisers, adopting Western models of governance, and educating young Thai elites, including their own children, in Western languages and knowledge. As the Thai state grew stronger, its mandala grew smaller. Chulalongkorn bowed to imperial pressures and ceded territories to France in Laos and Cambodia and to Britain in Malaya. But the kingdom itself survived, even as its rulers transformed it to resemble the Western colonial states that dominated the rest of the region. Thai monarchs were not unique among Southeast Asian kings in executing self-strengthening strategies to stave off the West. They were unique in succeeding.

High colonialism in Southeast Asia

By the late nineteenth century, Southeast Asia was no longer a mosaic of colonial territories and mandalas. Aside from Siam, Western colonies wholly dominated the region. It was a period of almost total white supremacy. As political projections from Europe and the United States, the Southeast Asian colonies illustrated Karl Marx's 1848 prediction in the *Communist Manifesto* that the Western bourgeoisie would "create a world after its own image." In this the Western colonies did not utterly succeed. But they changed Southeast Asia profoundly.

Colonial states such as the Dutch East Indies, British Burma, and the American Philippines were not mandala states. Their borders were fixed on maps, surveyed, and monitored. In the islands, the British and Dutch marked their coastlines with lighthouses and patrolled them with marine police. Colonial administrators endeavored to fill in the state's once-vague edges with an apparatus of power so that, now, there actually was a place—a line—at which the authority of one colony stopped and that of another one began. In practice, these borders were notoriously porous where smuggling, trafficking, and migration was concerned. But they were understood to exist and to demarcate fully bounded states. This included Siam, too, as one of the many adjustments to life in a neighborhood of European powers entailed fixing its borders.

These new states were governed, at the senior level, by white officials sent from Europe and employed in increasingly specialized bureaucracies. The most senior official was ordinarily a governor-general who, following the collapse of the East India companies, reported to a senior minister at home, usually a minister of colonies (but in the United States the secretary of war). These ministers reported, in turn, to their prime ministers and were also called upon to testify before parliament or congress, one of the great ironies of the era being that the colonial powers of Southeast Asia were all democracies.

Metropolitan control also determined the nature of the colonial states' relationships to each other. In the mandala world, neighbors were enemies. In the colonial world the relationship between, say,

British Malaya and the Dutch East Indies was fixed in Europe. If Britain and the Netherlands were on good terms at home, they also strove to cooperate in Southeast Asia, despite aggressive economic competition.

Generally speaking, colonial policies were established in the metropolitan centers and executed in the colonies. Great debates occurred on colonial issues in London, Paris, and the Hague. In fact, however, white colonial officials located on the ground in Southeast Asia were powerful. The governor-general of the Dutch East Indies ruled a territory forty-three times larger than the Netherlands itself. Provincial governors and district officers often had omnibus responsibilities for governing large numbers of subjects and for supervising the projects of the colonial state.

This was possible because beneath the top—the white tiers of colonial administrations—stood tiers and tiers of Southeast Asians who performed the day-to-day work of governance. They included district-level administrators recruited from indigenous elites and aristocracies as well as tax collectors and police and office clerks and, in the twentieth century, modern specialists such as surveyors, paramedics, foresters, and school teachers. With rare exceptions, only the officers of colonial armies were British, French, Dutch, and American (or other European ethnicity); the rank and file were generally made up of Native minorities.

In the colonies small white heads rested upon large Native bodies. This explains how such a small number of Europeans and Americans managed to dominate and govern Southeast Asian populations so much larger than their own numbers. In the Dutch East Indies at the peak of Dutch power in 1930, there were 250 Natives for every European (a census category that included Eurasians, Turks, Filipinos, and Japanese). In French Indochina the figure was 665. The superiority of whites was often fixed in colonial law codes and was universally understood. The protocols of colonial social life made this clear as retinues of Southeast Asian servants now served in white households as nannies, cooks, sweepers, launderers, gardeners, and drivers. In the rijsttafel (rice table smorgasbord) of Dutch Java, a dozen Native waiters stood in line to serve a single white diner.

In the early centuries of European and Southeast Asian interaction, intermarriage across status and color lines was common; in places, large and prominent mestizo clans emerged. But in the age of high colonialism in the late nineteenth and early twentieth centuries, children of mixed race made for awkward accommodations. Depending upon the status and legal initiatives of the parents, some were elevated into the ruling class, others became Natives. In mature colonies, stable social categories formed in which Eurasians were explicitly identified, as in the Spanish mestizos of the Philippines. Among the "pure" whites, demeaning stigmas usually applied. (Anxieties surrounding persons of mixed race are frequently depicted in stories of the times by Western authors such as George Orwell, Somerset Maugham, Louis Couperus, and Marguerite Duras.)

7. In the rijsttafel of Dutch Java, a dozen Native waiters stood in line to serve a single white diner. As a contemporary Jakarta advertisement reveals, these days everyone is welcome to enjoy the rijsttafel.

One of the great underlying purposes of the high colonial states was to draw an ever-escalating quantity of Southeast Asian resources to the West's hungry economies. The colonial states and Western capitalists took advantage of their overwhelming power to develop the region as a major global base of industrial-scale agribusiness and resource extraction. The Dutch began exporting large quantities of coffee, tea, and sugar after 1830 through a state-led system of forced cultivation. By the late nineteenth century, however, private plantations were the norm. Everywhere in Southeast Asia great swaths of land were opened to grow coffee, tea, and sugar as well as tobacco, palm oil, abaca, and rubber. Southeast Asians became menial wage laborers as plantation workers—planting, tending, and tapping rubber trees; picking tea leaves; cutting cane and working under the eyes of white European overseers and ultimately for large agribusiness companies such as Michelin (rubber), Dole (fruits), and Schimmelpenninck (tobacco).

In the Philippines, great sugar haciendas arose in Luzon and the Visayas. Mining companies flourished throughout the colonial world, yielding Malayan tin, Philippine gold, Vietnamese coal, and Burmese gems to global markets alongside petroleum from Burma, Sumatra, and Borneo. Royal Dutch Shell dominated oil production in the Dutch East Indies. Facilitating the movement of these commodities were new steamship lines, roads and railroads, and harbors. At the intersections of the new traffic patterns linking commodities to markets appeared bustling new towns, hubs of dynamic exchange that attracted merchants, artisans, and workers of all kinds. At the same time, the region's larger cities blossomed into major international trade hubs and colonial administrative centers, spreading beyond their historical cores into new suburbs and satellite towns: Manila, Saigon, Singapore, Batavia, Rangoon.

Populations soared during the period, and they also spread out. Responding to the opportunities and pressures of the colonial economies, indigenous Southeast Asians shifted to the new plantation zones for wage work, sometimes as indentured laborers. (Slavery was now forbidden in the colonies and also in Siam.) They also swept out of population-pressed home territories into large fertile spaces of as-yet-unopened land in places such as the southern delta lands of Burma and Vietnam and the Luzon plains, to grow wet rice for the market. Many prospered as farmers and cash-crop producers and also learned the hard lessons of the global economy when commodity prices plummeted.

As the region's remaining forests and swamps were cleared to make way for plantations and homesteading farmers, and as the land filled with people, primordial ecological equations began to shift, a process exacerbated by logging and mining in the forested hills. Animal and plant habitats diminished. By the end of the colonial era, Southeast Asia's environment had been almost wholly reshaped by humans.

Newcomers from China

Southeast Asia's age of colonies also brought legions of newcomers from China. Chinese merchants had traversed the region for centuries, and permanent settlements of Chinese had long existed in many Southeast Asian cities. But now the numbers increased dramatically. Pushed by dearth and disorder in China and pulled by Southeast Asia's burgeoning colonial economy, poor Chinese men by the hundreds of thousands fled China to find work and opportunity in the British, French, Dutch, and Spanish/American colonies—indeed everywhere in the region, including Thailand.

Many Chinese men came as menial coolies and did the dirty work of tin and gold mining, of lifting and loading at the wharves, and of sweeping and cleaning. Others found work in the businesses of already established Chinese migrants and became tinkers and tailors and carpenters and itinerant peddlers of consumer merchandise. Some started multipurpose shops and began to collect the local vegetables, fruits, and eggs of local farmers in exchange for credit to buy seeds, tools, carts, and draft animals. Chinese shops like these proliferated.

In time, small Chinese businesses became larger Chinese businesses. Carpenters and masons became contractors. Shopkeepers became moneylenders and bankers. Entrepreneurs became tycoons. By the early twentieth century, every colony had produced Chinese businessmen of immense fortune and influence. More significantly, in virtually every colony the Chinese had come to occupy the essential urban middle echelons of the regional economies. From whom could you buy a pair of scissors, mops, watering cans, pots, and pans? Gold and silver jewelry? A time piece, a bicycle, a water pump? Who could organize a work crew to move cane from the fields to the mill? To build a house? A church? To whom could you sell surplus rice, eggs, and fruit or rattan, resins, and honey collected from the forest? In most places and cases, by the early twentieth century in Southeast Asia, the answers to these questions involved someone of Chinese descent.

8. In the age of colonies, hundreds of thousands of men fled China to find opportunity in Southeast Asia. Migrants such as these pose for a photograph around 1890 in Dutch Borneo.

The impact of these migrations from China was uneven. Far greater numbers, relative to local populations, amassed in British Penang and Singapore and in the British Malay States, where the Chinese population rose to half the total and more. But all Southeast Asian cities now had substantial Chinatowns and the colonies and Thailand had large numbers of Chinese residents, from 2 to 4 percent in the Dutch East Indies and French Indochina to 10 to 12 percent in Thailand and the Philippines. Burma was an exception in the sense that it also drew large numbers of migrants from India, as did Malaya, Penang, and Singapore to a lesser degree.

The European regimes in Southeast Asia found the hardworking, money-savvy Chinese useful. Until the late nineteenth century, the British, Dutch, and French relied on them as revenue farmers who paid for the privilege of selling opium and collecting tolls. But they feared them, too. In most colonies Chinese were forbidden to buy agricultural land and confined to urban areas and urban occupations. There were periodic crackdowns (and in earlier centuries anti-Chinese massacres in Manila and Batavia). As the numbers of Chinese rose, so did talk of the Yellow Peril. For indigenous Southeast Asians the Chinese were also problematic. As suppliers of goods and credit, they were welcome; but as debt collectors and marketplace tricksters (a common stereotype), they were mistrusted and despised. The king of Siam, Vajiravudh, Chulalongkorn's Oxford-educated son, famously published an anti-Chinese pamphlet in 1914. Despite some intermarriage and assimilation, this ambivalence became rooted in Southeast Asia's new plural societies as they evolved toward the present.

New borrowings

These powerful changes in the economy, demography, and social composition of Southeast Asia during the age of colonies was accompanied by equally profound cultural changes. In a new wave of borrowing and adapting that mirrored the earlier periods of

Indianization and Islamization, Southeast Asians now encountered, and selectively embraced, the West.

White colonizers disagreed about whether it was a good idea to educate Natives as Westerners. The civilizing mission—creating a world after the West's own image—was complicated by racism. The idea, for example, of Burmese and Indonesians and Vietnamese mimicking the British, French, and Dutch was not all that attractive to many colonial whites. In most Southeast Asian colonies, Western education, that is, education in Western languages following a Western school curriculum, was strictly limited to Native elites and certain other well-to-do subjects. Some schools were designed to train Native officials in Western bureaucratic practices. For everyone else, the regimes offered a modicum of vernacular-language primary education, the quality and availability of which varied widely. (In British Burma in the 1920s only 4 percent of Native children advanced beyond grade four.) In places, missionary schools offered an alternative to this pattern. In the Philippines, American colonizers applied models of "industrial education" designed for racial minorities (e.g., at the Tuskegee Institute in Alabama) and introduced English-language education at a popular level, although in practice not universally.

Generally speaking, only a tiny handful of Southeast Asians were offered Western educations, and fewer still, university or professional-level degrees. As the colonial era matured, the Western regimes opened new slightly more advanced schools for health workers, surveyors, and teachers. Graduates of these schools formed the basis of a nascent professional middle class, part of a rising tide of people literate in the vernacular languages and the region's first true generation of readers.

As a small few learned English, French, and Dutch, words from these languages flooded into Southeast Asian vernacular languages, just as Sanskrit, Arabic, and Chinese words had done in earlier periods. English words now punctuated colloquial

Burmese, Malay, and Tagalog. French words became Vietnamese words. In the Dutch East Indies, people now went to the *bioskoop* and enjoyed *pikus-nikus* and *dansa-dansi*. They took photographs with a *kodak* and used Dutch words for car parts such as clutch, gears, and mufflers. (They still do.) Filipinos put food in the "fridge."

It was largely through the vernacular-language press that Southeast Asians learned of the wider world. Newspapers and magazines catering to the region's rising class of literates featured stories from the world round—revolution in China, war in Europe, radical reforms in Muslim Turkey under Kemal Atatürk. Southeast Asians read Western books in translation (*The Three Musketeers!*) and avidly watched European and American movies. Western popular music also swept into the region and already in the 1920s and 1930s there were local Southeast Asian versions of Western band music and jazz.

Likewise, urban Southeast Asian men began wearing jackets and trousers and Panama hats; women adopted skirts and dresses and coiffed their hair Hollywood-style and tried lipstick and rouge. Despite some disapproval, this was true of many urban Southeast Asians and their elites and also of the region's now-large population of Chinese. Family photographs of the period document these changes vividly.

More profoundly, both through the elite Western-language educations of the few and the mass vernacular learning of the many, a body of new ideas entered Southeast Asia. These included the fundamentals of Western science, geography, and economics; popular theories, including social Darwinism; and biographies of historical figures such as George Washington. By the 1920s, new political ideas such as democracy, socialism, and communism were the subjects of passionate popular discussion, debate, and action. The civilizing mission of colonialism thus bore within it the seeds of its own destruction.

The high point of Western colonialism occurred in the early twentieth century. This is when Western rule seemed permanently secure. (Keep in mind that Asia's own great radiating civilizations were both deeply compromised at the time—India as a colony of Britain and China undergoing a tumultuous political revolution.) But World War I weakened the Western powers and new political ideas and movements began to undermine their empires from the inside. By the 1930s, all of Asia and Southeast Asia was astir with nationalism.

The colonial powers reacted differently. Britain, faced with a sophisticated nationalist movement in India, yielded to nationalists in Burma by granting a high degree of home rule that involved an elected Burmese government and prime minister by the late 1930s. The United States also promised home rule in the Philippines. Under the Commonwealth of the Philippines of 1935, Filipinos wrote their own constitution and elected the entire national government and a president.

France and the Netherlands were much less willing to ease their colonies toward home rule. Despite permitting certain elected councils and elite collaborative bodies, they found it harder to consider the end of empire. In 1931, Bonifacius Cornelis de Jonge, governor-general of the Dutch East Indies, predicted confidently that the Netherlands would remain in the Indies for another three hundred years. The following year, Pierre Pasquier, governor-general of French Indochina, predicted that, in Vietnam, France could look forward to "the flowering and the expansion of one of the most beautiful branches that has sprouted from her genius."

However, nationalism and Japanese imperial armies changed everything. And sooner than anyone expected, Southeast Asia's colonies became nations.

Chapter 4
Nations

Most of Southeast Asia's colonies had been created by conquest and coercion. European rule was not welcome. Almost everywhere, Southeast Asians attempted to fend it off in every way possible. The sultan of Melaka rallied allies from neighboring states to drive away the Portuguese. Sultan Agung launched huge assaults against the Dutch fortress at Batavia. Burmese and Vietnamese kings went to war to save their kingdoms from the British and the French. And so it went across the region in encounters large and small.

The odds were against them, given the overpowering edge possessed by Europeans in weaponry and the logistics of wielding power. Even so, the sultanate of Aceh kept the Dutch at bay for thirty years. And elsewhere violent resistance made colonial conquests expensive and painful for advancing Westerners. (Referring to the British conquest of Burma, Kipling wrote of "the dead beneath our awnings…on the road to Mandalay.") When the dust settled and subjugation became a fact of life, memories of heroic resistance fueled the popular imagination and kept alive the dream of freedom.

Being colonized was a humiliation. It subjugated Southeast Asians to laws, regulations, and institutions of authority that were foreign. It relegated elites to second-class status in the colonial social hierarchy and to subordinate places in colonial bureaucracies. It rendered kings throneless or converted them into puppets who reigned in splendor but who had no power to rule.

Colonialism was also an insult to the region's religions. The builders of the British Empire in Burma nonchalantly entered Buddhist shrines with their shoes on and belittled the *sangha*, or monkhood. Muslims felt rage and humiliation under the thumb of the Dutch—nonbelievers for whom Islam was a medieval religion worthy of scorn.

Being colonized also interfered with the routines and customs of ordinary men and women. Colonial tax collectors pressed upon scarce resources, imposed new fines and fees, and interfered with traditional patron-client practices that had softened the burden of rents and taxes in lean years. New rules and regulations also limited people's access to traditional sources of sustenance, including forests and other commons that colonial governments claimed as state land.

For all of these reasons, resistance and rebellion were constant phenomena in the colonial world. Peasants rose against colonial tax collectors and their Native agents. Religious and cult leaders led bands of followers against infidel officials. And members of the nobility and upper classes struggled to restore their kings and princes to power. At times, all of these elements were in play simultaneously. These outbursts kept colonial regimes on edge but inevitably failed in the face of overwhelming force. Even so, they kept alive a spirit of resistance. Their leaders became figures of lore.

Embracing nationalism

In time, a new form of resistance emerged. It grew first among the new classes of Western-educated Southeast Asians, the young Filipinos, Indonesians, Vietnamese, and Burmese who spoke

Spanish, Dutch, French, and English. For this small group, education led to agency. From among their ranks arose the first generation of modern Southeast Asian men and women of prowess. Their educations and experience exposed them to Western Enlightenment ideas of reason and science, to the concepts of liberty and democracy, and to the revolutionary appeals of the American and French Revolutions and of Karl Marx. They became reformers and critics of the colonial state. They came to discern the difference between the kingdoms of the past and the modern nations of the West. And they began, some of them, to visualize their own colonized societies as nations-in-the-making. Hence they became *nationalists.*

This new concept was based not on the mandala states of old or of legitimacy borne of religious authority or, as in Vietnam, of a classical patrimonial Asian philosophy, but upon the notion of legitimacy residing within a body of citizens. And who, exactly, would these citizens be? None other than the subjects of the colonies. What would constitute the territories and boundaries of the new nations? The answer: They would be exactly co-terminus with those of the colonies. The new nation of Burma, for example, would embrace all the territory claimed by Britain as part of British Burma; Indonesia, the name chosen in the early twentieth century to convey the idea of a nation born within the Dutch East Indies, would be the same size and shape as the Indies itself. And so on. Colonies would become nations. And Natives would be citizens.

This was a fine dream, but given the strength of the colonial states, how could it be achieved? Beginning in the first decades of the twentieth century, Western-educated Southeast Asians began to organize movements for political reform and independence. Southeast Asia's proto-nationalists were a varied lot. Some were cautious and concentrated their efforts on self-strengthening—on improving themselves as better Buddhists and Muslims or on defending the positions of certain beleaguered groups, such as

Java's aristocratic priyayi. They founded clubs and schools and published journals. Others complained loudly, agitated, and became openly revolutionary. Some organized movements centered on religion. Others harkened to the example of Asian nationalists such as Mohandas K. Gandhi in India, Sun Yatsen in China, or the Meiji-era nation builders in Japan. And some became communists. Asia's first Communist Party was formed in 1920 in the Dutch East Indies, a year before such a party was founded in China. Indeed, for Southeast Asians, colonialism inadvertently ushered in a new era of protean possibilities.

A few examples will illustrate the complexity of the process. In Burma, the first acts of resistance occurred in the immediate wake of the British seizure of Mandalay in 1885, where royal officials and Buddhist monks mobilized armed support in a failed attempt to restore the king and the old order. (It took several years for Britain to quell the resistance.) By 1906, a group of English-educated students had organized the Young Men's Buddhist Association, the YMBA, whose self-improving members agitated for reforms, not rebellion. They protested against shoe-wearing in Buddhist shrines, colonial schools that promoted Western values, and Burma's colonial identification as a province of British India.

As Britain opened Burma to incremental home rule in the 1920s, many elite Western-educated young people entered public life as members of advisory and legislative councils and, eventually, by the late 1930s, a full-fledged elected Burmese government. (In step with these changes, Britain finally separated Burma from India in 1937.) An English- and French-educated lawyer, Ba Maw, was elected prime minister. Political actors like Ba Maw were passionate nationalists but nationalists who chose to advance their cause incrementally within the colonial state, agitating for new doors to be opened and, when they opened, walking through them. This was a common pattern in other colonies, too. But in Burma and elsewhere, more revolutionary forces were also in play.

By the time Ba Maw became prime minister in 1937, Britain's colony in Burma had been rocked profoundly by the global depression, which rendered many of its once-prosperous small farmers landless and which led to deadly interethnic riots targeting moneylenders from India and other foreigners. Amid troubling stirrings like these, in 1930 a large millenarian rebellion surfaced in which politicized peasants and nascent urbanites rose against the colonial state in an attempt to reestablish the "kingdom of Burma." The rebellion's charismatic leader and would-be king, Shaya San, was captured by the British, defended in the colonial courts by Ba Maw, and hanged. As these alarming events brought the harsh underlying realities of British Burma to light, a new generation of elite nationalists turned in a radical direction. Under Aung San, the We Burmans Society, or Thakins, declared themselves socialists, spurned Ba Maw and other collaborating gradualists, and organized for revolution.

Just as Buddhism provided a public identity around which Burmese opponents of Britain could rally, in Indonesia Islam became a rallying call. Among the earliest politicized movements in the Dutch East Indies were Muhammadiyah (the way of Muhammad) and Sarekat Islam (Islamic Union), both launched in 1912. Whereas Muhammadiyah focused on Muslim self-strengthening through education, community organizing, and the propagation of a stream of reform-minded Islam that embraced modernity, Sarekat Islam took a more agitational approach and stirred the anti-Dutch feelings of its followers. It boasted two million members by 1919. One of its branches, influenced by Dutch socialists on the spot (including an early Comintern agent), declared itself a Communist Party in 1920.

It was about this time that the word *Indonesia* was gaining currency as the name of the colony's nation-to-be. "Indonesia" became a beacon for a proliferating number of nationalist and proto-nationalist groups. In 1928, following a failed uprising by the young Communists, a congress of elite young nationalists pledged themselves, in the Youths' Oath, to Indonesia: one country, one nation, one language. Wholly in sync with this spirit, a young Dutch-educated engineer named Sukarno proposed that nationalism itself could bring together the colony's diverse peoples, religions, and ideologies, including Islam and communism. Sukarno's proactive stand of noncooperation was further than many of the colony's activists wanted to go, and it provoked the Dutch, who arrested him and kept him out of circulation for years, along with many of his like-minded colleagues. Nevertheless, by the 1930s, the dream of a free Indonesia animated the hopes of virtually all the colony's politicized organizations, revolutionary or not.

Opposition to the French in Vietnam was vociferous from the beginning. In the early twentieth century, Phan Boi Chau was already conspiring for revolution on the models of Meiji Japan and Sun Yatsen in China. Chau failed but inspired others. By the 1920s, the colony supported several parties with openly proto-nationalistic or nationalistic agendas. These included the reform-oriented Constitutional Party, which lobbied the French for municipal councils and more opportunities for Vietnamese to become French citizens, and the openly revolutionary Vietnam Nationalist Party (VNQDD) modeled on the Guomindang in China. The VNQDD's abortive uprising in 1930, crushed by the French, created an opening for yet another stream of Vietnamese nationalists, the Communists.

As a young man, Ho Chi Minh fled Vietnam when anti-French feelings were running high. In Britain and France and eventually in the new Soviet Union, he discovered socialism and then communism, whose unequivocal denunciation of colonialism he could heartily embrace. He became an early agent of the Comintern and in 1925 founded a revolutionary organization (Youth), the precursor of Vietnam's communist movement. Ho's subsequent maneuvering succeeded in uniting the colony's disparate Marxists and establishing a coherent party in 1930. His astute leadership combined with a talented group of adjutants—including Pham Van Dong and Vo Nguyen Giap—and France's suppression of their anti-Marxist nationalist rivals, account for the fact that, in Vietnam, Communists ultimately seized the leadership of the colony's national revolution.

Southeast Asia's first genuine nationalist revolution occurred in the Philippines in 1896, inspired by the reformist propagandizing of Jose Rizal and the revolutionary anger of Andres Bonifacio. In 1899, Filipino nationalists founded the first Republic of the Philippines, whose president, Emilio Aguinaldo, led the doomed effort at the turn of the twentieth century to fend off invading American armies. Once securely in power, the United States told its new Southeast Asian subjects that it was holding the colony in trusteeship; one day it would be theirs. It opened positions of senior leadership to elite Filipinos who soon became provincial governors and elected members of the colony-wide Philippine Assembly. By 1916 there was an elected senate as well. The colonial bureaucracy was also rapidly Filipinized.

In this way, elite Filipino families of the late Spanish era morphed into a new Americanizing elite under the United States. This situation muted revolutionary tendencies (some trade-union radicalism and a nascent communist movement notwithstanding) and created a class of wily collaborating nationalists who found their agency by clamoring for independence while at the same time reaping the benefits of public office. The Commonwealth of the Philippines, inaugurated in 1935 by the U.S. Congress, brought this process to a new stage. Manuel Quezon, archetypal politician of his day and leader of the Nacionalista Party, was elected president and led an entirely Filipino government under the watchful eyes of a U.S. high commissioner. As war clouds threatened in the late 1930s, Quezon hired U.S. general Douglas MacArthur to prepare for the defense of the colony. In the Philippines, nationalist hopes rested to the end with the Americans.

In the rest of Southeast Asia, nationalist sentiments were muted. Among the Malays in British territories, young men from princely families learned English and Western ways in school and came to see themselves as modern exemplars of their people; meanwhile, graduates of Malay vernacular-language schools harkened with some excitement to the nationalist movement in the nearby Dutch East Indies. But no one among either group emerged as dynamic nationalist leaders with politicized followings on a par with Sukarno, Aung San, Ho, or Quezon. The large Chinese populations of Malaya and the Straits Settlements were more politicized, but their concerns lay with the fate of China, not Southeast Asia. It was much the same elsewhere in Laos and Cambodia, where modern political stirrings were confined to a small group of French-educated elites and intellectuals whose concerns focused on Buddhism and on threats posed by Chinese and Vietnamese migrants. Tellingly, the party Ho Chi Minh founded in 1930 was the *Indochinese* Communist Party, but most of its members were Vietnamese.

And what about Siam, Southeast Asia's only sovereign state? Here the self-strengthening efforts of the Chakri kings Mongkut and Chulalongkorn succeeded in exposing a new generation of elite Thais to modern Western ideas. King Vajiravudh, Rama VI (r. 1910–1925), had been educated at Sandhurst and Oxford. Inspired by the heated nationalism of Europe, he propagated a jingoistic popular nationalism at home, complete with uniformed paramilitary scouts and anti-Chinese diatribes. Subsequently, as Siam's Westernized classes grew larger and more influential, their sense of being modern began to clash with the kingdom's absolute monarchy. Europe's monarchies were *constitutional* monarchies. In 1932, a conspiracy involving military and civilian activists orchestrated a bloodless coup d'état in which Siam's king Prajadhipok (Rama VII, r. 1925–1932) was subordinated to a constitution and parliament. The civilian and military governments that assumed power thereafter presided over an independent state that increasingly resembled the nations modeled on the West that other Southeast Asian nationalists were striving to achieve. In that spirit, in 1939, they adopted a conspicuously Western name for their country: Thailand.

A Japanese intervention

As the year 1940 approached, much of Southeast Asia was astir with nationalist hopes. In Burma, Indonesia, Vietnam, and the Philippines political movements with brilliant leaders were in play. And yet, aside from the Thais, already free, only Filipinos had any concrete hope for independence; the United States had promised it for 1946. Strive as they might, the others faced untold years of waiting and struggle.

Japan changed everything. Japan's modern march to empire had begun in the late nineteenth century as the Meiji government embarked on its quest to make Japan the equal of the world's great powers, namely, the Western empires. First in Taiwan (1895), then in Korea and Manchuria (1910 and 1931), and then in a large swath of the Chinese mainland (1937), the Japanese empire grew. As a rapidly industrializing and militarizing power, Japan drew essential raw materials from the colonies in Southeast Asia: copper, coal, iron ore, chromium, and petroleum.

In 1940, Japan's militarists established a beachhead in Indochina, where local French officials were collaborating with the Fascist-aligned Vichy government in France. After allying themselves with Germany and Italy in the Tripartite Pact of September 1940, they began planning to seize the rest of Southeast Asia.

In December 1941, Japan launched its attacks on two American colonies in the Pacific—Hawaii and the Philippines—as well as on British Malaya, British Burma, and Thailand. The Thais quickly capitulated and allied themselves with Japan. In Burma, young nationalists under Aung San and the Thakins led Japanese invaders into the British colony. In late 1941 and early 1942, forces of Imperial Japan swept triumphantly through British Malaya to Singapore and defeated the forces of the Netherlands in the Dutch East Indies. By April, General Douglas MacArthur and his Filipino-American forces in the Philippines had capitulated. For the first and only time in history, all Southeast Asia now fell under a single political domain. Japan called its new empire the Greater East Asia Co-Prosperity Sphere. It was to be *Asia for Asians*.

Some Southeast Asians welcomed the Japanese sincerely, others warily. Despite its appealing propaganda, Japan's urgent wartime priorities and military rule led to appalling brutalities. As British, Dutch, and Americans languished in improvised prison camps, ordinary Southeast Asians also suffered badly due to shortages of food, clothing, and common necessities such as soap. The Japanese forced some local women into sexual servitude and tens of thousands of Southeast Asian men into slave-like menial labor building roads, bridges, and railroads in distant sites.

The Japanese relied on Southeast Asian elites to continue functioning as officials. In places, they invited them to form whole governments. This occurred in Burma where Ba Maw became premier again under Japanese auspices, as his nationalist rival Aung San became minister of war and head of the new national army. In the Philippines, Jose Laurel, a Yale-educated member of the Philippine Supreme Court, headed another Japan-sponsored government as president. Both Ba Maw and Laurel met ceremoniously with Japan's war chief Hideki Tojo in Tokyo in 1943 on the occasion of the official "independence" of their occupied countries within the Co-Prosperity Sphere. Prince Wan Waithayakon of Thailand also attended the event in Tokyo. In Indonesia, Sukarno and a great many of his nationalist colleagues, including prominent Muslim leaders, lent their support to Japan's New Order in Asia as members of advisory bodies and propagandists for the empire in massive outdoor rallies.

In the occupied territories, collaboration with Japan was both an opportunity and a duty. If respected leaders did not come to the fore, local populations would be at the mercy of Japanese officers and unscrupulous opportunists. Remaining at the helm during wartime was also a way of sustaining one's place in society as larger power equations shifted unpredictably. A close relationship with Japanese officers could also provide useful leverage in strictly local power struggles.

But what if the Japanese were to lose the war? This became an issue after 1943 when news of the American advance across the Pacific began seeping into Southeast Asia. Some Southeast Asian collaborators appear to have placed all their hopes in Japan's promises. This was the case in Indonesia. But elsewhere, Southeast Asia's wartime leaders and elite actors responded strategically. In the Philippines, elite-connected anti-Japanese guerrillas were in contact with underground American agents throughout the war, alongside members of the Marxist-led Hukbalahap anti-Japanese peasant movement. Moreover, many in Manila's Japanese-sponsored government had close prewar ties to Americans and were well positioned to claim, later, that they accepted their wartime roles out of duty, not pro-Japanese sentiments. As for President Jose Laurel himself, one of his sons had been trained in the Japanese military academy and served with him in Manila during the war; another was serving with the Philippine government in exile in Washington.

In Burma, Aung San eventually used his wartime position as head of the Burmese national army to develop a clandestine anti-Japanese mass movement in collaboration with British and American agents. In Thailand, an underground Free Thai movement led by Pridi Banomyong, a prominent architect of Thailand's shift to constitutional monarchy and now regent to the underaged king, fostered ties with the British while the formal government kept up its public collaboration with Japan. As the winds of war blew evermore forcefully against Japan, these underground movements moved to the fore and assisted the Western Allied powers in their reconquest of the region.

In some parts of Southeast Asia, however, opposition to Japan was passionate from the outset. In Malaya, where the Malays and their sultans acquiesced to the occupation (with some supporting it enthusiastically), communist-leaning members of the local Chinese community formed the Malayan People's Anti-Japanese Army and struck out against the occupiers throughout the war in collaboration with British agents. And in Vietnam, Ho Chi Minh and his nascent communist movement mobilized a broad, popular armed movement to fight both the Japanese and the French. Under Ho's leadership, the Vietminh waxed strong amid wartime uncertainty and dearth, including a million-dead famine that struck Vietnam in 1945. That same year it collaborated with underground American agents in the final months of the war as it positioned itself for national leadership at war's end.

The Japanese occupation brought an end to the myth of white superiority. Not one Western power had withstood Japan, and Southeast Asians witnessed personally the humiliation of their former white bosses as they languished in wartime prison camps. In the meantime, many Southeast Asians welcomed the opportunity to rise to higher official positions by replacing now-absent whites and to undergo "can do" military training under the Japanese. Despite the deprivations of the war and the imminent return of Europeans, they faced the postwar years with heightened expectations. Nationalists stood poised to seize the moment.

Nations emerge

In some places, the region's colonizers acquiesced quickly. In the Philippines, the United States fulfilled its promise of independence on July 4, 1946. On that symbolic day, Manuel

Roxas, a member of the prewar elite of the American Philippines (and of the Japanese-sponsored wartime government) who had recently been elected president, stood before a crowd in Manila and declared that the Republic of the Philippines would henceforth "follow in the glistening wake of America's mighty prow." In Burma, Aung San's wartime mass movement, the Anti-Fascist People's Freedom League, emerged in the vanguard of independence efforts after the war. Aung San negotiated successfully with Britain and in 1947 was elected to lead the soon-to-be-independent government. His assassination by rivals that summer meant that someone else would claim this honor. On January 4, 1948, Aung San's longtime ally U Nu became premier of the Union of Burma.

Independence aspirations in Malaya were complicated by the absence of a passionate nationalist movement among Malays before the war and the presence of a communist-led, British-affiliated, Chinese independence movement during the war. Britain returned to Malaya with a blueprint for independence that aimed radically to alter the prewar status quo. Under the Malayan Union Plan, the old sultanates would be abandoned and all of Britain's subjects on the peninsula—Malay, Chinese, and Indian—would enjoy equal political rights in a unitary state. This plan acknowledged an important demographic truth, that by the late 1940s, Malaya's Chinese residents outnumbered (or at least equaled) the number of Malays.

Britain's plan for a Malayan Union catapulted the Malays into political action at last. Beginning in 1946, the colony's English-educated Malay elites mobilized around the United Malays National Organisation (UMNO) to rally Malays against the union plan and to lobby Britain for an alternative. They succeeded. A new plan in 1948 favored Malays in citizenship and official leadership and restored the nine historical states as well as their sultans, who would become constitutional monarchs in the planned parliamentary Federation of Malaya. The colony's communist-led Chinese activists immediately struck back in an armed rebellion that rattled the colony-in-transition for several years. Britain called it the Emergency and deployed its imperial armies to defeat the rebels with the support of UMNO and its Indian and Chinese partners—for many of Malaya's prosperous Chinese residents also opposed the radicals. Britain organized elections even as the fighting continued. The UMNO-led alliance prevailed, and on August 31, 1957, UMNO's Tunku Abdul Rahman, the newly elected premier, proclaimed freedom for the Federation of Malaya. In his speech he thanked Britain for "the assistance which we have received . . . along our long path to nationhood." Britain, Tunku said, "will ever find in us her best friend."

The French and the Dutch returned to Southeast Asia after the war as weakened states for whom empires still mattered dearly. Their postwar plans for Southeast Asia envisioned global federations of quasi-independent member states in which they would be the senior partners. This is not at all what Indonesian and Vietnamese nationalists had in mind.

In the final years of World War II, Sukarno and other leading Indonesian nationalists participated in Japan-fostered meetings to prepare for independence. A draft constitution was already in place on August 17, 1945, two days after Japan's surrender, when Sukarno seized the moment and declared Indonesia free. Soon afterward, partisans of the new Republic of Indonesia found themselves fending off returning Dutch troops, who occupied key urban areas as Sukarno and the Republic established free territories of their own. The often-violent standoff between the Republic and the Dutch—called the Indonesian Revolution— lasted four years and involved vexing negotiations interspersed with open warfare in which the Dutch army's superior weapons were poised against Indonesia's passionate cause and the home-ground advantage of its fighters. At first, the United States supported the Netherlands, but the exposure of Dutch atrocities and the Sukarno-led defeat of an internal Communist putsch

9. Sukarno was a Dutch-educated engineer who became Indonesia's first president. He believed that the force of nationalism itself could bring together the country's diverse peoples, religions, and ideologies.

gained favor for the Republic. In 1949, the Netherlands relinquished power to a federation of Indonesian states that gave way within a year to a unitary republic. Under the leadership of a relatively small group of Dutch-educated nationalists, the gargantuan tropical colony ruled for centuries by the Netherlands now became a nation.

In Vietnam the process of forming the nation was longer and bloodier. Like the Netherlands, France was loath to relinquish its colonies. Its postwar plan for a French Union ran headlong into the new Democratic Republic of Vietnam, whose independence Ho Chi Minh had proclaimed on September 2, 1945, quoting the American Declaration of Independence that "all men are created equal," with U.S. soldiers at the scene. By this time, Ho's organization, the Vietminh, controlled much of northern Vietnam and key areas of the center and south. France's return was enabled by its wartime ally, Britain, which occupied southern Vietnam as the Japanese departed. Instead of opting immediately for war, Ho agreed to place his government within France's French Union, but this arrangement broke down within a year.

The nine-year-long guerrilla war that followed was not precisely between the Vietnamese and the French. Despite the popular support and organizational acumen of the Vietminh—and the mantle of nationalism it bore—France had Vietnamese supporters as well. These included members of the colony's moneyed and propertied classes, its French-educated middle classes including military officers, and many Vietnamese Catholics and members of local religious sects. Significantly, Bao Dai, heir to the throne in Vietnam's Nguyen dynasty, agreed in 1949 to be head of state on the French side.

The Vietnamese on both sides of this conflict were nationalists, but they were nationalists with contrary hopes for the future of the nation. Communism divided them. This passionate disagreement drew the Vietnamese into the global crucible of the Cold War.

France's colonial armies and Vietnamese allies could not contain the surging Vietminh. By the early 1950s, the United States was subsidizing 80 percent of their flagging efforts as part of its postwar global mission to contain "the Reds" (as Ho and his followers now became in American propaganda). When Vietminh armies defeated France decisively in 1954 in the Battle of Dien Bien Phu, global Cold War factors more than local ones determined what happened next: the division of the country by the big powers (in the Geneva Accords) into Communist-led and non-Communist-led zones. Meant to be temporary, pending elections that were never held, these opposing zones hardened and prolonged Vietnam's decolonization for another twenty years.

In the north, the Democratic Republic under Ho Chi Minh and the Communist Party received support from the Soviet Union and China but claimed its legitimacy on the basis of its historical revolutionary achievement. It had many partisans south of the Geneva line, where the Republic of Vietnam, or South Vietnam, was blatantly beholden to its foreign sponsor, the United States. This significantly compromised its legitimacy. Even so, South Vietnam called upon the sincere loyalty of a great many Vietnamese for whom a Communist Vietnam was anathema and also upon the qualified and calculated support of many others for whom it was the better of two flawed options.

The hopeful project launched by the United States in South Vietnam unraveled quickly. The revolution soon reawakened in the south. Through the sustained, disciplined action of its highly committed partisans, the National Liberation Front (to Americans, the "Vietcong") ate deeply into the fragile body politic of the southern state. As the struggle intensified, the northern government and its guiding party engaged the fight in the south at ever-increasing levels, just as the United States escalated its military intervention in defense of its Cold War client. The carnage was stupendous for soldiers and civilians alike; between two and three million died. In the end, neither the efforts of the

South Vietnamese government nor the deployment at the war's peak of more than half a million U.S. soldiers nor the largest bombing campaign in history (against North Vietnam, Laos, and Cambodia) prevented the collapse of South Vietnam in April 1975.

The reunification of Vietnam that year marked the end of the country's decolonization. The dreams of nationhood planted long ago and proclaimed by Ho Chi Minh in 1945 had now come fully to fruition. The nation was claimed by its most successful nationalists, the Communists. Ho Chi Minh himself had died in 1969, but his party ruled on.

Inevitably, Vietnam's wrenching path to independence affected the fortunes of its Indochina neighbors, Laos and Cambodia. As its imperial fortunes waned in the early 1950s, France deftly relinquished its control in both would-be nations to their residual elites: in Cambodia to King Norodom Sihanouk, whose grand uncle (King Norodom) had invited the French into the kingdom ninety years before, and in Laos to a Royal Lao government led by Prince Souvanna Phouma, a neutralist, who together with his half-brother and ideological rival Prince Souphanouvong, dominated the small country's nascent political movements.

In the spirit of Cambodian nationhood, the French-educated Sihanouk abandoned the throne to become head of state and led his own political party as he fended off opponents from the left and the right. Brooking little opposition, he attempted to steer his country through the dangerous shoals of the Cold War through the 1950s and 1960s. Clashing bitterly with the United States, he refused to take sides in the war exploding next door in Vietnam, which inevitably bled across his borders; the Communist command center for the war in South Vietnam (COSVN) lay *just* within Cambodia, for example. The United States maneuvered for regime change and, in 1970, Sihanouk was overthrown by one of his generals; Lon Nol immediately led Cambodia into war on the U.S. and South Vietnamese side. Intensive U.S. bombing inside the country now accompanied chaotic ground fighting. All this led to a bitter end in 1975 with the capture of the state by the surging Khmer Rouge.

In Laos, the war in Vietnam penetrated early and deeply. The northeast plateau became an important part of the clandestine corridor through which the North Vietnamese fostered the revolution in the south. In collaboration, Prince Souphanouvong led the Pathet Lao, or Lao Communists. To push back, the United States recruited Laotian hill peoples, such as the Hmong, into clandestine anti-communist armies that fought a "secret war" alongside American agents throughout the long struggle. Meanwhile, in Vientiane, neutralist and pro-U.S. regimes (with Souvanna Phouma as the key player) by turns attempted to hold the center together. Amid this chaotic web of power struggles the Pathet Lao advanced. And it was they who assumed power at war's end in 1975. All former French Indochina was now reconfigured into Marxist-led nations of one sort or another.

By this time, the fledgling Federation of Malaya had expanded to incorporate two remaining pieces of Britain's erstwhile Southeast Asian empire: Sarawak, once the British-protected private domain of the Brooke family, and Sabah, formerly the private commercial domain of the British North Borneo Company. In 1963 these Borneo territories were folded into a new national entity named Malaysia, along with Singapore, the richest and most populous of Britain's Chinese-populated Straits Settlements. Singapore's highly politicized population was led by Lee Kuan Yew, the dynamic Cambridge-educated trade-union lawyer and head of the colony's left-leaning People's Action Party (PAP). Lee and his aroused Chinese constituents were not a good fit in the expanded Malay-led federation of Malaysia. In 1965, Singapore withdrew and, with Lee and his party at the helm, embarked upon its own future as an independent nation.

A few years later, in 1984, the Sultanate of Brunei relinquished its protected status under Britain and became, once again, a sovereign kingdom under its Sandhurst-educated sultan, an absolute monarch.

The nature of nations

As in the kingdoms of the past, in Southeast Asia's nations indigenous leaders once again took their places at the top of the social and political pyramid. New men and women of prowess rose to become elected politicians, political party bosses, power-seizing generals, and dictators, as well as leaders in fields encompassing education, health, law, journalism, and business. The anomaly of foreign rule was past. But the legacy of foreign rule was deep. In many respects, the new nations resembled the former Western colonies much more than they resembled the region's bygone kingdoms.

To begin with, both the spatial and the conceptual configurations of Southeast Asia's nations followed that of the colonies. The nations were geo-bodies, whose territories were mapped and whose official authority extended fully to the borders instead of attenuating away from the capital, mandala-style. For the most part, the maps of the colonies prefigured the maps of the nations, so that outlying rings of the old mandalas that had been captured and colonized by Western powers became part of the new nations—just as nationalists had envisioned.

In the islands, the impact of colonial conquest and mapping was radical. Unlike the mainland where modern nations overlay historic mandalas in Burma, Thailand, and Cambodia, in the islands the new nations represented wholly novel configurations created by Western empires. Although modern Indonesians like to think of their country as a modern incarnation of the great mandala kingdom of Majapahit, nothing remotely like the Dutch East Indies existed in Southeast Asia before the Dutch created it. Yet it was this exact colonial geo-body that Indonesian nationalists dreamed of as their own nation. The modern Philippines is

Nations

another obvious example. As a geo-body, Las Philipinas was a Spanish creation.

Malaysia is an extreme case. Britain became the hegemon in Malaya partly as a result of its treaty with the Netherlands in 1824 identifying the Melaka Straits as the borderline between English and Dutch spheres of influence. Malaya became "British" and subsequently Malaysian. Sumatra, the home of a great number of Malays, became "Dutch" and therefore Indonesian. That the north coast of Borneo would be colonized by Britain-affiliated privateers was largely serendipitous. But when Sarawak and North Borneo (Sabah) were orphaned by their private owners following World War II, Britain took them over and, seventeen years later, arranged for them to join Malaysia, a wholly accidental configuration that is unquestionably a nation today.

Finally, tiny East Timor underscores the point. Its half of the remote island of Timor (plus another small enclave) was a Portuguese presence that the Dutch let stand even as the Dutch East Indies grew all around it. It remained separate when the Indies became Indonesia and remains so today, despite a brutal twenty-four-year-long attempt by the dictator Suharto to make it part of Indonesia after Portugal withdrew in 1975. East Timor proved indigestible and became its own sovereign nation in 2002. Its nationalist leaders named Portuguese as the national language. Even in this small place, empire was destiny.

Colonialism shaped the new nations in other ways as well. Southeast Asia's nationalists longed for independence but embraced Western political ideas and other lessons of their colonizers. They created governments that built upon British, French, Dutch, and American models for their bureaucracies and for ministries of education, public works, finance, and foreign affairs. They created parliamentary democracies, presidential democracies, and Leninist one-party states. They established militaries with service branches, titles, and uniforms similar to those of the West.

They wrote constitutions. And they created educational systems based on textbooks, schoolrooms, and curriculums mirroring those of Western schools, including instruction in Western languages. All of these things enabled them to place their new states within the global matrix of modern nations.

Other legacies of colonialism were more problematic. Beyond a thin layer of Western-educated elites, most of Southeast Asia's new nations possessed large populations of poorly educated, semiliterate citizens. (In 1950, only Thailand and the Philippines possessed literacy rates above 50 percent.) Few were prepared to staff their ballooning bureaucracies with qualified personnel or their schools with qualified teachers. Moreover, the economies of Southeast Asia were overwhelmingly agricultural and industrially primitive. A total of 50 to 70 percent or more of the region's population was rural. The Western regimes had introduced little in the way of manufacturing and processing. Southeast Asia exported rubber, tin, coffee, tea, sugar, and the like and imported practically all its manufactured consumer goods and machinery, including cars, trucks, pumps, and printing presses.

The new nations of Southeast Asia had inadequate electric power, a poor network of roads and railroads, and few hospitals and doctors. In 1960, Indonesia counted one doctor for every 70,000 people. Poverty was widespread and in many places the norm. On average, the GDP per capita in Southeast Asia in the early postwar years was well under U.S.$300 dollars a year. In the eyes of the West, Southeast Asia was backward. It was the Third World.

Yet another legacy of colonialism weighed heavily. The fact that colonial maps became national maps meant that most of the new nations included within their boundaries territories occupied by ethnic groups that, historically, had been rivals or enemies of the nation's ruling group. These animosities flared anew after independence in Burma, Indonesia, the Philippines, and elsewhere.

The Cold War and authoritarianism

Many of these issues were complicated by ideology. The Cold War placed Southeast Asians, inadvertently, within one of the world's great contested arenas. China's revolutionary embrace of communism, the subsequent war in Korea, and the leading role of Ho Chi Minh in Vietnam's national revolution raised fears in the West and especially in the United States that all Southeast Asia would potentially "fall." This is what lay behind the long, losing campaign of the United States in Vietnam and in nearby Laos and Cambodia.

Elsewhere things played out differently. In the Philippines, a communist-led anti-Japanese movement known as the Hukbalahap grew strong during the Japanese occupation and mobilized peasants around a land-to-the-tiller program. After independence, the new nation's elite politicians criminalized the Huks and blocked their elected representatives from the legislature. In the subsequent campaign to defeat their armed movement, the United States found a compelling political ally in Ramon Magsaysay. As national defense chief and subsequently president, Magsaysay orchestrated aggressive anti-insurgency strategies alongside sociopolitical measures to address Huk grievances (including opening homesteading land to poor farmers). Magsaysay was unabashedly pro-American and told Filipino voters that their vulnerable nation was safer with the United States as a friend.

The post–World War II leaders of Thailand agreed. Under Field Marshal Sarit Thanarat and the generals Thanom Kittikachorn and Praphat Charusathien, Thailand fell into step with American Cold War policy, joining the Southeast Asia Treaty Organization (SEATO) in 1954 and steadfastly supporting American policy in Indochina while fiercely suppressing its own communist and left-wing students and activists. In Malaya, the Communist-led insurgency was also defeated. In each of these cases, substantial amounts of Cold War foreign aid flowed to the collaborating regimes. By the mid-1960s, Thailand, Malaysia, Singapore, and the Philippines were firmly in the anticommunist group as the fates of Vietnam, Laos, and Cambodia were still being contested.

Sihanouk's strategy of remaining free of Cold War conflicts by declaring neutrality in Cambodia found adherents in Burma and Indonesia. General Ne Win, who seized power in Burma in 1962, and Sukarno, Indonesia's founding president, both favored nonalignment. Indeed, Sukarno hosted the first world summit of nonaligned countries in Indonesia in 1955. At Bandung, he spoke for the "voiceless ones in the world" who were now coming into their own.

Unlike Ne Win, who led his country into isolation, Sukarno accepted aid from both sides, exasperating both in the process. As president, he presided over a striking array of political parties, from conservative Muslims on the one side to Communists on the other. His embrace of the surging Communists as political allies in the late 1950s and early 1960s, along with his anti-imperialist, anti-American rhetoric, won him the animosity of the United States. Washington supported a rebellion against him in 1958 and subsequently conspired with members of his officer corps to eliminate the Indonesian Communists. The Communist Party was legal in Indonesia and by 1963 claimed as many as two million members and ten million affiliates. Its annihilation in the army-led massacres of 1965–1966 removed communism as a political factor in Indonesia, ended Sukarno's career, and brought a pro-United States military dictatorship to power under Suharto. He ruled for thirty-three years.

Indonesia's turn to dictatorship exemplified a trend. By this time the early postindependence experiments in parliamentary democracy had also failed in Burma, where General Ne Win would rule even longer than Suharto. Generals ruled in Thailand, too. The Philippines soon shifted in an authoritarian direction as well when, in 1972, the two-term elected president Ferdinand Marcos declared martial law—to contain a communist threat, he said. Marcos ruled with American support until 1986.

The turn to authoritarian government in Southeast Asia, including the triumph of one-party rule in the Indochina states and in Singapore under Lee Kuan Yew, is perhaps a reflection of the enormous task of transforming colonies into nations. Many of the region's formative nationalists entertained visions of national societies in which citizens governed themselves through a process of democratic consensus. This proved romantic. They had not accounted for the power of lingering ethnic and regional animosities, for the corrosive impact of poverty, for the explosive appeal of utopian ideologies and their disciplined movements, nor for the machinations of great outside powers. Nor had they accounted for the visceral appeal of power itself as they and their elite peers competed with each other in the uncharted seas of nationhood.

The neighborhood matures

Many Southeast Asians alive in the late 1970s had lived through the entire transformation of their societies from colonies to nations. Surveying the region, they might have despaired. By 1975, the dust had settled in Vietnam but the trauma had yet to end as refugees by the tens of thousands fled the newly reunited country for years to come. Neighboring Cambodia was lost to atrocity behind the bloody veil of the Khmer Rouge, who murdered or otherwise caused to die about one-third of the country's population. A thousand miles away in East Timor, the inhabitants were reeling in resistance to an armed invasion by Indonesia. Burma languished under a military dictator, Ne Win, and the Philippines under a civilian one, Marcos. Suharto and the army dominated Indonesia. And in Thailand, a student-led movement for democracy in the mid-1970s brought about three years of civilian government only to be brutally overtaken by military rule once again. Moreover, with the exception of Singapore, Southeast Asia remained an archetypal Third World region, still poor and still in the throes of its own halting creation.

Yet at this very time, Southeast Asia stood on the verge of region-changing events. In 1976, ASEAN's members signed the groundbreaking Treaty of Amity and Cooperation in Southeast Asia, paving the way for region-wide cooperation. In late 1978, Vietnam launched its ten-year occupation of Cambodia that brought an end to the Killing Fields and inaugurated Cambodia's return to coherency. Only a few years later, Vietnam inaugurated the *doi moi* reforms that opened its economy to market forces and rapid growth. Almost simultaneously, the People Power Revolution of 1986 led by Corazon Aquino overthrew the Marcos dictatorship in the Philippines and restored the country's vibrant oligarchic democracy. Two years later, in 1988, a democracy movement in Burma led by Aung San's daughter, Aung San Suu Kyi, openly defied Burma's military junta and set into motion a series of events leading to consequential reforms in coming decades.

Next, the collapse of the Soviet Union in 1991 brought the Cold War and its distorting impact to an end. This major event made it possible for Southeast Asia's nations led by Communist and non-Communist parties to focus more on their similarities than on their differences. By 1999, Vietnam, Laos, Cambodia, and Burma had all joined the neighborhood association, ASEAN. Meanwhile, beginning in 1978, the ascendance of Deng Xiaoping in China set off a series of reforms that would soon transform China and have colossal repercussions for Southeast Asia.

Southeast Asia soon experienced its first postindependence boom. Beginning around 1990, new investment from Japan, North America, and Europe began lifting the regional economies, especially those of Malaysia, Thailand, Indonesia, and the Philippines, where economies began expanding at rates between 5 and 10 percent a year. Export processing zones and investor-friendly laws brought high-tech manufacturing into the region alongside a rise in low-tech, low-wage manufacturing. Cities blossomed with new construction as L-shaped cantilever cranes dominated the rising skylines of Bangkok, Jakarta, and Manila. Property values rose. So did incomes and opportunities for the rising number of the region's high school and university graduates. Middle classes expanded. Upper classes luxuriated—new golf courses sprouted everywhere. The region took on a new glow. People spoke of Southeast Asia's New Tigers, meaning Singapore, Malaysia, and Thailand. The Philippines called itself a "cub."

This exuberant period came crashing to an end in 1997. Beginning in Thailand, a monetary crisis swept the region. The decline of Japan's yen alongside Southeast Asia's poorly regulated banks, risky loans, and endemic corruption all fostered the crash. Southeast Asia was soon littered with bankruptcies and empty high-rise apartments. Abandoned half-built hotels and office buildings stood exposed like skeletons as legions of hopeful young MBAs, engineers, and professionals lost their jobs.

The impact of the crash was not permanent but it had consequences. In Indonesia it contributed to the fall of President Suharto, for example, who resigned in the face of popular protests in 1998. This surprising event led to a dynamic new period of democratization in Indonesia, known as *reformasi*. (The country's latest two presidents, Bambang Susilo Yudhoyono and Joko Widodo were both popularly elected.) The end of military dictatorship in Indonesia also paved the way for East Timor's independence. In a 1999 popular referendum authorized by Suharto's successor, the people of East Timor voted overwhelmingly in favor of separation from Indonesia. Indonesia's withdrawal was vengeful and bloody, but in 2002 East Timor became a fully sovereign nation, Southeast Asia's eleventh.

After 1997, the region slowly recovered, faltered again in the early 2000s, and recovered again in a pattern that continues. Each small boom intensifies the region's links to the larger world economy and brings new levels of economic diversity and sophistication to its manufacturing and financial sectors, as well as to its huge and still expanding agribusiness and mining sectors. This growth is asymmetrical. Southeast Asia has both very rich and very poor countries. In all but Malaysia, Singapore, Thailand, and Brunei, the very poor (people earning less than U.S.$3.10 a day) still account for more than 30 percent of the national populations.

Even so, Southeast Asia today is a far cry from Southeast Asia of early independence. Over the decades, a stable region has taken shape. The new states are intact. And, along with the rest of Asia—including India, Japan, South Korea, Taiwan, and China— they are wholly engaged with and embraced within today's global matrix of nation-states and the world capitalist economy.

Nations

Chapter 5
The past is in the present

Today's fast-changing Southeast Asians seem utterly engaged with the present. Among them, 45 percent are under fifteen years of age. Like young people everywhere, they participate in a mixing of popular culture that fuses global elements with local ones; social media links them to each other and to the world as never before. The lucky and ambitious ones are definitely learning English.

Meanwhile, the great stone monuments and temple complexes that marked the centers of old mandala kingdoms are tourist attractions today. So are the once-grand colonial hotels that were havens of luxury for world-traveling Westerners during the high age of colonies; think of the Raffles in Singapore, the Strand in Yangon (the former Rangoon). Many of the imperial government buildings and gracious ruling-class homes of the colonial era have been repurposed as museums, shops, and restaurants or remodeled as residences for today's elites. Dense populations and traffic jams are a given. Even in provincial cities and towns, motorbikes and noisy motorized tricycles and minicabs clutter the streets, jostling with a growing number of automobiles. Nationalities are taken for granted. One is Singaporean, Malaysian, Filipino, Thai. These identities feel permanent, eternal. ASEAN gatherings featuring ritual photographs of Southeast Asian heads of state standing side by side emblemize the coherence of the ten-nation neighborhood. Other facts of life include the cities' dirty air and filthy water and shorelines and beaches awash with the world's trash. Such is Southeast Asia of the moment.

What remains today of the past? Of Southeast Asia's kingdoms and colonies and its first-draft nations? Despite the distractions of the busy present, the answer is quite a lot.

The extraordinary heterogeneity of Southeast Asia has not changed. Beneath the skin of the region's national identities— Filipinos, Indonesians, Singaporeans, and so on—thousands of separate ethnicities and languages and dialects remain, playing a role in local power struggles and sometimes in national ones. In places, ethnic competitions have led to violence, especially where migrating outsiders compete with long-established residents and where ethnic differences are compounded by religious ones. This has occurred in eastern Indonesia, for example, where in-migrant Javanese Muslims have clashed with Christian Malukans and Papuans. The Muslim Rohingya are a despised minority among

10. Southeast Asian leaders meet at the 2016 ASEAN-UN Summit. The ten members of ASEAN have pledged to respect each other's sovereignty and to renounce the use of force in their relations with each other.

Buddhist Burmans. And so on. Everywhere, power-wielding majorities lord it over regional minorities in a hierarchy of size and influence. These big-fish–small-fish rivalries are much discussed and figure in countless stereotypes and jokes—as when Filipino Tagalogs speak about Cebuanos, or the other way around. In multiethnic Indonesia, the possibilities are legion.

Hill peoples are still thought of as backward by ethnic-majority lowlanders and are subjected to predatory policies by national governments that have opened their ancestral lands to logging, mining, and agribusiness. These days the hills are no longer apart. Southeast Asia's swidden farmers have been pinched into ever smaller pockets of the decreasing forests, just as wildlife has been. Hill farmers and their children have become wageworkers. Many now live in logging camps and mining towns and in the burgeoning provincial cities that flourish as exchange centers for logs, palm oil, coffee, copper, and a slew of other commodities. When they don their traditional finery of brightly dyed textiles, beads, feathers, and metalwork, it is likely to be for a special ritual or festival, or for world-traveling backpackers. In places where these changes have not yet occurred, as in upland Laos, national governments are committed to bringing them about quickly.

The plains are also changing. In the region's vast, flat lowlands, rice paddies still stretch into the distance. Rice is still the staple food for most Southeast Asians. But the economic disadvantages of farming and the region's prospering cities and towns continue to draw people from farms into the expanding urban economy, including the gray economy of city slums. (By 2010, some 42 percent of Southeast Asians had become urbanites.) The urban invasion of rice-paddy land is striking. On the outskirts of Southeast Asian cities, now replete with housing subdivisions, industrial parks, and pop-up commercial centers with fast food and petrol stations, one sees everywhere the earthen remains of former paddy-field bunds.

Power is money

Southeast Asians were early participants in commerce. The region's men of prowess—its kings, rajas, and sultans—amassed power by controlling large numbers of people who channeled resources toward their capitals. Throughout the mainland and the islands, they built and enriched their mandala centers by managing, taxing, and participating in trade.

Colonialism interrupted this pattern as Western colonial regimes and capitalists seized these opportunities for themselves. This was blatantly obvious in the behavior of the East India companies, but the crusading Iberians also created fortified trade hubs in Melaka and Manila for the same purposes. Later, more mature colonial states left commerce to private companies—think Michelin, British Petroleum, American Tobacco—and raised revenues from the taxes, levies, and fines they imposed upon their subjects.

The colonial apparatuses for managing and taxing trade and for revenue collection were inherited by the leaders of Southeast Asia's nations at independence. They enabled the region's new leaders to begin recapturing the profits of regional trade and local natural resources for the nation itself, and also for themselves. Southeast Asia's new men of prowess—elected politicians, dictators and strongmen, party leaders, and generals in power—imposed new tariffs and joint-venture laws, licensing requirements, and facilities fees; they cut profit-sharing deals with major agribusiness and mining companies; and, in some cases, they expropriated foreign-owned companies and strategic sectors of the economy altogether. Indonesia's Sukarno nationalized petroleum, for example.

In a similar way, new laws strove to marginalize Chinese participation in national economies and to redistribute Chinese wealth. Conspicuous examples of this include Indonesia and the

Philippines, where ethnic Chinese merchants were driven from their rural shops in the 1950s, and Malaysia, where the New Economic Policy beginning in 1971 sought to move more of the nation's potential wealth into Malay hands. Southeast Asia's ruling elites also used their influence to garner private fees, gifts, and bribes for opening doors to some business suitors and closing them to others. In many formal and informal ways, they have enriched themselves and their cronies and followers (including their citizens) in a pattern reminiscent of rulers in the age of kingdoms. Then as now, in Southeast Asia, power is money.

The lion's share of goods that enter and leave Southeast Asia, from tea, coffee, and sugar to petroleum, copper ore, coal, and every sort of consumer good, still goes by ship. As in the past, the harbor towns of Southeast Asia do a brisk business. To get a modern sense of the historic importance of classic maritime entrepôts such as Melaka, one can do no better than visit today's Singapore, the second busiest seaport in the world. Here immense container docks go on and on for miles on the island's south shore.

Singapore, famously free of the every-hand-is-out sort of corruption that plagues other countries in the region, illustrates the connection between political power and wealth accumulation. In this prosperous one-party state led by the People's Action Party (PAP), average citizens have done very well. Singapore is a First World country with a higher per capita gross domestic product (GDP) than the United States. The island nation's political elites have also done very well. Singapore's non-bribe-taking senior ministers and bureaucrats are paid salaries that surpass those of their regional peers by many multiples. Lee Hsien Loong, the current prime minister and son of founder Lee Kuan Yew, is the highest paid head of state in the world. Members of elite ruling-party families including the Lees have placed themselves comfortably among the island's business, financial, and professional top tier. In Singapore, everything is strictly legal. (Still, power is money.)

Sleeping mandalas

Southeast Asia's Western colonies and its new nation-states imposed upon the region a well-delineated matrix of states with clear borders; they are geo-bodies. What remains, then, of the mandalas of old? The impressive survival of the new states since independence and their formal incorporation into a web of international organizations, including ASEAN, suggest that Southeast Asia's nations are here to stay. Nation-building has succeeded in Southeast Asia. Nationalism is a force. And yet, Southeast Asia remains rife with conflict. Borders are porous. Certain regions remain astir. Others lie uneasily within the nation. Often, sleeping mandalas provide an explanation.

Thailand illustrates this point. Under the Chakri kings of the nineteenth century, Siam's mandala stretched deeply into the Malay Peninsula and embraced a wide swath of territory in western Cambodia. In typical mandala fashion, this huge domain had grown at the expense of others.

To the south, the Thais had subjugated several small Malay Muslim kingdoms that had once been part of the great mandala centered at Melaka. These included Patani, Kedah, Perlis, Trengganu, and Kelantan and their Malay-Muslim subjects. By the mid-nineteenth century, these mini-states were all under Thai sway. In 1909, however, the king of Siam, Chulalongkorn, ceded four of them to Britain, and they became part of British Malaya. Patani remained part of the Thai state; its Malay-Muslim subjects therefore remained on the Thai side of the border.

To the east, the immense mandala of Angkor had once included much of eastern Thailand. In the nineteenth century, the Chakri kings were reversing this process, aggressively attaching Battambang and Siem Reap and neighboring Khmer territories to the Thai mandala. This was one reason that King Norodom of Cambodia accepted French protection in 1863; in 1904, the French wrested the territories back when King Chulalongkorn ceded them to French Cambodia.

During World War II, Japan rewarded its Thai allies by allotting the Malay and Cambodian territories to Thailand, but they were restored to the British and French at war's end. This arrangement became fixed in the region's new nations. Today, Patani and other Malay-Muslim territories lie in Thailand, while Kedah, Trengganu, Perlis, and Kelantan are part of Malaysia. Meanwhile, Battambang and Siem Reap lie within Cambodia's geo-body. In short, the national borders of today's Malaysia, Thailand, and Cambodia lie athwart ancient mandala cusps that have been fluid as recently as seventy years ago.

Flash forward. Today, about 1.5 million Malay-speaking Muslims live in Thailand's "Muslim south," an area long awash in conflict and violence between its Malay-descended residents and the Thai authorities. These conflicts are usually described in religious terms—Muslim rebels, extremists, and separatists act out against the Buddhist Thai state. But the deeper roots of conflict lie in colonial-era border fixing and subsequent nation-building, which have interrupted the more fluid mandala patterns of classical Southeast Asia and rendered the Malays of southern Thailand a restless Muslim minority within a modern Buddhist nation.

Tensions of a different kind have arisen on the border between Thailand and Cambodia. Following the back-and-forth territorial shifts during World War II, this area remained problematic during the turbulent years of the Khmer Rouge and its aftermath in Cambodia. Beginning in the 1970s, refugee camps sprang up all along the long, mountainous Thai-Cambodian border as wave after wave of people fled the unfolding violence and atrocities. In a rugged garland of disparate refugee camps, tens of thousands of displaced people lived in limbo awaiting new homes abroad or an opening to return to Cambodia. The formal jurisdiction of both the Thais and Cambodians was highly compromised in this violent and fluid frontier along an age-old Southeast Asian mandala cusp.

Tensions flowed along this same border in 2008 over the ownership of Preah Vihear Temple. This one-thousand-year-old temple was one of thousands of Hindu/Buddhist cult temples that the Khmers of Angkor built throughout their giant mandala that penetrated deep into today's Thailand. This one lies along the current border. According to old French maps and a 1962 judgment by the International Court of Justice, Preah Vihear Temple lies in Cambodia.

In 2008, however, Cambodia's application to UNESCO to designate Preah Vihear a World Heritage Site aroused Thai politicians to claim the temple site for Thailand. Tempers flared, and in the next few years fighting broke out sporadically between Thai and Cambodian soldiers along the border. Passionate nationalist feelings stirred around the conflict, which was finally resolved in 2013 when the International Court of Justice declared the area a demilitarized zone. Why did this small temple and its ambient site matter so much? For both sides, the conflict recalls mandala contests that go back many centuries. This is remembered, even though, these days, the fight is cast in terms of national sovereignty. Like the conflict in southern Thailand, this one still simmers. More than a dozen similarly contested areas exist along the same long border.

We can identify another sleeping mandala in the Sulu Zone of maritime Southeast Asia. In the age of kingdoms, the Sulu Sea was a great field of mandala contestation, with small sultans and rajas and local big men dominating its island and riverine states. Spain took much of this territory out of competition by the 1600s, leaving Mindanao and its neighboring polities in play. This vast maritime theater of trading and raiding was famous for pearls, tortoise shells, and sea delicacies, and it was also the center of

Southeast Asia's maritime slave market with its center at Jolo. It was here that the sultan of Sulu held sway. He claimed a mandala that included most of the islands and small polities of the zone and that stretched to the northeast coast of Borneo. This area was also claimed by a competing sultan whose capital was in Brunei. Northeast Borneo thus lay on a mandala cusp, with one mandala pulling it toward Jolo, the other toward Brunei.

When the North Borneo Company acquired northeast Borneo in 1881 as the site for its agribusiness enterprises, it signed arrangements with both sultans. North Borneo came under British protection and was later absorbed directly into the British Empire. As a result, it subsequently became Sabah, a constituent state of modern Malaysia. Meanwhile, American colonizers in the Philippines brought the sultan of Sulu to heel, and his subordinate territories eventually became part of today's Republic of the Philippines.

This mandala-world and colonial-era backstory explains the repeated attempts by Filipino politicians to "reclaim" Sabah. The sultan of Sulu, they say, only *leased* North Borneo to the North Borneo Company; he did not sell it. Such efforts stir nationalist feelings but inevitably fail. In today's world the national geo-bodies are stronger than the underlying mandalas. Still, the Sulu Zone remains an arena where goods and people flow freely across soft borders. And Sabah is still on the cusp—close to a million Filipinos now live there.

The mandala dynamics of the Sulu Zone also help to explain the unrelenting violence and political conflict of the southern Philippines. Recall that this area was already Muslim when Spain arrived in the 1500s and that Spain never wholly controlled it. Instead, a variety of ethnic groups, including the seafaring Badjau, Tausug, and Sama Dilaut, competed for followers and resources among themselves, and, at times, they deferred to regional mandala centers. Large and small, they were led by proud sultans and warrior chiefs and clans claiming royal status.

American armies quelled these independent societies in the late 1800s, and they became part of the American Philippines. When the Republic of the Philippines became independent in 1946, these Muslim territories were involuntarily folded into the Christian nation. Most of the conflicts of the past seventy years, including wars of succession, movements for autonomy, and the penetration of the region by radical Islamists, can be traced to this event and to its postindependence consequences. These include the migration of Christian Filipinos into once majority-Muslim areas and the repeated and sometimes violent attempts by the Philippine government to integrate its Muslim South into the geo-body of the nation.

Another arena of contemporary unrest in Southeast Asia that can be understood in part through mandala dynamics is the catastrophe of the Rohingya in Myanmar. Their homeland in Arakan lies over an old mandala cusp dividing Muslim Bengal and Buddhist Burma. Britain's colonization of both areas led Arakan into the geo-body of British Burma and, hence, subsequently in 1948, into the independent Union of Burma, today's Myanmar.

As a consequence, the Muslim Arakanese, or Rohingya, became unwanted subjects within a nation that defined itself as Buddhist. This led to years of harassment by the group's Buddhist neighbors in Rakhine State (as Arakan is known today) and repression by the Burmese government itself: in 1982 dictator Ne Win denied them citizenship as Bengali "foreigners." (Currently this applies to more than eight hundred thousand people.) Buddhist-Muslim hostilities, rebellion, and reprisals ensued, all leading to the crisis of 2015 and after, in which tens of thousands of desperate, stateless Rohingya refugees have fled Myanmar for uncertain futures in Bangladesh, Malaysia, Indonesia, and Thailand.

Like the Rohingya, the Shans, Karen, and Kachin of Myanmar are also restless within the nation. Their territories, once small mandala polities in their own right, were also included within the huge mandala of the Konbaung kings that Britain seized in the nineteenth century. They, too, became part of British Burma and were subsequently included in the official geo-body of the Union of Burma at independence in 1948. Almost immediately, rebellions erupted in these outlying non-Burman territories, challenging the new nation's fragile parliamentary government and leading to, among other things, the triumph of the army as the dominant institution in Burma.

Throughout the ensuing decades, entities such as the Shan State Army, the Chin National Front, the Kachin Independence Army, the Karen National Union, the United Wa State Army, and others governed their territories in defiance of the Union of Burma, sometimes funding their armies and shadow states with profits from opium grown in the Golden Triangle. War between the armies of the center and the armies of the periphery dragged on and on, leaving a record of appalling brutality in its wake, plus waves of refugees who made their way into neighboring Thailand. Myanmar's current membership in ASEAN may serve to reinforce the nation's territorial claims, and new governments since 2011 have been negotiating an end to the long wars with more than a dozen armed groups. (Eight such groups signed a cease-fire agreement in 2015). Yet as Myanmar moves gingerly away from military rule, it remains to be seen whether the nation will succeed in its efforts to unify.

Myanmar's fragility is exceptional. Even as sleeping mandalas stir beneath today's geo-bodies and underlie certain contemporary disturbances, Southeast Asia's nations show every sign of enduring.

India and China

Thinking of the deep structures of Southeast Asia's formation, what can we observe about India and China, the two radiating civilizations from which Southeast Asians borrowed so much?

Of these two, India was formative, shaping the major societies of most of the mainland and islands over centuries as Hindu- and Buddhist-inflected civilizations and contributing to the Islamization of the islands as well. A great deal of India's influence remains in layer upon layer of language, culture, and custom throughout the region. Millions of Southeast Asians bear names from the classical Indian story cycles; in Indonesia, many a young couple gets married in regalia that harken back to the epics. Buddhism and Islam are the hegemonic religious cultures; in Bali, a brilliant Southeast Asian Hinduism survives.

But it is hard to find examples of contemporary borrowing from India, aside from the popularity of Bollywood films. Southeast Asians are not learning Indian languages—unless you mean English—although they will still sometimes reach into Sanskrit to find an appropriate-sounding name for something modern (as an alternative to using an English word). Trade between India and Southeast Asia pales in comparison to the region's trade with others. The South Asian community in Southeast Asia tends to be small and concentrated in Malaysia and Singapore, with expatriates scattered about elsewhere. As India rises to prosperity and influence, this will surely change. But as of now, it is Asia's other great radiating civilization that looms large in Southeast Asia's present: China.

The impact of China's long ties and waves of migration to Southeast Asia is permanent. Today, the Southeast Asian Chinese control a large swath of the regional economy, despite the ever larger participation of indigenous Southeast Asians. Overcoming stigmatizing stereotypes and a variety of laws and policies designed to curb their influence in the region's independent nations, they have continued to thrive. One key to their success is a region-wide network of families and interconnected businesses that transcends the national economies. Links of kinship, dialect, and mutual trust foster business ties and expedite transactions across a vast "offshore" Chinese matrix that has flourished even in times when China itself has languished.

After its reunification under Mao Zedong and the Communist Party, China began wielding influence in Southeast Asia by supporting Ho Chi Minh's revolution in Vietnam and, to a lesser degree, fostering other communist movements in the region. In 1955, Chou Enlai made a point of attending Sukarno's nonaligned summit at Bandung.

Yet the People's Republic of China remained largely preoccupied with itself until after the Cultural Revolution and Mao's death in 1976. As China subsequently began to ratchet up its market economy under Deng Xiaoping, the offshore Chinese community in Southeast Asia came rapidly into play. Money being held in Bangkok, Jakarta, Singapore, Manila, and Kuala Lumpur could now be invested profitably in China. And money being generated in China could be invested in Southeast Asia.

In the 1990s, capital flows between Southeast Asia and China began to rise. In the next decade they soared. The existence of a region-wide matrix of Chinese families and businesses made this possible. For the first time in centuries, the economy of China became a driving variable in the economy of Southeast Asia. Today Chinese money and goods are pouring into the region. Like the Walmarts of the United States, the shopping centers and markets of Southeast Asia are chock-full of Chinese-made consumer goods, from nuts and bolts and pins to light bulbs, electric fans, air conditioners, television sets, and motorcycles. These products are imported by long-established Chinese-owned companies already on the spot. At the same time, investments from China are funding hydroelectric dams, hotels and casinos, agribusiness plantations, factories, and mines, and ambitious railway projects connecting Southeast Asian cities to Chinese cities.

A very large shift is underway. After two centuries of decline and turmoil, China is re-staking its historical claim to preeminence in Asia. The country's startling new wealth is making this possible, combined with the political coherence of the Chinese state in the years following Mao. This new China is still evolving; many large variables, including the ultimate role of the ruling party, are still up in the air. But China's power is clear. China today claims a geo-body commensurate with the farthest reaches of the Qing dynasty and is asserting itself aggressively on its fringes. Along the once-soft, multiethnic border connecting Southwest China and the northern tier of Southeast Asian mini-states, the Chinese state has abandoned long-practiced strategies of indirect governance and pushed state institutions and programs of Sinicization to the very border. These include militarized agricultural farms producing export commodities, especially rubber.

China's aggressive advance into the South China Sea, where several Southeast Asian countries claim maritime rights and island clusters and reefs that China also claims, is proving much more worrisome. With its newfound strength, China is now occupying some of these islets and converting them into larger ones with landfill and adding airstrips, ports, and military outposts. In the Spratly Islands, for example, these initiatives are especially alarming because, in spite of China's large presence in Southeast Asian history, it has rarely attempted to place itself physically within the region in this way.

Southeast Asian governing elites feel the pressure and, by way of a response, are balancing rather than resisting. On the one hand, they are accommodating the Chinese. In 2015, for example, all the ASEAN countries pledged to join China's new alternative to the World Bank, the Asian Infrastructure Investment Bank (AIIB). And in 2017, they hastened to attend the gala summit of China's ambitious Belt and Road initiative, which seeks to link Asia to Europe and Africa through a vast web of Chinese-built ports, industrial parks, roads, and rails. On the other hand, Southeast Asia's leaders are beefing up their ties to the West and the United States, welcoming recent U.S. economic and strategic initiatives under the Barack Obama administration and in-your-face U.S. naval exercises near China-occupied islands under the Donald Trump administration. In a case decided in 2016, the Philippines persuaded the Permanent Court of Arbitration in The Hague that China has no historical basis for its claim to waters in the West Philippine Sea.

China's new power and its growing presence in Southeast Asia empowers the region's large Chinese-descended minority, as they now form part of China's vastly expanding economy in the region. Connections to China are valuable. The stigma attached to Chinese descent that lingers in parts of Southeast Asia—in Indonesia, for example, where President Joko Widodo was slandered by his political opponents as being Chinese during the elections of 2014—may wane as the status of China itself rises. Or it may intensify if people in Southeast Asia come to feel that a rich, powerful China poses a threat and undermines national loyalties among its China-descended citizens.

Lessons of the West

Despite the remarkable rise of China in recent decades and Asia's other robust economies in Japan, South Korea, and Taiwan, Southeast Asia remains today in an age of Westernization. To be sure, in the realm of popular culture Southeast Asians savor Japanese manga and cosplay and are riveted by television dramas from South Korea. They enjoy foods and music from around the world. As always in history, they are outward looking. But when it comes to learning foreign languages, it is still English that confers status and provides entrée to the global conversation. It is still to Western universities that elite and aspiring Southeast Asians flock. (Yale, Duke, and Stanford Universities all have Singapore-based programs, alongside Wharton, INSEAD, MIT, and others.) These same universities serve as models for Southeast Asia's own burgeoning university sector, its technical institutions, and its teaching and nursing academies. And although computer technology and high-tech manufacturing are global phenomena and are fields in which many companies across Asia excel, Silicon Valley still glitters.

Moreover, Southeast Asia's nations continue to follow the Western models of government with which they began at independence, with ministries and departments and constitutions that resemble those of the West. Even the region's dictators have clothed their thuggish regimes in the language and apparatuses of democracy. Suharto arranged to have himself reelected every seven years in festive Indonesia-wide "democracy parties." Marcos held "people's referendums" in martial-law Philippines. In Thailand, power-seizing generals inevitably speak of returning the kingdom to elected governments and eventually do so. Authoritarian Singapore also holds elections regularly to relegitimize the highly disciplined and domineering People's Action Party.

Southeast Asians today are adapting what is new, attractive, and powerful in the wider world just as they once yielded to the appeal of Hinduism, Buddhism, and Islam. And just as they adopted these infusions selectively in the past—fusing what was new and exciting with what was old and comfortable—they are doing the same thing today.

Take democracy, for example. The introduction of democratic ideas and structures has altered how political power struggles occur in Southeast Asia. But it has not really altered the power structures and social hierarchies that determine who competes for power. In modern Malaysia, for example, elite Malays dominate the nation just as their ancestors dominated Malay kingdoms of old. Sultans and their titled officials and loyal chiefs have made way for the party politicians of UMNO and for prime ministers and tiers of modern elected and appointed officials (although feudal titles remain popular). Today's Malay men of prowess compete politically. And yet certain deep structures remain. Recall that all but one of Malaysia's prime ministers to date have been descendants of Malay royal families. And note that in the modern nation, as in Malay kingdoms of the past, Chinese actors play significant but subordinate roles.

The Philippines hosts a wildly popular democratic culture. Filipinos believe in elections and, despite the familiar candidate's cry of "I was cheated," honor the outcomes. They flock to the polls. But with very few exceptions, the people who run for office and win are members of an old class of prominent families whose social position and wealth date to the Spanish period. The same clans have dominated the same districts and provinces from generation to generation. Democracy has not displaced the oligarchy. It has provided a machinery for organizing the competition among its members and for legitimizing elite rule in the modern republican nation. At the same time, Philippine elections occasionally provide an opening for modern celebrities such as movie stars and athletes—huge vote-getters—to join the governing class.

Indonesia's elite Western-educated founders attempted to form a parliamentary democracy and led the new nation through its first elections. Democracy soon foundered, however, and in 1965 it was wholly overtaken by Suharto's military dictatorship. The fall of Suharto restored hopes for democracy; in fact, in the years since 1998 Indonesia has elected thousands of officials high and low, including several presidents. Despite this, many elite players under the former dictatorship continue to wield power under the new election-driven system. Political parties facilitate elite competition and serve as conduits for patronage and the spoils of office. In local elections across Indonesia, voters often favor candidates from old elite and aristocratic families. Much like the Philippines, in Indonesia, democratic elections appear to have provided a means for privileged groups to maintain their influence in a new guise. National elections in Indonesia also reveal the enduring power of Java: all but one of the country's seven presidents have been Javanese.

We can observe something similar in the region's armies and navies. From the Philippines to Thailand to Burma and Indonesia, the structure of modern militaries follows that of Western militaries, with tiers of familiar ranks and divisions of duty, i.e., infantry, ordnance, intelligence, and so on. But lurking just below the surface of the formal chain of command are structures of a personal nature that link leaders to followers and, among officers, faction to faction. (These factions often arise among graduating classes at military academies, much like fraternities.) In Southeast Asia, commanders of regional-based units and special operations foster bonds of personal loyalty with their men, making special efforts to provide for their families. These bonds endure. Patron-client ties and personal relationships like these can be activated in political crises and power struggles, pulling whole divisions one way or another. Quarreling factions in Sukarno's army led directly to his downfall in 1965; Suharto's well-cultivated following aided his rise. In 1986, General Fidel Ramos mobilized his personal ties in the Philippine military to shift support away from dictator Marcos to Marcos's rival, Corazon Aquino. The power structures of military dictatorships are riven with internal factions of this sort. In armies, too, borrowed Western structures disguise social dynamics that are deeply Southeast Asian.

Where social mobility is concerned, however, militaries and especially military dictatorships have provided new avenues for social mobility in the region. In many countries, including Indonesia and Myanmar, military officers emerged as new elites in the postindependence era. This occurred partly because military officers replaced or supplanted civilian officials in key senior functions and, significantly, because families of officers were accorded opportunities for education, travel, and experience unavailable to many ordinary people. They emerged not only as people with access to power but also as well-educated people with useful skills. Thus, to be affiliated with an officer-corps family became a distinct advantage.

Something similar is true in one-party states. In Singapore, membership in the PAP is the steppingstone to elite status in the republic. It is the same in Vietnam and Laos, where

Communist Parties still rule despite having abandoned much of communism itself.

The tension between borrowed ideas and local ones has been debated passionately from the beginning of the modern era. Southeast Asia's rising Western-educated nationalists all grappled with the problem of seizing what was best from the West without forfeiting their own hallowed beliefs and cultural identities. This led many of them to revisit their own traditions. Young Burmese radicals discovered that the teachings of modern socialism were already to be found in classical Buddhist teachings. Sukarno argued that the roots of democracy in Indonesia lay deep in the consensus-forming practices of traditional Javanese villages. Others found democracy in the Qur'an.

In more recent times, Southeast Asian leaders wishing to restrain unfettered popular democracy have also appealed to tradition. Sukarno did exactly that when he suppressed his new country's quarreling political parties in favor of "Guided Democracy." Mahathir Mohamad, the authoritarian prime minister of Malaysia from 1982 to 2003, appealed to "Asian Values." In a similar vein, Singapore's founder Lee Kuan Yew defended his predilection for elite-led authoritarianism and his critique of Western individualism in Confucian terms. And what is "Thai democracy"? In Thailand, power-seizing generals and their elite civil-society supporters in recent years have overthrown popularly elected civilian governments on the grounds that they violated Thai values honoring religion, monarchy, and the nation.

Religious identities

Religion is another arena where resistance to the West's influence is strong. Flourishing movements among Southeast Asian Buddhists and Muslims emphasize reasserting religious values in the face of the highly individualistic values of the West. This is especially strong among the region's Muslims, who make up

37 percent of the population. Keep in mind that, today, virtually all Muslim young people yearn to use computers and high-tech smartphones. They are avid consumers of Western culture in the forms of music, films, and television shows. In these ways they are thoroughly modern. But they are also emphatically Muslim.

Throughout Muslim Southeast Asia today, mosques are full; young people and their elders regularly gather to study and pray; people increasingly use Arabic salutations in social encounters and public events; Muslim self-improvement books, videos, and television shows proliferate; and Muslim women wear head scarves and appropriately modest clothing in accordance with conservative practices. (For the youth, blue jeans are often part of the ensemble.) These phenomena emphasize the positive identity of Islam.

Embedded within this larger phenomenon are social and ideological movements that are politically assertive, including political parties in Malaysia and Indonesia that campaign for making the laws of Islam (Sharia) the laws of the land. In a handful of provinces they have succeeded, but by and large they have not. The debate remains a lively one. Meanwhile, national governments have stepped up their support for Islam in the realms of education and mosque building and in facilitating the Hajj. In Malaysia especially, the ruling party has increasingly adopted the mantle of Islam as part of the country's Malay identity.

At the same time, more extreme Muslim subcultures have also penetrated Southeast Asia, recruiting small numbers into exclusionist cults and jihadist movements associated with global assaults aimed at the West, such as al-Qaeda and ISIS (Islamic State). Extremists have been identified in Malaysia, Indonesia, and the southern Philippines. In Indonesia sporadic terrorist attacks have occurred, including the infamous Bali bombings of 2001 and others, more recently, in Jakarta. This radical fringe does not speak for the vast majority. Still, it puts the region's Muslims on edge and acts as an alarm factor for Christian minorities, who in today's Malaysia and Indonesia are already inclined to feel beleaguered in the face of an assertive Islam. An unfortunate consequence of this has been Muslim-Christian violence in several places in Indonesia.

Across the mainland, Buddhism remains the religious discourse through which most Thais, Burmese, Lao, and Cambodians understand and interpret the contemporary world. This can take multiple forms, from the purely contemplative to the politically engaged. Buddhism is invoked with respect to every issue, from poverty, crime, and gender to kingship and democracy. New sects flourish. In places, Buddhism is highly politicized, especially in Myanmar, where Buddhists are an empowered majority. As noted, longstanding tensions and rivalries between Buddhists and Muslims in some areas lie behind recent bloody outbursts and the flow of Muslim refugees abroad.

Meanwhile, Christianity is growing in Southeast Asia. Significant populations of Christians have been present in the region for a long time in the Philippines, Vietnam, East Timor, and parts of eastern Indonesia. Christian missionaries during the high colonial period created further pockets of Christians in Burma and Indonesia. In the years since independence, Catholicism has advanced among the region's ethnic Chinese populations in Indonesia and elsewhere, and Protestant sects have advanced generally, especially Pentecostal and evangelical denominations that have evangelized the region's now-exposed hill peoples and restless urbanites in places like Singapore. Today, a quarter of all Southeast Asians are Christian.

Yet, even as world-religion identities grow stronger in Southeast Asia, the region's cultures of fusion and tolerance survive. In one telling example, two thousand-year-old Hindu temples recently unearthed on the campus of the Islamic University of Indonesia will not be destroyed or covered up but will instead be displayed prominently on the Muslim campus. As for Southeast Asia's primordial spirits, they live on comfortably embedded within the everyday spiritual habits of millions of the region's Buddhists, Muslims, and Christians. Spirits rarely make the news but, in 2015, they did so when the deputy chief minister of Sabah, Malaysia, blamed a deadly earthquake on foreign tourists who had stripped naked on Mount Kinabalu and disturbed the local spirits. To appease them, rituals were duly held.

A beleaguered habitat

Visitors to Southeast Asia today from outside the region arrive at swanky international airports in or near a capital city and many will not stray far from these megacities—Bangkok, Singapore, Manila, Jakarta—and their five-star hotels, modern office buildings, fashionable restaurants, and chic shopping malls or from well-traveled tourist pathways that lead to museums, monuments, and beaches. Yet even privileged travelers cannot altogether escape the profound environmental forces that impact ordinary Southeast Asians.

The human habitat of today's Southeast Asia has been shaped by the region's accelerating participation in global trade, leading growing numbers of people to press into the region's forests, wetlands, and hills to reap subsistence and profits from the land. Much of the region's old-growth forest has succumbed to loggers and agribusiness companies and, in places, to needy farmers. Some of the land has been converted into industrial tree plantations and other monocultures, but much has simply been degraded. Silted rivers and downstream floods are other common consequences of this transformation, along with declining biodiversity and animal habitat and the loss of the climate-regulating benefits of forests.

Efforts to convert remaining forests in Kalimantan and Sumatra to oil palm and paper-wood plantations are so aggressive that companies induce massive fires to clear the land. Smoke from these fires rolls across the earth, creating sickening fumes in Jakarta, Singapore, Kuala Lumpur, and southern Thailand. People wear face masks in defense. Otherwise, it is the exhaust from the surging numbers of cars, trucks, buses, and motorbikes that dirties the air of the region's cities. Asthma, bronchitis, and lung disease plague millions of urbanites. The water is not clean either, as unchecked human and industrial waste, not to mention simple trash, flows into the rivers, lakes, bays, and city canals. In Southeast Asia the rule has become bottled water only, please.

Southeast Asians are justly alarmed about this. Activists are vocal, and conscientious politicians are enacting sensible laws. Forest rangers and air-quality inspectors are at work. Indeed, ASEAN task forces, scientists, technocrats, ministers, government officials, and nongovernmental organizations (NGOs) are urgently trying to turn the tide. They are succeeding here and there. But by and large they are no match for the huge global forces driving the world's economy or for the powerful local interests in Southeast Asia who have much to gain from their failure. The hard truth is that the assault on Southeast Asia's environment continues largely unabated today.

The situation is scarcely different in China or India or much of the developing world. The impact of globalization, climate change, and the scramble for the earth's resources is universal. As a habitat for humans and other living things, Southeast Asia is inextricably part of these larger forces. Its fate is also the fate of the earth.

References

Chapter 2: Kingdoms

The essential point about power arising from control of people is emphasized by Anthony Reid in *Southeast Asia in the Age of Commerce, 1450–1680*, vol. 1, *The Land below the Winds* (New Haven, CT: Yale University Press, 1988). The description of Southeast Asian warfare and of early-modern Southeast Asian commerce also largely follows Reid, *Southeast Asia in the Age of Commerce, 1450–1680*, vol. 1, *The Land below the Winds*, and vol. 2, *Expansion and Crisis*.

For mandalas, see Stanley J. Tambiah, "The Galactic Polity in Southeast Asia," *Hau: Journal of Ethnographic Theory* 3.3 (2013): 503–534; and O. W. Wolters, *History, Culture, and Region in Southeast Asian Perspectives* (Ithaca, NY: Cornell Southeast Asia Program, 1999). Wolters introduced the term "men of prowess."

For patron-client ties, a good place to begin is James C. Scott, "Patron-Client Politics and Political Change in Southeast Asia," *The American Political Science Review* 66.1 (1972): 91–113.

The idea that Southeast Asians chose to live in inaccessible uplands to be free, is presented in James C. Scott, *The Art of Not Being Governed: An Anarchist History of Upland Southeast Asia* (New Haven, CT: Yale University Press, 2010).

The term "mystic synthesis," to describe Java's Hindu-Buddhist-Islamic ways, comes from M. C. Ricklefs, *Mystic Synthesis in Java: A History of Islamization from the Fourteenth to the Early Nineteenth Centuries* (Norwalk, CT: EastBridge Signature Books, 2006).

Chapter 3: Colonies

Conrad quotation is from Joseph Conrad, *Outcast of the Islands* (London: J. M. Dent, 1949), 57.

Swettenham quotation is from Frank Swettenham, *British Malaya: An Account of the Origin and Progress of British Influence in Malaya* (London: John Lane, 1907), 345.

Chapter 4: Nations

Kipling quotation is from Rudyard Kipling, "Mandalay," in *Barrack-Room Ballads and Other Verses* (London: Methuen, 1892).

On nations as geo-bodies, see Thongchai Winichakul, *Siam Mapped: A History of the Geo-body of a Nation* (Honolulu: University of Hawaii Press, 1994).

Chapter 5: The past is in the present

On Southeast Asian democracy, see, inter alia, Edward Aspinall, "The Surprising Democratic Behemoth: Indonesia in Comparative Asian Perspective," *Journal of Asian Studies* 74.4 (2015): 889–902; and Mark R. Thompson, "Democracy with Asian Characteristics," *Journal of Asian Studies* 74.4 (2015): 875–887.

On Thailand's Muslim south, see Michael Montesano and Patrick Jory, eds., *Thai South and Malay North: Ethnic Interactions on a Plural Peninsula* (Singapore: National University of Singapore Press, 2008).

On Sulu Sea issues, see Katrina Navallo, "Filipino Migrants in Sabah: Marginalized Citizens in the Midst of Interstate Disputes," Academia.edu, 2015.

On the fate of the hills, see Jefferson Fox, Yayoi Fujita, Dimbab Ngidang, et al. "Policies, Political-Economy and Swidden in Southeast Asia," *Human Ecology* 37.3 (2009): 305–322.

Further reading

Chapter 1: What is Southeast Asia?

Beeson, Mark, ed. *Contemporary Southeast Asia*. London: Palgrave Macmillan, 2009. See especially Greg Felker, "The Political Economy of Southeast Asia," 46–73.

Dayley, Robert, and Clark D. Neher. *Southeast Asia in the New International Arena*. Boulder, CO: Westview, 2013.

Duncan, Christopher R. *Civilizing the Margins: Southeast Asian Government Policies for the Development of Minorities*. Ithaca, NY: Cornell University Press, 2004.

Jones, Gavin W. "The Population of Southeast Asia," Asia Research Institute, Working Paper 196. Singapore: National University of Singapore, 2013.

Robison, Richard, ed. *Routledge Handbook of Southeast Asian Politics*. London: Routledge, 2014. See especially Jeffrey A. Winters, "Oligarchs and Oligarchy in Southeast Asia," 53–67.

Scott, James C. *The Art of Not Being Governed: An Anarchist History of Southeast Asia*. New Haven, CT: Yale University Press, 2010.

Chapter 2: Kingdoms

Andaya, Barbara Watson, and Leonard Y. Andaya. *A History of Early Modern Southeast Asia*. Cambridge, UK: Cambridge University Press, 2015.

Coedès, George. *The Indianized States of Southeast Asia*. Translated by Susan Cowing. Honolulu: Hawaii East-West Center Press, 1968.

Lieberman, Victor. *Strange Parallels: Southeast Asia in Global Context, c800-1830*. 2 vols. Cambridge, UK: Cambridge University Press, 2003-2009.

Reid, Anthony. *Southeast Asia in the Age of Commerce*. 2 vols. New Haven, CT: Yale University Press, 1988-1993.

Tarling, Nicholas, ed. *The Cambridge History of Southeast Asia: From Early Times to c1500*. Vol. 1. Cambridge, UK: Cambridge University Press, 1999.

Wolters, O. W. *History, Culture, and Region in Southeast Asian Perspectives*. Ithaca, NY: Cornell University Southeast Asia Program, 1999.

Woodside, Alexander. *Vietnam and the Chinese Model: A Comparative Study of Nguyen and Ch'ing Government in the First Half of the Nineteenth Century*. Cambridge, MA: Harvard University Press, 1971.

Chapter 3: Colonies

Brocheux, Pierre, and Daniel Hémery. *Indochina: An Ambiguous Colonization, 1858-1954*. Berkeley: University of California Press, 2009.

Conrad, Joseph. *An Outcast of the Islands*. 1896. Reprint, Cambridge, UK: Cambridge University Press, 2016.

Conrad, Joseph. *Lord Jim*. 1900. Reprint, Cambridge, UK: Cambridge University Press, 2011.

Couperus, Louis. *The Hidden Force*. 1900. Translated by Alexander Teixeira de Mattos. Amherst: University of Massachusetts Press, 1985.

Duras, Marguerite. *The Lover*. Translated by Barbara Bray. New York: Pantheon Books, 1985.

Cribb, Robert, ed. *The Late Colonial State in Indonesia: Political and Economic Foundations of the Netherlands Indies, 1880-1942*. Leiden, The Netherlands: KITLV Press, 1994.

Furnivall, J. S. *Netherlands India: A Study of a Plural Economy*. Cambridge, UK: Cambridge University Press, 1944.

McCoy, Alfred W. *Policing America's Empire: The United States, the Philippines, and the Rise of the Surveillance State*. Part 1. Madison: University of Wisconsin Press, 2009.

Orwell, George. *Burmese Days*. 1934. Reprint, London: Penguin, 2014.

Owen, Norman G. *Prosperity without Progress: Manila Hemp and Material Life in the Colonial Philippines*. Berkeley: University of California Press, 1984.

Phelan, John Leddy. *The Hispanization of the Philippines: Spanish Aims and Filipino Responses, 1565–1700*. Madison: University of Wisconsin Press, 1959.

Reid, Anthony, ed. *Sojourners and Settlers: Histories of Southeast Asia and the Chinese*. Sydney: Allen & Unwin, 1996.

Ricklefs, M. C., Bruce Lockhart, Albert Lau, Portia Reyes, and Maitrii Aung-Thwin. *A New History of Southeast Asia*. Basingstoke, UK: Palgrave Macmillan, 2010.

Tagliacozzo, Eric. *Secret Trades, Porous Borders: Smuggling and States along a Southeast Asian Frontier, 1865–1915*. New Haven, CT: Yale University Press, 2005.

Thongchai Winichakul. *Siam Mapped: A History of the Geo-body of a Nation*. Honolulu: University of Hawaii Press, 1994.

Chapter 4: Nations

Anderson, Benedict R. O'Gorman. *Imagined Communities: Reflections on the Origin and Spread of Nationalism*. London: Verso, 2006.

Bradley, Mark Philip. *Vietnam at War*. Oxford: Oxford University Press, 2009.

Chandler, David P. *The Tragedy of Cambodian History: Politics, War, and Revolution since 1945*. New Haven, CT: Yale University Press, 1991.

Edwards, Penny. *Cambodge: The Cultivation of a Nation, 1860–1945*. Honolulu: University of Hawaii Press, 2007.

Elson, Robert E. *The Idea of Indonesia: A History*. Cambridge, UK: Cambridge University Press, 2008.

Evans, Grant. *A Short History of Laos: The Land in Between*. Chiang Mai, Thailand: Silkworm Books, 2002.

Kahin, George McTurnan. *Nationalism and Revolution in Indonesia*. Ithaca, NY: Cornell University Press, 1952.

McCoy, Alfred W., ed. *Southeast Asia under Japanese Occupation*: New Haven, CT: Yale University Southeast Asia Studies, 1980.

Marr, David. *Vietnamese Anticolonialism, 1885–1925*. Berkeley: University of California Press, 1971.

Robinson, Geoffrey. *The Dark Side of Paradise: Political Violence on Bali*. Ithaca, NY: Cornell University Press, 1995.

Shiraishi, Takashi. *An Age in Motion: Popular Radicalism in Java, 1912–1926*. Ithaca, NY: Cornell University Press, 1990.

Taylor, Robert H. *The State in Myanmar*. Honolulu: University of Hawaii Press, 2009.

Zinoman, Peter. *The Colonial Bastille: The History of Imprisonment in Vietnam, 1862–1940*. Berkeley: University of California Press, 2001.

Chapter 5: The past is in the present

Anderson, Benedict R. O'Gorman. *The Spectre of Comparisons: Nationalism, Southeast Asia, and the World*. Manila: Ateneo de Manila University Press, 2004.

Hefner, Robert W. *Civil Islam: Muslims and Democratization in Indonesia*. Princeton, NJ: Princeton University Press, 2000.

Ricklefs, M. C. *Islamization and Its Opponents in Java, c1300 to the Present*. Honolulu: University of Hawaii Press, 2012.

Schober, Juliane. *Modern Buddhist Conjunctures in Myanmar: Cultural Narratives, Colonial Legacies, and Civil Society*. Honolulu: University of Hawaii Press, 2011.

Sidel, John T. *Capital, Coercion, and Crime: Bossism in the Philippines*. Stanford, CA: Stanford University Press, 1999.

Good feature writing about current affairs in Southeast Asia can be found on the *Wall Street Journal, New York Times*, and BBC websites alongside those of many regional newspapers and article aggregators / new portals, e.g., the Philippines-based Rappler and the Australia National University–based *New Mandala*. Economic data and reports on contemporary issues, such as poverty, human trafficking, the environment, etc., can be found on several United Nations websites, such as the United Nations High Commissioner for Refugees (UNHCR), United Nations Development Programme (UNDP), United Nations Environment Programme (UNEP), United Nations Children's Fund (UNICEF), United Nations Economic and Social Commission for Asia and the Pacific (ESCAP), and UN News Centre; see also the World Bank, Asian Development Bank (ADB), Association of Southeast Asian Nations (ASEAN), World Resources Institute (WRI), Amnesty International, and World Wildlife Fund (WWF). Useful academic journals include *Contemporary Southeast Asia, Asian Survey, Sojourns*, and the *Journal of Southeast Asian Studies*.

Index

Index

"Clearly written and inviting, even to readers who may not at first consider themselves scientific, *The World According to Physics* is a book that should be read and appreciated by many."

—Jocelyn Bell Burnell, University of Oxford

"A clear, simple, and fascinating account of what physics tells us about our universe, and— crucially—what evidence supports that view, from one of the most talented, inspiring, and informative popularizers of science. A triumph!"

—Ian Stewart, author of *Do Dice Play God?*

"This book presents a comprehensive account of modern physics, weaving together a tapestry of new and familiar topics. Al-Khalili has a distinctively light voice that comes across throughout and works incredibly well."

—Pedro G. Ferreira, author of *The Perfect Theory: A Century of Geniuses and the Battle over General Relativity*

THE WORLD ACCORDING TO PHYSICS

THE WORLD ACCORDING TO PHYSICS

JIM AL-KHALILI

PRINCETON UNIVERSITY PRESS
PRINCETON AND OXFORD

Requests for permission to reproduce material from this work
should be sent to permissions@press.princeton.edu

Published by Princeton University Press
41 William Street, Princeton, New Jersey 08540
6 Oxford Street, Woodstock, Oxfordshire OX20 1TR

press.princeton.edu

ISBN 978-0-691-18230-8
ISBN (e-book) 978-0-691-20167-2

British Library Cataloging-in-Publication Data is available

Editorial: Ingrid Gnerlich and Arthur Werneck
Production Editorial: Mark Bellis
Text and Cover Design: Chris Ferrante
Production: Jacquie Poirier
Publicity: Sara Henning-Stout and Katie Lewis
Copyeditor: Annie Gottlieb

This book has been composed in Adobe Text and Futura PT

Printed on acid-free paper. ∞

Printed in the United States of America

10 9 8 7 6 5 4 3 2

CONTENTS

This book is an ode to physics.

I first fell in love with physics when I was a teenager. Admittedly, this was partly because I realised I was good at it. The subject seemed to be a fun mix of puzzle-solving and common sense, and I enjoyed playing with the equations, manipulating the algebraic symbols, and plugging in numbers so that they revealed the secrets of nature. But I also realised that if I wanted satisfying answers to the many deep questions about the nature of the universe and the meaning of existence bubbling up in my teenage mind, then physics was the subject I had to study. I wanted to know: What are we made of? Where do we come from? Does the universe have a beginning, or an end? Is it finite in extent, or does it stretch out to infinity? What was this thing called quantum mechanics that my father had mentioned to me? What is the nature of time? My quest to find answers to these questions has led to a life spent studying physics. I have some answers to my questions now; others I am still searching for.

Some people turn to religion or some other ideology or belief system to find answers to life's mysteries. But for me, there is no substitute for the careful hypothesising, testing, and deducing of facts about the world that are the hallmark of the scientific method. The understanding we have gained through science—and physics in particular—of how the world is made up and how it works is, in my view, not just one of many equally valid ways of reaching the 'truth' about reality. It is the *only* reliable way we have.

No doubt many people never fell in love with physics, as I did. Perhaps they were turned off from studying science because they decided, or perhaps were told by others, that it is a hard—or a geeky—subject. And to be sure, getting to grips with the subtleties of quantum mechanics can bring on a headache. But the wonders of our universe can and should be appreciated by everyone, and gaining a basic understanding doesn't take a lifetime of study. In this book, I want to describe why physics is so wonderful, why it is such a fundamental science, and why it is so crucial to our understanding of the world. The grand scope and sweep of physics today are breathtaking. That we now know what (almost) everything we see in the world is made of and how it holds together; that we can trace back the evolution of the entire universe to fractions of a second after the birth of space and time themselves; that through our knowledge of the physical laws of nature we have developed, and continue to develop, technologies that have transformed our lives—this is all pretty staggering. I still find myself thinking, as I write this: How can anyone *not* love physics?

This book is intended to serve as an introduction to some of the most profound and fundamental ideas in physics. But the topics I cover are not ones you will likely have encountered at school. For some readers, the book may be a first invitation into physics—one that will entice you to learn more about it, maybe even pursue it as a lifelong journey of study and discovery, as I have. To others, who may have gotten off on the wrong foot with physics early on, it may serve as a gentle reintroduction. For many, it may provoke wonder at just how far humanity has come in its quest to understand.

To convey a working knowledge of what physics tells us about the nature of our world, I have selected an array of the most important concepts in modern physics and attempted to show how they link together. We'll survey the vast range of this conceptual landscape, from the physics of the largest cosmic scales to that of the smallest quantum level; from physicists' quest to unify the laws of nature to their search for the simplest possible physical principles governing life; from the speculative frontiers of theoretical research to the physics that underpins our everyday experiences and technologies. I will also offer readers some new perspectives: ideas that we physicists have learnt to accept, but which we haven't done a very good job of conveying to those outside our innermost circles of experts. For example, down at the subatomic scale, separated particles communicate with each other instantaneously despite being far apart, in a way that violates common sense. This property, called nonlocality, may force us ultimately to revise our entire understanding of the structure of space itself. But, sadly, many non-physicists—and indeed some physicists— misunderstand or misinterpret what this really means.

A criticism levelled (usually by theoretical physicists) at many popular science books covering fundamental concepts in physics is that they don't always help the lay reader grasp what these concepts actually mean. In my view, this is because the physicists who truly understand the concepts, and who write the research papers and come up with new theories, are not necessarily the best at explaining their own ideas to non-physicists. But, in turn, those who may have more experience and success with communicating their work to the public may not understand certain concepts deeply enough themselves to go beyond simple analogies. Even if one understands the physics and can successfully (I hope) communicate with non-physicists, it is not a small challenge to explain terms like gauge invariance, duality, eternal inflation, the holographic principle, conformal field theories, anti-de Sitter spaces or vacuum energy in a way that conveys real insight into the physics involved, without involving complex mathematics. I have done my best, but there may well be some readers who feel I could have done better. And, of course, this will be true.

Nevertheless, if you wish to delve more deeply into any particular topics which I only touch on briefly here, then there are many books that do this brilliantly. I list at the end of the book some of those I believe you would find the most accessible and enlightening. Many of the books on this list describe the journey of scientific progress—how physics has developed over the millennia since the ancient Greeks, how discoveries were made, and how theories and hypotheses were proposed and discarded. These books often focus on the revolutions that have overturned previously held views about the universe and describe the leading players in these historical accounts. In this short book, however, I won't look back on how far we've come; nor will I say too much about how far we have yet to go (since I don't know, and also because I suspect it is still a long way), although I will focus in chapter 8 on what we *know* we don't know.

I have no particular theory to plug, either. For example, when it comes to reconciling quantum mechanics with general relativity (the holy grail of modern theoretical physics), I do not subscribe to either of the two main camps working towards this goal: I am neither a string theory advocate nor a loop quantum gravity fan,[1] since neither theory falls within my particular specialism; and when it comes to interpreting the meaning of quantum mechanics, I am neither a 'Copenhagenist' nor a 'many worlds' enthusiast.[2] But, this won't stop me from being somewhat polemical about these issues now and then.

I will also try not to become too embroiled in philosophical or metaphysical musings, even though there is a temptation to do so when one is discussing some of the more profound ideas at the forefront of physics, whether on the nature

---

1 I will of course explain what these ideas involve later.

2 Again, I will explain later.

of space and time, the various interpretations of quantum mechanics, or even the meaning of reality itself. I do not mean by this that physics does not need philosophy. To give you an idea of how philosophy feeds into my subject at the most fundamental level, you may be surprised to know that physicists cannot yet even agree on whether the job of physics is to figure out how the world *really* is, as Einstein believed—to reach some ultimate truth that is waiting out there to be discovered—or whether it is to build models of the world and to come up with our best current stab at *what we can say* about reality, a reality that we may never truly know. On this matter, I am on the side of Einstein.

To put it simply, I would argue that physics gives us the tools to understand the entire universe. The study of physics is a search for explanations, but to embark on that search we must first ask the right questions, something philosophers are very good at.

And so, we will begin our journey in a suitably humble frame of mind, one that, if we're honest, we all share—as children, as adults, and with generations past and future: one of not knowing. By thinking about what we don't yet know, we can think about how we can best find out. It is the many questions we have asked over the course of our human history that have given us an ever-more-accurate picture of the world we know and love.

So, here is the world according to physics.

THE WORLD ACCORDING TO PHYSICS

CHAPTER 1

THE AWE OF UNDERSTANDING

While stories will always be a vital part of human culture, even in science—and our lives would be the poorer without them—modern science has now replaced many of the ancient mythologies and accompanying superstitious beliefs. A good example of how we have demystified our approach to understanding the world is the creation myths. Since the dawn of history, humankind has invented stories about the origins of our world, and deities that were instrumental in its creation, from the Sumerian god Anu, or Sky Father, to the Greek myths about Gaia being created out of Chaos and the Genesis myths of the Abrahamic religions, which are still believed as literal truths in many societies around the world. It may appear to many non-scientists that our modern cosmological theories about the origins of the universe are themselves no better than the religious mythologies they replace—and, if you look at some of the more speculative ideas in modern theoretical physics, you might agree that those who feel this way have a point. But through rational analysis and careful observation—a painstaking process of testing and building up scientific evidence, rather than accepting stories and explanations with blind faith—we can now claim with a high degree of confidence that we know quite a lot about our universe. We can also now say with confidence that what mysteries remain need not be attributed to the supernatural. They are phenomena we have yet to understand—and which we hopefully will understand one day through reason, rational enquiry, and, yes . . . physics.

Contrary to what some people might argue, the scientific method is *not* just another way of looking at the world, nor is it just another cultural ideology or belief system. It is the way we learn about nature through trial and error, through experimentation and observation, through being prepared to replace ideas that turn out to be wrong or incomplete with better ones, and through seeing patterns in nature and beauty in the mathematical equations that describe these patterns. All the while we deepen our understanding and get closer to that 'truth'— the way the world *really* is.

There can be no denying that scientists have the same dreams and prejudices as everyone else, and they hold views that may not always be entirely objective. What one group of scientists calls 'consensus', others see as 'dogma'. What one generation regards as established fact, the next generation shows to be naïve misunderstanding. Just as in religion, politics, or sport, arguments have always raged in science. There is often a danger that, all the while a scientific issue remains unresolved, or at least open to reasonable doubt, the positions held by each side of the argument can become entrenched ideologies. Each viewpoint can be nuanced and complex, and its advocates can be just as unshakable as they would be in any other ideological debate. And just as with societal attitudes on religion, politics, culture, race, or gender, we sometimes need a new generation to come along, shake off the shackles of the past, and move the debate forward.

But there is also a crucial distinction to science, when compared with other disciplines. A single careful observation or experimental result can render a widely held scientific view or long-standing theory obsolete and replace it with a new worldview. This means that those theories and explanations of natural phenomena that have survived the test of time are the ones we trust the most; they are the ones we are most confident about. The Earth goes around the Sun, not the other way around; the universe is expanding, not static; the speed of light in a vacuum always measures the same no matter how fast the measurer of that speed is moving; and so on. When a new and important scientific discovery is made, which changes the way we see the world, not all scientists will buy into it immediately, but that's *their* problem; scientific progress is inexorable, which, by the way, is *always* a good thing: knowledge and enlightenment are always better than ignorance. We start with not knowing, but we seek to find out . . . and, though we may argue along the way, we cannot ignore what we find. When it comes to our scientific understanding of how the world is, the notion that 'ignorance is bliss' is a load of rubbish. As Douglas Adams once put it: 'I'd take the awe of understanding over the awe of ignorance any day.'[1]

WHAT WE DON'T KNOW

It is also true that we are constantly discovering how much more there is that we don't yet know. Our growing understanding yields a growing understanding of our ignorance! In some ways, as I will explain, this is the situation we have in physics right now. We are currently at a moment in history when many physicists see, if not a crisis in the subject, then at least the building up of a head of steam. It feels as though something has to give. A few decades ago, prominent physicists such as Stephen Hawking were asking, 'Is the end in sight

---

1 Douglas Adams, *The Salmon of Doubt: Hitchhiking the Galaxy One Last Time* (New York: Harmony, 2002), 99.

for theoretical physics?'[2] with a 'theory of everything' potentially just around the corner. They said it was just a matter of dotting the 'i's and crossing the 't's. But they were wrong, and not for the first time. Physicists had expressed similar sentiments towards the end of the nineteenth century; then along came an explosion of new discoveries (the electron, radioactivity, and X-rays) that couldn't be explained by the physics known at the time and which ushered in the birth of modern physics. Many physicists today feel that we might potentially be on the verge of another revolution in physics as big as that seen a century ago with the birth of relativity and quantum mechanics. I am not suggesting that we are about to discover some fundamental new phenomenon, like X-rays or radioactivity, but there may yet be a need for another Einstein to break the current deadlock.

The Large Hadron Collider has not yet followed up on its 2012 success in detecting the Higgs boson, and thereby confirming the ex-

2 This was the title of an article Hawking wrote in 1981: S. W. Hawking, *Physics Bulletin* **32**, no. 1 (1981): 15–17.

istence of the Higgs field (which I will discuss later); many physicists were hoping for the discovery of other new particles by now, which would help resolve long-standing mysteries. And we still don't understand the nature of the dark matter holding galaxies together or the dark energy that is ripping the universe apart; nor do we have answers to fundamental questions like why there is more matter than antimatter; why the properties of the universe are so finely tuned to allow for stars and planets, and life, to exist; whether there is a multiverse; or whether there was anything before the Big Bang that created the universe we see. There is still so much left that we cannot explain. And yet, it is hard *not* to be dazzled by our success so far. While some scientific theories may turn out to be connected to each other at a deeper level than we thought, and others may turn out to be entirely wrong, no one can deny just how far we've come.

Sometimes, in the light of new empirical evidence, we realise that we were barking up the wrong tree. Other times we simply refine an idea that turns out not to be wrong, but just a rough approximation that we improve upon to gain a more accurate picture of reality. There are some areas of fundamental physics that we might not be entirely happy with, where we know deep down that we've not heard the final word, but which we nevertheless continue to rely on for the time being because they are useful. A good example of this is Newton's universal law of gravitation. It is still referred to, grandly, as a 'law' because scientists at the time were so confident that it was the last word on the subject that they elevated its status above that of a mere 'theory'. The name stuck, despite the fact that we now know their confidence was misplaced. Einstein's general theory (note that it's called a theory) of relativity replaced Newton's law, because it gives us a deeper and more accurate explanation of gravity. And yet, we still use Newton's equations to calculate the flight trajectories of space missions. The predictions of Newtonian mechanics may not be as accurate as those of Einstein's relativity, but they are still good enough for nearly all everyday purposes.

Another example that we are still working on is the Standard Model of particle physics. This is an amalgamation of two separate mathematical theories, called electroweak theory and quantum chromodynamics, which together describe the properties of all the known elementary particles and the forces acting between them. Some physicists think of the Standard Model as nothing more than a stopgap until a more accurate and unified theory is discovered. And yet, it is remarkable that, as it stands now, the Standard Model can tell us everything we need to know about the nature of matter: how and why electrons arrange themselves around atomic nuclei, how atoms interact to form molecules, how those molecules fit together to make up everything around us, how matter interacts with light (and therefore how almost all phenomena can be explained). Just one aspect of it, quantum electrodynamics, underpins all of chemistry at the deepest level.

But the Standard Model cannot be the final word on the nature of matter, because it doesn't include gravity and it doesn't explain dark matter or dark energy, which between them make up most of the stuff of the universe. Answering some questions naturally leads to others, and physicists continue their search for physics 'beyond the Standard Model' in an attempt to address these lingering but crucial unknowns.

HOW WE PROGRESS

More than any other scientific discipline, physics progresses via the continual interplay between theory and experiment. Theories only survive the test of time as long as their predictions continue to be verified by experiments. A good theory is one that makes new predictions that can be tested in the lab, but if those experimental results conflict with the theory, then it has to be modified, or even discarded. Conversely, laboratory experiments can point to unexplained phenomena that require new theoretical developments. In no other science do we see such a beautiful partnership. Theorems in pure mathematics are proven with logic, deduction, and the use of axiomatic truths. They do not require validation in the real world. In contrast, geology, ethology or behavioural psychology are mostly observational sciences in which advances in our understanding are made through the painstaking collection of data from the natural world, or via carefully designed laboratory tests. But physics can *only* progress when theory and experiment work hand in hand, each pulling the other up and pointing to the next foothold up the cliffside.

Shining a light on the unknown is another good metaphor for how physicists develop their theories and models, and how they design their experiments to test some aspect of how the world works. When it comes to looking for new ideas in physics, there are, very broadly, two kinds of researchers. Imagine you're walking home on a dark, moonless night when you realise that there's a hole in your coat pocket through which your keys must have fallen at some point along your route. You know they have to be somewhere on the ground along the stretch of pavement you've just walked, so you retrace your steps. But do you only search the patches bathed in light beneath lampposts? After all, while these areas cover only a fraction of the pavement, at least you will see your keys if they are there. Or do you grope around in the dark stretches in between the pools of lamplight? Your keys may be more likely to be here, but they will also be more difficult to find.

Similarly, there are lamppost physicists and searchers in the dark. The former play it safe and develop theories that can be tested against experiment—they look where they can see. This means they tend to be less ambitious in coming up with original ideas, but they achieve a higher success rate in advancing our knowledge, albeit incrementally: evolution, not revolution. In contrast, the searchers in the dark are those who come up with highly original and speculative ideas that are not so easy to test. Their chances of success are lower, but the payoff can be greater if they are right, and their discoveries can lead to paradigm shifts in our understanding. This distinction is far more prevalent in physics than in other sciences.

I have sympathy for those who get frustrated by the searchers and the dreamers, who often work in esoteric areas like cosmology and string theory, for these are the people who think nothing of adding a few new dimensions here or there if it makes their maths prettier, or to hypothesise an infinity of parallel universes if it reduces the strangeness in ours. But there have been some famous examples of searchers who have struck gold. The twentieth-century genius Paul Dirac was a man driven by the beauty of his equations, which led him to postulate the existence of antimatter several years before it was discovered in 1932. Then there's Murray Gell-Mann and George Zweig, who in the mid-1960s independently predicted the existence of quarks when there was no experimental evidence to suggest such particles existed. Peter Higgs had to wait half a century for his boson to be discovered and the theory that bears his name to be confirmed. Even the quantum pioneer Erwin Schrödinger came up with his eponymous equation with nothing more than inspired guesswork. He picked the right mathematical form of equation even though he didn't yet know what its solution meant.

What unique talents did all these physicists have? Was it intuition? Was it a sixth sense that allowed them to sniff out nature's secrets? Possibly. The Nobel Prize winner Steven Weinberg believes it is the aesthetic beauty in the mathematics that has guided great theoreticians like Paul Dirac and the great nineteenth-century Scottish physicist James Clerk Maxwell.

But it is also true that none of these physicists worked in isolation, and their ideas still had to be consistent with all established facts and experimental observations.

THE SEARCH FOR SIMPLICITY

The true beauty of physics, for me, is found not only in abstract equations or in surprising experimental results, but in the deep underlying principles that govern the way the world is. This is a beauty that is no less awe-inspiring than a breathtaking sunset or a great work of art such as a Leonardo da Vinci painting or Mozart sonata. It is a beauty that lies not in the surprising profundity of the laws of nature, but in the deceptively simple underlying explanations (where we have them) for where those laws come from.[3]

---

3 Of course, beauty need not only be associated with simplicity. Just as with great art or music, there can also be beauty in the sheer complexity of some physical phenomena.

A perfect example of the search for simplicity is science's long and continuing journey to discover the basic building blocks of matter. Take a look around you. Consider the sheer range of materials that make up our everyday world: concrete, glass, metals, plastics, wood, fabrics, foodstuffs, paper, chemicals, plants, cats, people . . . millions of different substances, each with its own distinctive properties: squidgy, hard, runny, shiny, bendy, warm, cold. . . . If you knew nothing of physics or chemistry, you might imagine that most materials have little in common with each other; and yet we know that everything is made of atoms, and that there is only a finite number of different kinds of atoms.

But our quest for ever-deeper simplicity does not stop there. Thinking about the structure of matter goes all the way back to the fifth century BC in ancient Greece, when Empedocles first proposed that all matter consisted of four fundamental 'elements' (his 'fourfold roots of everything'): earth, water, air, and fire. In contrast to this simple idea, and around the same time, two other philosophers, Leucippus and his pupil Democritus, proposed that all matter was composed of tiny indivisible 'atoms'. However, these two promising ideas conflicted with each other. While Democritus believed that matter was ultimately made of fundamental building blocks, he thought there would be an infinite variety of such different atoms; whereas Empedocles, who proposed that everything was ultimately made up of just four elements, argued that these elements were continuous and infinitely divisible. Both Plato and Aristotle promoted the latter theory and rejected Democritus's atomism, believing that its simplistic mechanistic materialism could not produce the rich diversity of beauty and form of the world.

What the Greek philosophers were doing was not true science as we understand it today—apart from a few notable exceptions, such as Aristotle (the observer) and Archimedes (the experimenter), their theories were often not much more than idealised philosophical concepts. Nevertheless, today, through the tools of modern science, we know that both of those ancient ideas (atomism and the four elements) were, in spirit at least, along the right lines: that all the stuff making up our world, including our own bodies, and including everything we see out in space—the Sun, the Moon, and the stars—is all made of fewer than a hundred different types of atoms. We also now know that atoms have internal structure. They are made of tiny, dense nuclei surrounded by clouds of electrons while the nucleus itself is made up of smaller constituents: protons and neutrons, which are in turn made of even more fundamental building blocks called quarks.

So, despite the apparent complexity of matter and the immeasurable variety of substances that can be made up from the chemical elements, the truth is that the ancients' quest for simplicity didn't go far enough. As we understand physics today, all the matter we see in the world is made up of not the four classical elements of the Greeks, but just three elementary particles: the 'up' quark, the 'down' quark, and the electron. That's it. Everything else is just detail.

And yet the job of physics is more than just classifying what the world is made of. It is about finding the correct explanations for the natural phenomena we observe and the underlying principles and mechanisms that account for them. While the ancient Greeks might have debated passionately about the reality of atoms or the abstract connection between 'matter' and 'form', they had no idea how to explain earthquakes or lightning, let alone astronomical events such as the phases of the Moon or the occasional appearance of comets—although this didn't prevent them from trying.

We have come a very long way since the Greeks of antiquity, and yet there is also plenty that we still have to understand and explain. The physics I will cover in this book is mostly the stuff we are confident about. Throughout, I will explain *why* we are confident and point out what is speculative and where there may be some wiggle room. Naturally, I anticipate that some parts of the story will become out-of-date in the future. Indeed, an important discovery might be made the day after this book's publication that revises some aspect of our understanding. But that is the nature of science. *Mostly*, what you will read about in this book is established beyond reasonable doubt to be the way the world *is*.

In the next chapter, I explore the idea of scale. No other science so brazenly addresses such a vast range of scales, of time, space, and energies, as physics does, from the unimaginably tiny quantum world to the entire cosmos, and from the blink of an eye to eternity.

After gaining an appreciation for the scope of what physics can explain, we will begin on our journey in earnest, starting with the three 'pillars' of modern physics: relativity, quantum mechanics, and thermodynamics. In order to paint the picture of our world that physics has given us, we must first prepare the canvas, and in this case the canvas is space and time. Everything that happens in the universe comes down to events that take place somewhere in space and at some moment in time. And yet, we will see in chapter 3 that we cannot separate the canvas from the painting. Space and time themselves are an integral part of reality. You may be shocked to discover just how different the physicist's view of space and time is from our everyday, commonsense one, for it relies on Einstein's general theory of relativity, which describes the nature of space and time and defines how we think about the fabric of the cosmos. Once this canvas is ready, we can proceed to prepare our paints. In chapter 4, I define what a physicist means by matter and energy, the stuff of the universe: what it consists of, how it was created, and how it behaves. One can think of this chapter as a companion to the previous one, because I also describe how matter and energy are intimately related to the space and time in which they exist.

In chapter 5, I plunge into the world of the very small, zooming in and shrinking down to study the nature of the fundamental building blocks of matter. This is the quantum world, our second pillar of modern physics, where matter behaves very differently from our everyday experiences, and where our grip on what is real becomes increasingly tenuous. And yet . . . our understanding of the quantum is far more than a flight of fancy or mere intellectual diversion; without an understanding of the rules governing the building blocks of matter and energy, we would not have been able to build our modern technological world.

In chapter 6, we zoom out of the quantum world to see what happens when we put many particles together to make up larger, more complex systems. What do physicists mean by order, disorder, complexity, entropy, and chaos? Here, we encounter the third pillar of physics, thermodynamics—the study of heat, energy, and the properties of matter in bulk. We are led inevitably to ask what makes life itself so special. How is living matter so different from non-living matter? After all, life must be subject to the same laws of physics as everything else. In other words, can physics help us understand the difference between chemistry and biology?

In chapter 7, I explore one of the most profound ideas in physics, the notion of unification: the way we have sought, and found, over and over again, universal laws that bring together seemingly disparate phenomena in nature under one unifying description or theory. I conclude the chapter with a look at some of the front-runners for an all-encompassing physical 'theory of everything'.

By chapter 8 we will have reached the limit of what we currently understand about the physical universe and can finally dip our toes in the vast ocean of the unknown. I explore some of the mysteries we are currently struggling with and speculate upon whether we are close to solving them.

In the penultimate chapter, I discuss how the interplay of theory and experiment in physics has led to the technologies on which our modern world is built. For example, without quantum mechanics, we would not have been able to understand the behaviour of semiconductors or invent the silicon chip, on which all of modern electronics is founded, and I would not be typing these words on my laptop. I will also take a look into the future and predict how current research into quantum technologies is going to revolutionise our world in unimaginable ways.

In the final chapter, I explore the notion of scientific truth, particularly in a 'post-truth' society in which many people remain suspicious

of science. How does the process of science dif-
fer from other human activities? Is there such a
thing as absolute scientific truth? And if the job
of science is to seek out deep truths about nature,
how should scientists convince wider society of
the value of the scientific enterprise: the forming
and testing of hypotheses, and rejecting them if
they do not fit the data? Will science ever come
to an end one day when we know all there is to
know? Or will the search for answers continue to
lead us deeper down an ever-expanding abyss?

I promised you in the preface that I would try
not to get too tangled up in philosophical musings, and yet here I am doing just that, and this is
still only the Introduction. So, I will take a deep
breath and start us off again, gently, with a sense
of scale.

CHAPTER 2

SCALE

Unlike philosophy, logic, or pure mathematics, physics is both an empirical and a quantitative science.[1] It relies on the testing and verification of ideas through reproducible observation, measurement, and experimentation. While physicists can sometimes propose exotic or outlandish mathematical theories, the only true measure of their efficacy and power is whether they describe phenomena in the real world against which we can test them. This is why Stephen Hawking never won a Nobel Prize for his work in the mid-1970s on the way black holes radiate energy, a phenomenon known as Hawking radiation: the Nobel is only awarded to theories or discover-

---

1 Just for completeness, I should add that during the past couple of decades a new discipline called experimental philosophy has emerged.

ies that have been confirmed experimentally. Likewise, Peter Higgs and others who made a similar prediction had to wait half a century for the existence of the Higgs boson to be confirmed at the Large Hadron Collider.

It is also the reason why physics as a scientific discipline only began to make truly impressive advances once the tools and instruments necessary to test theories—through observation, experimentation, and quantitative measurement—had been invented. The ancient Greeks may have been brilliant at abstract thinking, developing subjects such as philosophy and geometry to a level of sophistication that is still valid today, but—Archimedes aside—they were not particularly famous for their experimental prowess. The world of physics only really came of age in the seventeenth century, thanks to a large extent to the invention of the two most important instruments in all of science: the telescope and the microscope.

If we were only able to understand the world we can see with our naked eyes, then physics would not have got very far. The range of wavelengths that can be 'seen' by the human eye is just a sliver of the full electromagnetic spectrum, and our eyes are constrained to discerning only those objects that are not too small and not too far away. While we can, in principle, see out to infinity, provided a sufficient number of photons make it to our eyes (and given an infinite amount of time for them to reach us!), this would not likely provide us with much useful detail. But, once the microscope and the telescope were invented, they opened up windows on the world that dramatically increased our understanding, magnifying the very small and bringing closer the very far away. At last, we could make observations, and detailed measurements, to test and refine our ideas.

On the 7th of January 1610, Galileo pointed his modified and improved spyglass up towards the heavens and banished forever the notion that we were at the centre of the cosmos.[2] He observed

---

2 No doubt historians of science will dispute this simplistic claim. Galileo did not suddenly establish heliocentrism with his observations and really only offered suggestive facts (like Jupiter's moons).

four of the moons of Jupiter and correctly inferred that Copernicus's heliocentric model was correct—that the Earth goes around the Sun and not vice versa. By observing bodies in orbit around Jupiter, he showed that not all celestial bodies revolve around us. The Earth isn't at the centre of the cosmos, but is just another planet, like Jupiter, Venus, and Mars, orbiting the Sun. With that discovery, Galileo ushered in modern astronomy.

But it wasn't just a revolution in astronomy that Galileo would bring about. He also helped put the scientific method itself on a firmer foundation. Building on the work of the medieval Arab physicist Ibn al-Haytham, Galileo 'mathematised' physics itself. In developing mathematical relationships that describe, and indeed predict, the motions of bodies, he showed beyond doubt that, as he put it, the book of nature 'is written in mathematical language.'[3]

---

3 A quote from Galileo's famous book, *The Assayer* (Italian: *Il Saggiatore*), published in Rome in 1623.

At the opposite end of the scale to Galileo's astronomical observations, a very different new world was opened up by Robert Hooke and Antonie van Leeuwenhoek with the microscope. Hooke's famous book, *Micrographia,* published in 1665, contains stunning drawings of miniature worlds, from the eye of a fly and the hairs on the back of a flea to individual cells in plants, that no one had ever witnessed before.

Today, the range of scales open to exploration by humankind is astounding. With electron microscopes we can see individual atoms, just a tenth of a millionth of a millimetre across, and with giant telescopes we can gaze out to the furthest reaches of the observable universe 46.5 billion light-years away.[4] No other science studies such a span in scale. In fact, forget resolutions to the size of atoms, a team at the

---

4 The most distant light we can see, from the edge of the observable universe, has been travelling towards us for over 13 billion years and so shows us what the universe was like when it was very young. However, due to the expansion of space, the origin of this light is now much further away than 13 billion light-years.

University of St Andrews in Scotland recently showed me something mind-blowingly impressive when it comes to measuring the smallest length scales. They've come up with a way of measuring the wavelength of light using a device called a wavemeter, to an accuracy of a single attometre—or one-thousandth of the diameter of a proton. They did this by passing laser light through a short optical fibre, which scrambles the light into a grainy pattern called 'speckle', and then tracking how this pattern changes with the minutest of adjustments to the wavelength of the light.

And it is not only the range of *length* scales that physics embraces; we can also measure time from the minutest fractions of the twinkling of an eye to cosmic eternities. Here is a stunning example. In an experiment carried out in Germany in 2016, physicists measured a period of time almost too short to imagine. They were studying a phenomenon called the photoelectric effect, in which photons free up electrons by knocking them out of atoms. The process was first explained correctly by Einstein in 1905 in a famous paper for which he won the Nobel Prize many years later (and not for his work on the theories of relativity, as you may have thought). Today, this process of knocking electrons out of materials is called photoemission and is the way we turn sunlight into electricity in solar cells.

In the 2016 experiment, two special lasers were used. The first fired an almost unimaginably short pulse of ultraviolet laser light at a jet of helium gas. The duration of this pulse was a mere ten thousandth of a trillionth of a second, or 100 attoseconds (10^{-18} seconds).[5] The second laser was lower in energy (its frequency being in the infrared range) and its pulse duration was a little longer than the first. Its job was to capture the escaping electrons, allowing the researchers to calculate how long it had taken them to be knocked out. The researchers found that this was even quicker: a mere tenth of the duration of the first laser pulse. What is inter-

---

5 There are more attoseconds in a single second than there have been seconds since the Big Bang.

esting about this result is that the knocked-out electrons actually drag their heels a little. You see, helium atoms each contain two electrons, and the ones that are knocked out feel the influence of the partner they leave behind, which, ever so slightly, delays the ejection process. It is staggering to think that a physical process taking just a few attoseconds can actually be measured like this in the lab.

In my own field of nuclear physics, there are processes that are even faster than this, although these cannot be measured directly in the lab. Instead, we develop computer models to explain the different structures of atomic nuclei and the processes that take place when two nuclei collide and react. For example, the first step in nuclear fusion—when two heavy nuclei come together like coalescing drops of water to make an even heavier nucleus—involves the very rapid reorganization of all the protons and neutrons from both nuclei into the new combined nucleus. This quantum process takes less than a zeptosecond (10^{-21} seconds).

At the other extreme of the time scale, cosmologists and astronomers have been able to work out the age of (our part of) the universe so precisely that we are now confident that the Big Bang took place 13.8242 billion years ago (give or take a few million years). Our confidence in the accuracy of this value may sound arrogant to some—and even unbelievable to those who still cling to the medieval idea that the universe is only six thousand years old—so let me explain how we come to this figure.

Let me first make two important assumptions, which I will discuss in more detail later on, but will now just say that they are both supported strongly by observational evidence: (1) that the laws of physics are the same everywhere in our universe, and (2) that space looks the same in all directions (the same density and distribution of galaxies). This gives us confidence that we can use the observations we make from Earth, or via satellite observatories in orbit around the Earth, to learn about the entire cosmos. Doing this has allowed us to work out the age of the universe in several different ways.

For example, we can learn a lot by studying the stars in our galaxy. We know how long stars can live, depending on their size and brightness, which determines how fast they burn via thermonuclear fusion. This means we can work out the age of the oldest stars, which sets a lower limit on how old our galaxy is, which in turn gives us a lower limit on the age of the universe. Since the oldest stars are about 12 billion years, the universe cannot be younger than that.

Then, by measuring the brightness and colour of the light entering our telescopes from distant galaxies, we can work out how fast the universe is expanding, both now and in the past. The further out we look, the further back in time we are probing, since the light we see will have taken billions of years to reach us and is thus bringing us information about the distant past. And if we know how fast the universe has been expanding, we can wind back the clock to a time when everything was squeezed together in the same place: the moment of the universe's birth.

Quite separately, by studying the tiny variations in the temperature of deep space (the so-called cosmic microwave background) we can get an accurate snapshot of the universe as it was before any stars and galaxies had even formed, just a few hundred thousand years after the Big Bang. This allows us to pinpoint the age of the universe even more precisely.

While it is one thing to say that physics allows us to learn about the universe at the shortest and longest distance and time scales, what I find equally remarkable is that we have discovered laws of physics that apply across the entirety of these ranges. Maybe you do not find this surprising; maybe it is natural for you to assume that the laws of nature that operate on the human scale should also work on other scales of distance, time, and energy. But this should be far from obvious.

To explore this further, I will introduce three concepts that are not always taught to students of physics, but which most certainly should be: universality, symmetry, and reductionism.

UNIVERSALITY

The first 'universal'[6] law of physics was discovered by Isaac Newton.[7] Whether or not he saw an apple fall from a tree on his mother's farm, triggering him to develop his law of gravitation, or what the mathematical formula articulating this law looks like, are not of importance here. The crucial point is that Newton realised that the force that pulls an apple to the ground has the same origin as the force that keeps the Moon in orbit around the Earth—that a simple mathematical relation can describe both processes equally well. The way objects behave due to gravity here on Earth is the same as the behaviour of the

---

6 I am using the word here in a very general sense and not in the more specific way as understood by some physicists working in the field of statistical mechanics. There, the term 'universality', as introduced by the American physicist Leo Kadanoff in the 1960s, is the observation that there are properties for a class of physical systems that do not depend on their detailed structure and dynamics but can instead be deduced from a few global parameters.

7 In fact, Robert Hooke's work on gravitation preceded that of Newton.

Moon around the Earth, the planets around the Sun, and the Sun around the centre of the Milky Way galaxy. The gravitational force that shapes life on Earth is the same force that has shaped the entire universe since the Big Bang. The fact that Newton's description of gravity was superseded by Einstein's more accurate one more than two centuries later does not detract from this insight about the *universality* of gravity.

Einstein's general theory of relativity, which improved on the predictions of Newton, also gave us an entirely new description of reality, which I will explore in greater depth in the next chapter. Indeed, Einstein's theory demonstrates a universality that is quite astonishing, and I will mention just one aspect of it here to highlight what I mean. The beautiful mathematical construct that Einstein presented to the world in 1915 is also still our current best theory on the nature of space and time, and it is extremely accurate. It also correctly predicts that a gravitational field will *slow down* the passage of time: the stronger the field, the slower time runs. This effect has the strange consequence that time ticks by ever so slightly slower in the Earth's core (deep within its gravitational well) than it does on the surface. This difference in age that has accumulated over the four and half billion years of our planet's existence means that the core is in fact two and a half years younger than the crust. Put another way, for every sixty years of Earth's history, its core has aged one second less than its crust. This figure has been calculated using the formula from general relativity, and it is not at all obvious how we might go about checking it experimentally, but such is our trust in the formula that no physicist is in any real doubt about its veracity.

If you think about the above prediction, you might find it somewhat paradoxical. After all, if we were to drill a hole through the Earth, then travel down to its centre, we would no longer feel the effects of gravity since the Earth would be pulling us equally in all directions—we would feel weightless. However, the effect on time is not due to the strength of the gravitational *force* at the centre of the Earth, which is zero, but rather to the gravitational '*potential*' there. This is the amount of energy needed to pull a body from that location out to a place far from Earth's gravity entirely. A physicist would say that the core of the Earth is in the deepest part of the Earth's potential well, where the slowing of time is greatest.

We can even measure the difference in the rate of flow of time over a height of just a few metres. A clock upstairs in your house is in a slightly weaker gravitational potential (further from the Earth's core) than a clock downstairs, and so runs ever so slightly faster. But this effect is extremely tiny: the two clocks would be out of sync by just one second every hundred million years.

If you are feeling sceptical about all this, let me assure you that the quantitative effect of gravity on time is very real indeed; if we didn't take it into account in modern telecommunications, the smartphone in your pocket would not be able to pinpoint your location anywhere nearly as accurately. Where you are on Earth relies on your phone receiving signals from several GPS satellites in orbit. The time it takes for these electromagnetic waves to cover the distance has to be known to within just a few hundredths of a microsecond (so that your location can be pinpointed to within a few metres). But this doesn't work if we assume that time runs at the same rate everywhere. In fact, the highly precise atomic clocks on board satellites gain around 40 millionths of a second each day and so must be deliberately slowed down in order to match the rate of slower Earth-bound clocks. Without this, satellite clocks would gain time and your GPS location would drift by over ten kilometres each day—rendering the information useless.

What is also remarkable is that those same equations of general relativity that predict the way gravity causes tiny modifications to the rate at which clocks tick can also tell us about the longest time scales imaginable, mapping the history of the universe over billions of years all the way back to the Big Bang, and even predicting its future. Einstein's theory of relativity applies equally well at the shortest and longest intervals of time.

But this universality only stretches so far. We know that, at the very tiniest of length and time scales, the physics of our everyday world (whether according to Newton or Einstein) breaks down and must be replaced by the predictions of quantum mechanics. Indeed, as I will explain in the coming chapters, the very definition of time according to quantum theory differs dramatically from the way it enters into general relativity, which is just one of the many challenges still facing physicists in their attempts to combine relativity and quantum mechanics into one unified theory of quantum gravity.

SYMMETRY

The universality of the laws of nature has fascinating mathematical origins and is linked with one of the most powerful ideas in science: symmetry. At a rudimentary level, everyone understands what is meant by a geometric shape that is symmetrical. A square is symmetrical because if you draw a line vertically down its centre, splitting it in half (or doing the same thing with a horizontal or diagonal line), then swapping the two halves around doesn't alter its shape. You also achieve the same result if you rotate it in multiples of 90 degrees. A circle has even more symmetry, because you can rotate it by any angle without changing its appearance.

In physics, symmetries can tell us something much deeper about reality than just the invariance of certain shapes when they are rotated or flipped. When physicists say that a physical system has a symmetry, they mean that some property of that system stays the same when something else changes. This turns out to be a very powerful concept. 'Global' symmetries are when laws of physics remain the same (there is no change in the way they describe some feature of the world) as long as some other change, or 'transformation', is applied equally everywhere. In 1915, Emmy Noether discovered that, wherever we see such a global symmetry in nature, we can be sure to find an associated law of conservation (a physical quantity remaining the same). For example, the fact that the laws of physics don't change when you move from one place to the next gives us the law of conservation of momentum, and the fact that the laws of physics don't change from one time to the next gives us the law of conservation of energy.

This has proven to be an extremely useful idea in theoretical physics and has deep philosophical consequences. Physicists are always on the look-out for deeper, less obvious symmetries that are hidden in their mathematics. Noether's theorem tells us that we don't 'invent' the mathematics in order to have a way of describing the world, but rather, as Galileo observed, that nature speaks the language of mathematics, which is 'there', ready and waiting to be discovered.

The search for new symmetries has also helped physicists in their quest to unify the forces of nature. One such mathematical symmetry—that is not so easy to explain—is called supersymmetry. We do not yet know if this is a true property of nature, but if it is, then it could help us solve a number of mysteries, such as what dark matter is made of and whether string theory is the correct theory of quantum gravity. The problem is that this symmetry predicts the existence of a number of as yet undiscovered subatomic particles. Until we have experimental verification, supersymmetry remains just a neat mathematical idea.

Physicists have also learnt a lot—and picked up a stack of Nobel Prizes for their efforts—by trying to find exceptions to the rules and laws that these symmetries give us, an idea known as 'symmetry breaking'. Have you ever sat at a circular dinner table in restaurant or at a fancy function and forgotten whether the side plate for your bread roll is to your left or your right? Before any of the guests at your table touches anything, the neatly laid out arrangement of plates, glasses and cutlery is symmetric. Etiquette aside, it doesn't really matter which side your bread plate is on, but as soon as someone makes a choice and (correctly) places a bread roll on the side plate to their left, the perfect symmetry is broken and everyone else can follow suit.

Symmetry breaking has helped physicists understand the building blocks of matter: the elementary particles, and the forces between them. The most famous example relates to one of the two types of force acting within the confines of atomic nuclei, known as the weak nuclear force. Until the 1950s, the laws of physics were thought to be exactly the same in a mirror reflection of our universe. This idea (swapping left and right) is known as 'parity conservation' and is obeyed by the other three forces of nature: gravity, electromagnetism, and the strong nuclear force. But it turns out that the weak nuclear force, which is responsible for protons and neutrons transforming into each other, breaks this mirror symmetry. It does not lead to exactly the same physics when left and right are switched over. This violation of reflection symmetry now forms an important ingredient in the Standard Model of particle physics.

REDUCTIONISM

Much of modern science has been built on the idea that to understand some complex property of the world, we need to break it down to its basic parts, like taking a mechanical clock apart to see how all the gears and levers fit together to make it work. This view, that the whole is no more than the sum of its parts, is known as reductionism, and it has been a staple of many disciplines in science to this day. The idea goes back to the Greek philosopher, Democritus, and his notion of atomism—that matter cannot be infinitely divided but is instead composed of basic building blocks. Later philosophers, like Plato and Aristotle, argued against atomism, believing that there had to be something missing, which they thought of as 'the form of the thing', and which had to be added to the substance itself. Take, for example, the form of a statue. Its meaning and its essence are more than just the stone it is made of. This vague metaphysical notion is not a part of modern physics. But thinking of things in this way helps to make a clearer argument against reductionism.

Let's take another example: water. We can study the properties of a molecule of H_2O as much as we want: the geometry of the bonds between the oxygen and hydrogen atoms and the quantum rules that govern this, the way water molecules stick together and arrange themselves, and so on. But we would not be able to *deduce* the property of 'wetness' of water by looking solely at its constituent parts down at the molecular level. This 'emergent' property only becomes apparent when trillions of water molecules come together in bulk.

Does this then imply that the whole is more than the sum of its parts, in the sense that there is some extra physics that we need to include to explain, for example, the bulk properties of matter? Not necessarily. The idea of emergence—that there are qualities of the physical world, like heat or pressure or the wetness of water, that do not have counterparts at the level of atomic physics— does not mean that there is more to a system than the sum of its parts, provided those emergent properties are still only built upon more fundamental concepts, such as the electromagnetic forces between subatomic particles in the case of water.

The reductionist enterprise continued when physicists in the nineteenth century attempted to understand the properties of complex systems that could not be explained by the simple laws of Newtonian mechanics. Towards the end of that century, James Clerk Maxwell and Ludwig Boltzmann developed two new subfields of physics—thermodynamics and statistical mechanics—which helped physicists to learn about systems made up of many pieces by looking at them 'in bulk'. (We will look at these areas of physics more deeply in chapter 6.) Thus, while it is true that we cannot measure the temperature or pressure of a gas by looking at how its individual molecules vibrate and bump into each other, we still know that temperature and pressure are due to nothing more than the collective behaviour of individual molecules. What else can there be?

But while this simplistic reductionist line of thinking is not wrong—in the sense that there is no extra physical process that magically appears when we zoom out from the molecular scale—it is of limited usefulness when trying to describe the properties of a complex system. What we require is not 'new' physics, but 'more' physics, in order to learn about and understand how certain properties can emerge in a system from the collective behaviours of its constituents. The Nobel laureate Philip Anderson summed this view up in the title of a famous paper: 'More is different.'[8]

---

8 In this paper, published in 1972 [P. W. Anderson, Science 177 (4047): 393–96}], Anderson made his argument

But knowing that more physics is needed when we put the constituent parts (the particles, atoms and molecules) together to make up bulk matter is not the same as saying we know what that missing physics is. This becomes clear if we try to find a unified picture of the physical universe. We are still unable to derive the laws of thermodynamics from the Standard Model of particle physics, for example—or indeed to do the reverse, since it is not obvious which of these two pillars of physics is the more fundamental. And we are even further away from understanding more-complex structures, such as what dis-

---

against extreme reductionism. He used as an example the hierarchy of scientific disciplines arranged in a linear order, from physics, as the most 'fundamental' science, to chemistry to biology to psychology to the social sciences. This hierarchy did not imply, he claimed, that one subject is just an applied version of the one below, since 'at each stage, entirely new laws, concepts and generalizations are necessary, requiring inspiration and creativity to just as great a degree as in the previous one. Psychology is not applied biology nor is biology applied chemistry.' As an argument against reductionism, I regard this as somewhat weak. Whether or not a concept is fundamental does not depend on how profound it is, or how much inspiration or creativity was required to understand it.

tinguishes life from non-life. After all, you and I are still only made up of atoms, yet being alive is clearly more than just a matter of complexity, for a living organism is no more complex in terms of its atomic structure than an identical but recently deceased organism.

And yet . . . maybe we can dream of a time when we are able to have a single unified physical theory that underpins all natural phenomena. Until then, suffice it to say, a reductionist line of thinking only gets us so far, and we need to use different theories and models depending on what we are trying to describe.

THE LIMITS OF UNIVERSALITY

Despite our quest for laws of physics that are universal, the limits of reductionism point to the fact that sometimes the world can behave very differently at different scales and needs to be described and explained using the appropriate model or theory. For example, on the scale of planets, stars, and galaxies, gravity dominates everything—it controls the structure of the cosmos. But it plays no role, that we can detect, down at the atomic scale where the other three forces (electromagnetism and the strong and weak nuclear forces) dominate. Indeed, probably the biggest unresolved problem in the whole of physics—one we will return to in chapter 5—is that the laws of physics that describe our everyday, so-called 'classical' world of matter, energy, space, and time simply don't work when we shrink down to the world of individual atoms, where the very different rules of quantum mechanics come into play.

Even at the quantum level, we often need to choose the appropriate model that is most applicable to the system we wish to study. We've known since the early 1930s, for example, that the atomic nucleus is made up of protons and neutrons; but in the late 1960s, it was discovered that these particles are not elementary, and are in fact made up of even tinier, more fundamental constituents: the quarks. This has not meant that nuclear physicists were forced to describe the properties of nuclei using quark models. A simplistic reductionist approach might suggest that this is necessary for a deeper, more accurate description of the atomic nucleus. But that would not be very helpful. To a very good approximation, when describing the properties of nuclei, protons and neutrons behave as though they are structure-less entities and not composite systems of three quarks. So, while their properties and behaviour *must* ultimately be due to their deeper structure, this is not apparent or necessary if we wish to understand properties like the shape or stability of a nucleus. In fact, even within nuclear physics itself, a number of very different mathematical models are employed—each applying best to a certain class of nucleus; there is not a universal theory of nuclear structure.

This is what I mean by the world behaving differently at different scales of size, duration, and energy. While two of the wonderful things about physics are the universality of many of its theories and the way we can understand more about a system by digging deeper and under-standing how its parts relate to the whole, it is also true that we often have to choose the most appropriate theory depending on the scale we are interested in. If you want to fix your washing machine, you do not need to understand the intricacies of the Standard Model of particle physics—even though washing machines, like everything else in the world, are ultimately made up of quarks and electrons. If we tried to apply our most fundamental theories about the quantum nature of reality to every aspect of our day-to-day lives, we wouldn't get very far.

Now that we have explored both the potential and the limitations of what physics can tell us— from the power of the mathematical symmetries underpinning our physical laws, to the sheer scale over which these laws can be applied, to the limitations of reductionism and universality—we are ready to get down to business. In the next chapter, I begin with the first of the three fundamental pillars of physics: Einstein's relativity.

CHAPTER 3

SPACE AND TIME

In such a short book I am unable to cover all areas of physics, fascinating though so many of them are. Instead, I have distilled our current understanding of the physical universe down to three central pillars: three pictures of reality that come from very different directions. The first of these, introduced in this chapter and the next, is built on the work of Albert Einstein in the early twentieth century. It lays out our present understanding of the way matter and energy behave within space and time on the very largest scales due to the influence of gravity—an understanding that is encompassed in his famous general theory of relativity.

In order to paint Einstein's picture of the world, we must start with the canvas itself. Space and time are the substrates in which all events take place. However, such concepts are slippery.

Common sense tells us that space and time should be in place from the start—that space is *where* events happen and the laws of physics are acted out, while the inexorable passage of time is, well, just *is*. But, is our commonsense view of space and time right? An important lesson physicists must learn is to *not* always trust common sense. After all, common sense tells us that the Earth is flat, but even the Ancient Greeks understood that its sheer size meant we could not easily discern its curvature, but that there were simple experiments they could perform to prove that it was in fact a sphere. Similarly, everyday experience tells us that light has the properties of a wave and therefore cannot also behave as though it were made up of a stream of individual particles. If it were, how could we explain interference patterns? And yet it has been proven beyond doubt, through careful experiments, that our senses can deceive us when it comes to the nature of light. And when it comes to the quantum world, we must abandon many everyday notions based on simple intuition if we are to truly understand what is going on.

Learning not to always trust our senses is a valuable skill that physicists have inherited from the philosophers. As far back as 1641, René Descartes argued in his *Meditations on First Philosophy* that in order to know things about the material world that were absolutely true, he first needed to doubt everything, often despite what his senses were telling him. This doesn't mean that we cannot believe anything we are told or shown, but that, according to Descartes, those material things he judges to be true 'demand a mind wholly free of prejudices, and one which can be easily detached from the affairs of the senses'.[1]

In fact, long before even Descartes considered this, the medieval scholar Ibn al-Haytham began a philosophical movement in the early eleventh century known in Arabic as *al-Shukuk* (The Doubts), and he wrote extensively, particularly on the celestial mechanics of the Greeks, that

---

[1] From the 1911 edition of *The Philosophical Works of Descartes* (Cambridge University Press), translated by Elizabeth S. Haldane, p.135.

one should question past knowledge and not take what one is told without evidence. This is why physics has always been an empirical science relying on the scientific method of testing hypotheses and theories through experimentation.

Nevertheless, some of the most important breakthroughs in physics have been the results of the logical conclusions drawn not from real experiments or observations, but from 'thought experiments', whereby the physicist considers some hypothesis and devises an imaginary experiment that can test its consequences. Such an experiment may or may not be possible to perform in practice, but it can still provide us with a valuable tool to learn about the world through the power of logic and reasoning alone. Some of the most famous thought experiments were conducted by Einstein and helped him develop his theories of relativity. Once his theories were fully developed of course they could be tested in real laboratory experiments.

When it comes to the meaning of space and time the difficulty we have is not surprising, for we are ourselves imprisoned within them, and it is hard to free our minds from their confines and 'see' reality from the outside. And yet, incredibly, this is possible to do. In this chapter, I will outline our current understanding of the nature of space and time—a celebration of the debt we owe to Einstein and his two beautiful theories of relativity.

HOW DOES A PHYSICIST DEFINE SPACE AND TIME?

An important characteristic of Newtonian physics is that space and time have a real existence independent of the matter and energy that exist within them. But philosophers the world over had contemplated this idea long before Newton. For instance, Aristotle believed that empty space did not exist in its own right—that without matter there can be no space. Much later, Descartes argued that space was no more than the distance (or 'extension') between bodies. According to these two great thinkers, the space inside an empty box only exists because of the confines of the box—take away the walls of the

box, and the volume that was inside it no longer
has any meaning.

But let us explore this example a little. What
if you subsequently discovered that the box was
sitting within the empty space of a larger one?
Does the space within the smaller box, after its
walls are removed, continue to exist now that
it forms a part of the volume in the larger box?
And must it therefore have been a real 'thing'
all along? Imagine now that the empty smaller
box—where, by empty, I mean truly devoid of
anything: a vacuum—is *moving* in a vacuum contained within the larger box. Is the empty space
inside the smaller box the same empty space as
it moves, or is it occupying different parts of the
space within the larger box? This is easy to answer if we replace the 'empty space' inside the
sealed smaller box with water. As the box moves
around within a larger volume of water, we can
accept that it keeps the same water molecules
inside it while displacing the water outside as it
moves. But what if there is no water? And what if
we now get rid of the physical walls of both boxes,
and everything else in this imaginary universe, so

that all that is left is nothingness? Is that nothingness still something? Does this empty space exist ready to be filled with matter, or to be contained within the confines of a box? Maybe I am just asking the same question in different ways, but only because it is by no means a trivial one.

Isaac Newton believed that space has to exist in order for matter and energy to be contained within it and for events to take place within it. But space exists, he argued, only as an empty nothingness, independently of the laws of physics that govern the behaviour of matter and energy within it. For Newton, space is the canvas on which reality is painted. For without space—and time, of course—to fix events to, how would we be able to assign coordinates to locate events? Surely, they must happen at 'some point' in space and at 'some moment' in time. Without absolute space and time in place, how can we hope to anchor reality?

But was Newton right? The answer we can give today is both yes and no. (Sorry.) He was correct in the sense that space *is* real—it is more than just the gaps between things, as Descartes had argued. But he was wrong about space having an absolute existence *independently* of what it contains.

These two statements sound contradictory . . . until you learn about Einsteinian relativity. Einstein proved that absolute space and absolute time do not exist as separate entities. But to appreciate why this notion is necessary, I need to introduce you to the first of his two theories of relativity.

EINSTEIN'S SPECIAL THEORY

Until Isaac Newton completed his work on the laws of motion, debates about the nature of time were considered to be the domain of philosophy and metaphysics rather than proper science. Newton described how objects move and behave under the influence of forces, and since all motion or change requires time to make any sense, time had to be included as a fundamental part of his mathematical description of the world. But Newtonian time is absolute and relentless; it flows at a constant rate, as though there were an imaginary cosmic clock ticking off the seconds, hours, days, and years independently of the events and processes taking place in space. Then, in 1905, Einstein brought the Newtonian world crashing down by revealing how time is connected to space at a deep level.

Einstein's conclusion was that time is not absolute: it doesn't run at the same rate for everyone. If I see two simultaneous events—say, two flashes of light from sources on either side of me—then someone else moving past me at that very moment will not see them happening at the same time, but rather one slightly after the other. This is because the rate of flow of time for each of us depends on our state of motion relative to each other. This weird notion is one of the very first lessons of relativity theory and is called the relativity of simultaneity. Let us take a step back and look at these concepts more carefully.

Consider how sound waves travel to your ears. Sound is, after all, nothing more than the vibration of air molecules that pass on energy through their collisions. Without matter (air) there would be no sound. In space, no one can hear you scream, as the byline to the 1980s movie *Alien* correctly pointed out.

Einstein's insight was to suggest that, unlike sound waves, light waves do not need a medium to carry them. His theory rested on two ideas (known as the principles of relativity). The first, originating with Galileo, states that all motion is relative and that there is no experiment that can be performed to show that someone or something is truly at rest. The second principle states that light waves travel at a speed that is independent of the speed of the source of the light. Both these ideas seem reasonable, until you dig a little deeper into their implications. Let us consider the second idea first—that light moves at the same speed for everyone—and carry out a simple thought experiment.

Imagine an approaching car on an empty country road. The sound waves from its engine will reach you ahead of the car since they are travelling faster, but their speed has to do with how quickly the vibrating air molecules can transmit them; they do not reach you any quicker if the car speeds up. What happens instead is that they get compressed to shorter wavelengths. This is the well-known Doppler effect that we recognise as the change in pitch of the car as it finally reaches you and goes past. When it is receding, the waves of sound are emitted from a progressively longer distance away and therefore reach us stretched to longer wavelengths, and hence a lower pitch. So, while the *wavelength* of sound waves depends on the speed of their source, the *speed* of the waves themselves relative to us (how long they take to reach us) does not change unless *we* start moving through the air towards the approaching car. So far, so good, I hope.

Light is different. It does not need a medium to travel through, and with respect to which we can measure its speed. This means that no one has a privileged position in which they can say they are truly at rest and therefore can reliably measure the 'true' speed of light. Einstein concluded from this that we should all measure light to have the same speed regardless of how fast we are moving relative to each other. (Provided, that is, we are not undergoing any acceleration or deceleration while measuring the speed of the light some distance away from us.[2])

Now consider two rockets approaching each other at constant speed close to that of light. But they have no reference point to argue over who is, or isn't, moving. An astronaut on board one rocket sends a pulse of light towards the oncoming second rocket, measuring the speed of the pulse as it travels away from him. Since he can quite legitimately claim to be at rest, floating in empty space, while the other rocket is doing all the moving, he should see the light moving away from him at its usual speed of just over one billion kilometres per hour,[3] and he does indeed see this. But at the same time, the astronaut in the second rocket can also legitimately claim to be floating stationary in space. She too

---

2 This is a technical detail. Basically, general relativity deals with non-inertial reference frames where spacetime appears curved due to gravity or acceleration. In such non-inertial frames, you only measure light to have a constant speed as it passes close to you.

3 The speed of light in empty space is 1.0792528488 billion km/hr.

will therefore expect to measure the speed of the light reaching her to be just over one billion kilometres per hour (since, like the sound waves from the car, the light's speed should not depend on the speed that its source is approaching her). And she does indeed measure light to have this speed. It would seem, therefore, that both astronauts measure the same light pulse to be travelling at the same speed, despite moving towards each other themselves at near light speed!

This strange nature of light turns out to be a property of the speed at which it can travel rather than of light itself—a speed that is the maximum possible in our universe and which stitches space and time together into one fabric. For the only way light can travel at the same speed for all observers regardless of how fast they themselves are moving relative to each other is if our concepts of distance and time change.

Here is another example. Imagine that you, on Earth, send out a series of light pulses, or flashes, into space to chase down a friend who has headed off in a very fast rocket—a powerful futuristic one that can travel at 99 percent of the speed of light. You will measure the light pulses to be travelling away from you at one billion kilometres per hour and therefore slowly overtaking your friend's rocket at just 1 percent of the speed of light, in the same way that a car in the fast lane of a motorway that is travelling just a little faster than one in the slow lane overtakes it at a speed that is the difference between their two speeds. But what does your friend in the rocket see if she tracks the overtaking light pulses? Relativity theory tells us that she will see them overtaking her at one billion kilometres per hour. Remember, the speed of light is constant, and all observers see it travelling at the same speed.

The only way for this to make sense is if time on board the rocket is ticking by at a slower pace than for you on Earth. That way, what you see as the slow overtaking of a light pulse past the rocket window, your friend sees as a light pulse flashing past, because very little time will have elapsed on the rocket's slower-ticking clock—although for your friend, the clock is ticking at a normal rate. Thus, one of the consequences of all observers seeing light moving at the same speed is that we all measure distances and times differently. And we do indeed see this: the constancy of the speed of light for all observers is a fact, verified experimentally over and over again, and without which our world wouldn't make sense.

The special theory of relativity resolves this counterintuitive situation beautifully by combining time and space in order to retrieve something that we can all agree on. Imagine the whole of space is contained within a vast rectangular three-dimensional box. To define an event taking place within the box we assign to it x, y, and z coordinates (indicating its position relative to the three axes of the box) along with a value for time (when the event took place). Common sense would tell us that the time value is quite different from the three numbers defining the event's location in space. But what if we could add a time axis to the three of space? It would need to be in a 'direction' that is at right angles to each of the three spatial axes, which is impossible for us to visualise. This would result in a combined four-dimensional volume of space-*plus*-time.

An obvious simplification to help us with this visualisation is to sacrifice one of the dimensions of space and collapse our 3-D volume onto a two-dimensional surface, leaving the freed-up third dimension to use as the time axis. Now, think of this static block of space and time as a giant loaf of sliced bread, where the time axis lies along the length of the loaf. Each slice of bread is a snapshot of the whole of space at a single moment, while successive slices correspond to successive times. This is known in physics as the block universe model. While it is only three-dimensional (two of space and one of time), we must not forget that it really represents a four-dimensional construct: 4-D spacetime. Mathematically, we don't have a problem dealing with four dimensions; it's just picturing them that is not possible.

Perceiving 4-D spacetime from the outside, we would experience the totality of existence, not only of all space, but of all times: past, present, and future, coexisting and frozen. It is an impossible viewpoint, an omniscient one, because in reality we are always trapped within the block universe and we experience the passage of time as a steady crawl along the time axis, moving smoothly from one slice of the loaf to the next, like frames in a movie stacked alongside each other instead of end to end on a reel. The reason the concept of the block universe is so useful is because it allows us to understand our different perspectives according to relativity theory. Two observers moving at high speed relative to each other might each record two events—say, flashes of light—but they will not agree on how far apart those flashes are or the time interval between them. This is the price we must pay if we are to all see light moving at the same speed. Viewed within the four dimensions of the block universe, spatial distances and time intervals can be combined, so the separation between any two events, called the spacetime interval, will be the same for all observers. Their disagreement about distances and times, if treated separately, turns out to be nothing more than different perspectives in spacetime. You and I can look at a cube from different angles so that what I see as its depth (the distance measured along my line of sight) will not appear the

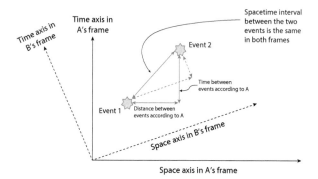

FIGURE 1. Events in spacetime—two observers, A and B, moving at high speed relative to each other, both see two events (flashes of light), which are separated in both space and time. They will not agree on the distance between the events, or on the time duration between them. This is because their space and time axes are different. But in 4-D spacetime (here two dimensions of space are ignored for simplicity) the (spacetime) interval between the two events in both frames is the same: the two right-angled triangles have the same hypotenuse even though each has a different space distance and time distance.

same to you if you see it face on. It depends on the angle at which we are looking at it. But we can nevertheless agree that it is a cube of equal-length sides, and that any differences are just down to our different perspectives. The same is happening in the 4-D block universe. We will always agree on spacetime intervals between events.

Einstein's relativity teaches us that we must view things within 4-D spacetime, in which both spatial and temporal distances become just a matter of perspective. No observer has the right to claim that their perspective of space and time is more correct than any other, because we will all agree once space and time are combined. Individual perspectives of space and time separately are relative, but combined spacetime is absolute.

EINSTEIN'S GENERAL THEORY

Just as the special theory merges space with time, Einstein's general theory of relativity links spacetime with matter and energy, which I will discuss further in the next chapter, to give a more profound explanation of the concept of gravity than that of Newton. According to Newton, gravity is an attractive force: an invisible rubber band between masses that pulls them together and acts instantaneously between them no matter how far apart they are. Einstein gives us a deeper and more accurate explanation: that the strength of the gravitational pull that a body feels is a measure of the curvature of spacetime around it.

Again, this curvature is not something we can visualise. It is impossible to imagine flat 4-D spacetime, let alone when it's curved. For most everyday purposes, Newton's depiction of gravity as a force is a good enough approximation to reality, but its shortcomings become ever more evident when gravity gets a lot stronger, such as when we approach a black hole, or if we need to measure distances and times very accurately, such as onboard GPS satellites. In such cases, we are forced to abandon the Newtonian picture and fully embrace Einstein's vision of curved spacetime.

Since gravity is defined by the curvature of spacetime, this means that it influences the passage of time as well as the shape of space. For us, embedded within spacetime, this effect manifests itself as a slowing down of time, in a similar way to what we see when objects move close to the speed of light. The stronger the gravity, the slower a clock will tick compared to one far from the source of the field, in a 'flatter' region of spacetime.

Unfortunately for those who prefer complex ideas explained in plain language rather than dense mathematics, most attempts by physicists to describe how and why time runs more slowly in stronger gravity fall short of either explaining the phenomenon correctly or explaining it at all. But I will try.

Just as two people moving relative to each other will, according to special relativity, measure each other's clock ticking at a slower rate, a similar situation arises between the two observers if they are a fixed distance apart, but one of them is feeling a stronger gravitational pull—say, on the surface of the Earth, while the other is hovering far out in space. Again, the two of them will disagree on the time interval between events. As before, their clocks will tick at different rates: being deeper within the Earth's gravitational well, where there is more spacetime curvature, the Earth observer's clock will tick more slowly. However, unlike in special relativity, the situation here is no longer symmetrical, as she would see the clock out in space ticking more *quickly*. In a very real sense, gravity slows the flow of time.

We can say that the reason that a body 'falls' to Earth is because it always moves to where time runs the slowest—it is trying to age more slowly. Isn't that beautiful?

So much, then, for the effect of gravity on time. But what about space? What does general relativity tell us beyond the somewhat unhelpful remark that gravity 'causes space to curve'? Remember how both Aristotle and Descartes argued that, without any matter to fill it, space did not have an independent existence? Well, Einstein would take this a step further. According to his general theory, matter and energy *create* a gravitational field, and spacetime is nothing more than the 'structural quality' of this field. Without the 'stuff' contained within spacetime, there is no gravitational field and hence no space or time!

This may sound somewhat philosophical, and I suspect even some physicists will be uncomfortable with it. The problem is, in part, down to the way we teach physics. We tend to start with special relativity and 'flat' spacetime (because it is easier to teach and because

Einstein hit upon it first), then we progress on to the more difficult general relativity, in which this flat spacetime is filled with matter and energy, causing it to curve. In fact, conceptually we should think of it the other way around, beginning with matter and energy within spacetime. This way, special relativity is just an idealised approximation that only works when gravity is so weak that spacetime can be regarded as 'flat'.

The point I wish to make is a subtle one, and you can take solace from the fact that even Einstein himself did not fully appreciate its implications to begin with. Two years after completing the general theory, he wrote a popular science book (or 'booklet', as he referred to it) entitled *Relativity: The Special and the General Theory (A Popular Exposition)*, which was first published in German in 1916. Over the next four decades of his life, as he honed his understanding of what the maths told him about the universe, he would add appendices to this booklet. In 1954, the year before he died, he wrote his fifth and final appendix: two dozen pages of prose containing some of the most profound ideas ever produced by the human mind.

To understand Einstein's thinking, we must understand the concept of a 'field' in physics. The simplest definition of a field is that it is a region of space containing some form of energy or influence, in which every point can be assigned a value that describes the nature of the field at that point. Think of the magnetic field surrounding a bar magnet. The field is strongest close to the poles of the magnet and becomes progressively weaker the further away in space from the magnet we get. The pattern of iron filings that arrange themselves along the magnetic field lines is simply their way of reacting to the field they are immersed in. But the point I wish to make sounds too obvious to warrant stating: *the magnetic field needs space to exist in*.

In stark contrast, the gravitational field, as described by Einstein and created by the mere existence of matter, is more than just a region of influence *within* space and time. It *is* spacetime.

Einstein went to great lengths in appendix 5 of his 'booklet' to clarify his thinking on this. In a new preface to the 1954 edition, he says:

> [S]pacetime is not necessarily something to which one can ascribe a separate existence, independently of the actual objects of physical reality. Physical objects are not in space, but these objects are spatially extended. In this way the concept of 'empty space' loses its meaning.

Then, in appendix 5, he clarifies this further: 'If we imagine the gravitational field . . . to be removed, there does not remain a space of the type (1) [i.e., flat spacetime], but absolutely nothing.' Flat spacetime, 'judged from the standpoint of the general theory of relativity, is not a space without field, but a special case . . . which in itself has no objective significance. . . . There is no such thing as an empty space, i.e., a space without field.' He concludes, 'Spacetime does not claim existence on its own, but only as a structural quality of the field.' Building on the ideas of Aristotle and Descartes, Einstein generalised the notion that there is no space without material bodies and showed that there is no spacetime without a gravitational field.

Just like our magnetic field, the gravitational field is a real physical thing—it can bend, stretch, and undulate. But it is also more fundamental than the electromagnetic field: the electromagnetic field needs the gravitational field to exist, since without a gravitational field there is no spacetime.

EXPANSION OF SPACE

There is one final point I wish to make before I move on. A common confusion many have with the idea of spacetime curvature becomes apparent when physicists describe the expansion of the universe. If spacetime is one big static four-dimensional block, what does it mean when physicists talk about it expanding? How can something that includes time embedded within it expand? After all, the word 'expand' suggests something changing with time, but that something *contains* time! The answer is that the expansion of space that we observe through our telescopes does not involve any stretching of the time coordinate too. It isn't spacetime that is stretching, but rather only the three dimensions of space expanding as time moves forward. Although spacetime is in some sense democratic, with time as just one of the four dimensions, we can algebraically manipulate the equations of general relativity (by which I mean recast them in a slightly different form) so that all distances will now be multiplied by a 'scale factor' that increases as time moves forward and only space expands.

Remember also that this expansion only happens in the vast expanses *in between* the galaxies, because within the galaxies themselves the gravitational field that holds them together is strong enough to withstand the overall cosmic expansion. Galaxies are like the raisins embedded within a loaf of rising bread in the oven. The loaf expands, but the raisins themselves remain the same size—they just become more separated from each other.

In terms of the block universe, imagine that our local spacetime sits within a 'bread universe' in which successive slices of the loaf, as we move along the time axis from past to future, get bigger. Floating outside of spacetime, you'd just see the static loaf with its increasing slice sizes. But from our vantage point trapped within the loaf (or within a figurative raisin within the loaf), all we can experience is successively larger slices, and so we see a point (a distant galaxy, say) moving further away from us as we move through the slices.

Despite all these deeply profound concepts, everything about spacetime that I have described in this chapter comes from just one of the three pillars of modern physics. But space, according to relativity theory, is smooth and continuous. If we zoom in, smaller and smaller, we will ultimately reach the domain of the second pillar of modern physics, quantum mechanics, where everything is fuzzy and subject to chance and uncertainty. What then happens to space and time at these tiniest of length scales and shortest of intervals? Will spacetime itself become grainy, like the pixels of an image magnified beyond its resolution? Maybe. We will come to that soon.

The block universe in relativity also says that we can think of time as static and unchanging, with past, present, and future coexisting as part of four-dimensional spacetime. But the third pillar of physics, thermodynamics, tells us that the idea of time as 'just another dimension' is inadequate. Thermodynamics describes the way systems change with time; more than that, it gives a directionality to time that is missing from the three dimensions in space. Independently of our own perception of time flowing in one direction only—born from the fact that we remember the past, live in the present, and anticipate the future—there exists an arrow of time that points from the past to the future, ruining the neat symmetry of the block universe.

But we are not yet ready to explore these next two pillars of physics. First we must fill our spacetime with stuff: matter and energy. The lesson from Einstein is that matter, energy, space, and time are all intimate companions. We will explore what this means in the next chapter.

CHAPTER 4

ENERGY AND MATTER

The general theory of relativity is mathematically encapsulated in what is known as Einstein's field equation (actually a set of equations that can be written together in a compact form on a single line). But equations always have two sides separated by an '=' sign, and the shape of spacetime is only half of the equation. I now wish to explore the other side.

Einstein's equation expresses how a gravitational field, or rather, the shape of spacetime, is determined by matter and energy. It is often said that his field equation shows how spacetime is curved by matter and energy and, at the same time, how matter and energy behave in curved spacetime. The point is that, just as matter and energy cannot exist without somewhere to exist *in*, there would, equally, be no spacetime without matter and energy. So, let us explore what we know about the 'stuff' of the universe.

ENERGY

Energy is one of those concepts we all feel we understand intuitively. For example, we say we feel 'low on energy' if we're hungry, tired or unwell; conversely, if we're fit and well, we may feel 'energetic' enough to head for the gym. Sometimes, people use the term in a very unscientific way in phrases like 'I could feel the positive energy in the room,' or 'You are giving off a lot of negative energy'. In physics, the concept of energy indicates the *capacity to do work*; thus, the more energy something has, the more it is able to do, whether that 'doing' means moving matter from one place to another, heating it up, or just storing the energy for later use. The notion of energy has been used widely in physics for a couple of centuries, ever since it was found to be more useful as a concept than the admittedly more tangible notion of 'force'—since we can feel forces, but we do not always have a direct sense of energy if it is not in the form of heat or light.

The definition of energy as the capacity to do work does nevertheless link it to the idea of a force, for when we use the term 'work' in physics, we generally mean the ability to move something against a resisting force. For example, I need energy to move a heavy piece of furniture along the ground against the force of friction, or to lift something above my head against the pull of gravity. Similarly, a battery expends energy pushing an electric current through a circuit against a conductor's resistance; and the heat energy stored in steam produces pressure to power turbines that transform this energy into electricity, which can then be used to produce mechanical work—or light and heat again.

Energy comes in many different flavours: a moving body has kinetic energy; a body in a gravitational field has stored potential energy; and a hot body has thermal energy due to the motion of its atoms. But while all of this is correct, it doesn't get to the heart of what energy actually is.

Let us begin with the *law of conservation of energy*, which states that the total amount of energy in the universe is constant. This follows, through Noether's theorem, from a deeper idea of time symmetry: that all the laws of physics are 'time translation invariant', which leads to the total energy of a physical process being conserved over time. This has led to profound new insights, such as the prediction of the existence of new elementary particles. The conservation of energy also tells us that perpetual motion machines are impossible, since energy cannot be continually conjured up from nowhere.

On the face of it, you might think that this is all there is to it: the total amount of energy in a system (indeed, in the entire universe) is conserved, even though it changes from one form to another. But there is something deeper about the nature of energy that I have not yet mentioned. In a rather loose sense, we can divide it into two types: *useful energy* and *waste energy*—a distinction that has profound consequences linked to the arrow of time. We know we need energy to run our world, to feed our transport and our industries, to generate the electricity we use to light and heat our homes, to run our appliances and to power all our electronic devices. Indeed, energy is required just to sustain life itself.

Surely this cannot last forever. So, will we one day run out of useful energy? Zooming out, we can think of the entire universe as a wound-up mechanical clock that is slowly running down. But how can this be so if energy is always conserved? Why can't energy circulate indefinitely, changing from one form to another, but always there? The answer turns out to be down to simple statistics and probability, and what is known as the second law of thermodynamics. But if you don't mind, I will save that discussion until chapter 6. For the moment let us move on, from energy to matter.

MATTER AND MASS

Whenever we talk about the nature of matter, we also need to understand the concept of mass. At the most basic level, the mass of a body is a measure of the amount of 'stuff' it contains.

In everyday language, mass is often taken to mean the same thing as weight. This is fine on Earth since the two quantities are proportional to each other: if you double a body's mass you will also double its weight. But out in empty space, a body has no weight, even though its mass stays the same.

However, even mass does not always remain constant. The faster a body moves, the more its mass increases. This is not something you will be taught at school, and Isaac Newton would have found it astonishing, because it is yet another consequence of the nature of spacetime as elucidated by Einstein's Special Theory of Relativity. If you are wondering why we don't see this in everyday life, it is because we do not typically encounter things moving close to the speed of light, where the effect becomes noticeable. For example, a body moving at 87 percent of the speed of light, relative to some observer, will be measured by that observer to have double the mass it has when it is not moving, and a body moving at 99.5 percent of the speed of light will have ten times the mass it had when it was 'at rest'. But even the fastest bullet only travels at 0.0004 percent of the speed of light, which means we generally do not experience relativistic effects or changes in moving bodies' masses.

The increase in the mass of a body as it reaches a significant fraction of the speed of light does not mean that it grows larger in size, or that the number of atoms it contains increases, but rather that it gains more momentum (making it harder to stop) than you might expect based simply on its 'at rest' mass. According to Newtonian mechanics, a body's momentum is the product of its mass and its speed, meaning that its momentum increases in proportion with its speed—you double its speed and its momentum doubles. But Newtonian mechanics says nothing about masses increasing when a body is moving. Special relativity gives us a different (and more correct) 'relativistic' formula for momentum, which is no longer proportional to a body's speed. In fact, momentum becomes infinite when a body reaches light speed.

This is a useful way of understanding why nothing can travel faster than light (another of the predictions of Special Relativity). Think of the energy needed to make a body move faster. At low speeds, this energy gets transferred into kinetic energy (energy of motion) as the body speeds up. But the closer the body gets to the speed of light, the harder it gets to make it go even faster, and the more of the energy being put into it gets used to increase its mass instead. This notion leads to the most famous equation in physics: $E = mc^2$, which links mass (m) and energy (E) together (along with the square of the speed of light, c) and suggests that the two quantities are transformable into each other. In a sense, mass can be thought of as frozen energy. And because the speed of light squared is such a large number, a small amount of mass can be converted into a large amount of energy, or conversely, a large amount of energy freezes into very little mass.

Therefore, we see that the law of conservation of energy is more accurately generalised to the law of conservation of energy *and* mass: the total amount of energy plus mass in the universe is constant over time. Nowhere is this notion clearer or more important than in the subatomic world, where $E = mc^2$ led to an understanding of nuclear fission and the unlocking of the energy of the atomic nucleus. And it is $E = mc^2$ that lies behind half a century of accelerator laboratories in which beams of subatomic particles are smashed together at ever higher energies to create new matter—new particles—out of the energy of the collision. But there are rules associated with what sort of matter particles can be created from energy, and we will discuss some of them in the next section.

THE BUILDING BLOCKS OF MATTER

From the moment, over a century ago, when Ernest Rutherford, with the help of Hans Geiger and Ernest Marsden, probed the interior of atoms for the first time, by aiming alpha particles at a thin gold leaf and watching how many passed through it and how many bounced back, physicists have been obsessed with delving ever deeper into the subatomic world. They first revealed the structure of atoms themselves—electron clouds surrounding a tiny, dense nucleus. Then, they looked inside the nucleus itself to discover that it is made of smaller building blocks, protons and neutrons. And eventually, they zoomed in even deeper to reveal the elementary quarks hidden within the protons and neutrons. To give you an idea of scale, if an atom were blown up to the size of a house, then the volume within a proton or neutron in which the quarks are confined would be the size of a single grain of salt. And remember that atoms themselves are incredibly tiny: you can fit more atoms into a single glass of water than there are glasses of water in all the oceans of the world.

At school, we learn about the electromagnetic force in the form of electrical or magnetic attraction or repulsion, but it plays an even more crucial role down at the atomic scale. Atoms bond together in all sorts of combinations, to make simple molecules and complex compounds and ultimately the huge variety of different materials we see around us. But how the atoms bind together comes down to the way their electrons arrange themselves around the nuclei, which is of course the very essence of chemistry, and this binding together of atoms to make up the stuff of our world is almost entirely due to the electromagnetic force between the electrons. In fact, together with gravity, the electromagnetic force is responsible, either directly or indirectly, for nearly all the phenomena we experience in nature. On the microscopic scale, materials are held together by the electromagnetic forces between atoms. On the cosmic scale, it is gravity that holds matter together.

Within the atomic nucleus is a very different world. Since nuclei are made up of two types of particles, positively charged protons and neutral neutrons (collectively called nucleons), electromagnetic repulsion between the protons should force nuclei apart; and gravity is far too weak at this tiny scale to be of any use. And yet the constituents of nuclei are held together tightly. This is thanks to a different force that works as a glue to stick protons to neutrons and even protons to protons, despite the repulsion of their positive charges. It is called the strong nuclear force and is felt most strongly between the even tinier constituents of protons and neutrons: the quarks themselves, which are bound together by 'force carrier particles' called gluons. Thus while quarks are attracted to each other by exchanging gluons, a quark and an electron interact via the electromagnetic force (because they both have electric charge) by exchanging photons.

The quantum rules governing the structure, shapes and sizes of atomic nuclei are very complicated and will not be discussed here. Ultimately, however, it is the interplay of the *repulsive* electromagnetic force between the positively charged protons and the *attractive* nuclear force between all nucleons (which is itself a remnant of the 'strong' force—the internal 'gluonic' attraction between the quarks within the nucleons) that contributes to the stability of nuclei, and hence of atoms, and hence of all the matter around us, including us.

There is also another force—the fourth and final (known) force of nature, which is also—mostly—confined within atomic nuclei. It is known simply as the weak nuclear force, and it arises from the exchange of W and Z bosons between certain particles (in the same way that quarks exchange gluons and electrons exchange photons). Like the strong nuclear force, this weak force also acts over very short ranges, and we do not to see its effects directly. However, we are very familiar with the physical processes triggered by this force, as it causes protons and neutrons to transform into each other, which in turn leads to beta radioactivity: charged particles ejected from nuclei. Beta particles come in two types: electrons and their antimatter partners, positrons, which are the same as electrons but with opposite charge. The process is quite simple: if a nucleus has an imbalance between the number of protons and neutrons it contains, leading it to become unstable, then one or more protons or neutrons will transform into the other to redress the balance. In the process, either an electron or a positron is created and ejected (ensuring that electric charge is conserved). Thus, a nucleus with too many neutrons will undergo beta decay in which a neutron will change into a proton, and an electron is emitted, its negative charge cancelling out the positive charge of the created proton as is required (since the original neutron had no charge). Conversely, an excess of protons prompts one of them to convert into a neutron plus a positron that carries off the proton's positive electric charge, leaving a more stable nucleus behind.

Protons and neutrons each contain three quarks, which come in two types (or 'flavours') known somewhat unimaginatively as 'up' and 'down'. These two flavours carry different fractions of electric charge. A proton contains two up quarks, each with a positive charge equivalent to two-thirds of the negative charge of an electron, and one down quark with negative charge that is just one-third of the electron's. Added together they make up +1, the correct positive charge of the proton. The neutron, on the other hand, consists of two down quarks and one up quark, so its total charge is zero.

In total, six different flavours of quarks exist, each with a different mass. As well as the up and down quarks that make up atomic nuclei, the other four are called 'strange', 'charm', 'top', and 'bottom'—all arbitrarily chosen names. These quarks are heavier than the 'up' and the 'down,' but only exist fleetingly. Finally, in addition to *electric* charge, quarks also have another property known as *colour* charge, which relates to the strong nuclear force and helps explain the way quarks interact with each other.[1]

Electrons belong to another class of particles, called leptons, of which there are also six types. Along with the electron, there is the muon and the tau (short-lived heavy cousins of the electron) and three types of neutrinos (very light, almost undetectable particles that are formed during beta decay). Leptons do not feel the strong nuclear force and do not carry colour charge.

To summarise, according to our current understanding, the Standard Model of particle physics tells us that there are, overall, two kinds of particles: the matter particles (the fermions), which include six flavours of quarks and six leptons; and the force carrier particles (the bosons),

---

1 As well as the threesomes of quarks making up nucleons, they can also come in pairs (strictly, quarks and antiquarks) to make up another class of particle called mesons. We still do not know for sure if quarks can combine to make more exotic composite particles, such as so-called tetraquarks, which would be made up of two quarks and two antiquarks, or pentaquarks, with four quarks and one antiquark.

which include the photon, the gluons, the W and Z, and of course the Higgs, which I will discuss later on.

If all this sounds unnecessarily complicated, then you'll be relieved to hear that for most practical purposes it needn't be so. Everything you see: all the stuff that makes up our world, including our own bodies, and everything we see out in space: the Sun, the Moon, and the stars, is all made of atoms, and all atoms are, in turn, made up of just two kinds of particles: quarks and leptons. Indeed, all atomic matter consists of just the first two quark flavours (the up and down), plus one of the leptons (the electron). Although you may be surprised to know that the most common matter particle is the neutrino.

A BRIEF HISTORY OF MATTER AND ENERGY

So how and when did all this matter come to be in the first place? To understand this we need to zoom back out again and explore the cosmos on the largest scales.

That our universe is expanding has been
known for almost a century. Astronomers observed the light from distant galaxies to be
stretched towards the red end of the electromagnetic spectrum (or, redshifted), indicating
that these galaxies are moving away from us. In
fact, the further away galaxies are, the greater the
redshift of their light and so the faster they must
be moving. However, seeing galaxies receding in
every direction does not mean that we occupy a
privileged position in the centre of the universe.
Rather, it means that *all* galaxies are moving away
from each other, because the space between them
is stretching. Note that this expansion does not
apply *within* clusters of galaxies, like our Local
Group: the Milky Way, Andromeda, and a handful of smaller galaxies, which are close enough to
each other to be gravitationally bound and thus
able to resist the expansion of space.

But what, you may ask, has the expansion of
the universe to do with the origin of matter and
energy? Well, this expansion is one of the most
compelling pieces of evidence we have for the
Big Bang—the moment 13.82 billion years ago

when our part of the universe was born in a state of incredibly high temperature and density. Put simply, if the universe we see is expanding now, with the galaxies flying apart, then everything must have been closer together in the past. At some point in time, if we go back far enough, all the matter, as well as the space containing it, must have been squeezed together. There is therefore no location in the universe that we could travel to, plant a flag, and claim that the Big Bang happened there. The Big Bang happened everywhere in the universe. And just to confuse you further, if the universe is infinite in size now (as it may well be), then it would have to have been already infinite in size at the Big Bang (since you cannot expand something finite to make it infinite—unless you have infinite time to do it!). That the Big Bang happened *everywhere* within already infinite space, rather than at some particular 'place', is an important concept to grasp.

A more up-to-date, and conceptually more logical, take on this notion is that the Big Bang we refer to is only a 'local' event. It created just the visible universe we are able to discern, whereas the entirety of the infinite universe contains other distant regions of space beyond what we could ever see, and which had their own big bangs. This is one of the ways of explaining the idea of a multiverse, which I will come to in chapter 8.

There is plenty of other evidence to support the Big Bang theory, too, such as the relative abundances of the light elements. About three-quarters of the mass of all the matter we see in the universe is in the form of hydrogen, and one quarter is helium (the next lightest element).[2] Only a tiny amount exists of all the other elements, most of which were made in stars long after the Big Bang. This dominance of hydrogen and helium in the universe is predicted by the Big Bang theory and is exactly what we observe. And the great thing is that we don't need to travel around the universe to determine this composition. The light we collect in our telescopes car-

---

2 Note that I used the word 'mass' here. In terms of numbers of atoms in the universe, about 92% are hydrogen and only 8% are helium (because helium is four times the mass of hydrogen).

ries within it the telltale signature of the distant atoms that have produced it or that it has passed through on its journey to Earth. The fact that we can learn about the ingredients of the universe just by studying the light that reaches us from space is one of the most beautiful notions in science.

The other piece of evidence in support of the Big Bang—the discovery of which in 1964 finally confirmed the theory beyond reasonable doubt—is the existence of the so-called cosmic microwave background (or CMB) radiation. This ancient light that fills all of space originated at a time, not long after the Big Bang, when neutral atoms first formed, during a period in the universe's history called the 'era of recombination'. It took place 378,000 years after the Big Bang, when space had expanded and cooled enough for positively charged protons and alpha particles[3] to capture electrons and form

---

3 Alpha particles are nuclei of helium, the next lightest element after hydrogen. They consist of four nucleons: two protons and two neutrons.

hydrogen and helium atoms. Before this, electrons would have been too energetic to stick to the protons and alphas to make neutral atoms; consequently, photons (the particles of light) couldn't travel very freely without bumping into and interacting with these charged particles, so the whole of space would have taken on a foggy glow. But, once the universe cooled enough for atoms to form, space became transparent and the photons were set free. This light has been travelling across the universe in all directions ever since.

This first light has also been losing energy as space expands, but not by slowing down, since light always travels at a constant speed. Instead, it is the wavelength of the light that has been stretched with the expansion of the space it is moving through, so that today, billions of years later, it is no longer in the visible part of the spectrum, but in the form of microwaves. Astronomers have measured this microwave radiation and found it to correspond to a temperature of deep space of a little less than three degrees above absolute zero, a value that agrees with the prediction of the Big Bang theory—which, by the way, was made before the measurement.

But let us go back to an even earlier time in our universe's life, long before atoms were even formed. It began as a stupendously hot bubble of energy and, within a trillionth of a second, had cooled enough for subatomic particles, quarks and gluons, to form—condensing out from this energy as space expanded. To begin with, these particles were very energetic and roamed around unconfined in a hot soup called the quark-gluon plasma, at a temperature of trillions of degrees Celsius. Then, when the universe was a mere millionth of a second old, they began to clump together to form protons and neutrons (along with other heavier particles). Matter then went through various stages of evolution in those first few seconds, with different particles forming and disappearing. It is here that we encounter one of the biggest outstanding unanswered questions in physics: the mystery of the missing antimatter.

A few years after Paul Dirac predicted its existence in 1928, antimatter was discovered by Carl Anderson in cosmic rays: high-energy particles from space that collide mainly with oxygen and nitrogen molecules in the Earth's upper atmosphere to produce a shower of secondary particles, including the electron's antiparticle, the positron. We now know that all elementary matter particles (the fermions) have mirror-image antimatter partners.[4] When an electron and positron come into contact, they completely annihilate each other with their masses combining and transforming into pure energy via $E = mc^2$.

The reverse of this annihilation process is also continuously taking place down at the tiniest scales. If we could magnify the quantum realm, we would see particles and their antiparticles popping in and out of existence all the time in a constant exchange between matter and energy. Thus, a photon, which is no more than a lump of electromagnetic energy, can transform itself into an electron and a positron in a process known as pair creation. But, in the very early, dense universe, when particles and antiparticles were

---

4 The other type of particle, the force carriers like photons, are called bosons and technically do not have antiparticles.

appearing and disappearing, matter for some reason came to dominate over antimatter. The fact that we are here at all indicates that this must have been so. We have yet to understand what happened to the 'missing antimatter' that, luckily for us, gave rise to the extra profusion of matter we see today.

A few minutes after the Big Bang, the conditions were right for protons (nuclei of hydrogen) to fuse together to make helium[5] plus a tiny amount of element number three, lithium. But as the universe expanded further, the temperature and pressure dropped below the threshold for heavier nuclei to be formed via the fusion of lighter ones. This is because, for nuclear fusion to take place, the fusing nuclei must be energetic enough to overcome the mutual repulsion of their positive charges, but below a certain matter density and temperature, this no longer happens.

A little later, after the era of recombination, atoms began to clump together under the

---

5 Technically, there are several steps here, including the beta decay of protons into neutrons.

influence of gravity—and I am holding back on the vital role played by dark matter here, but will say more about it in chapter 8—and primordial gas clouds (proto-galaxies) began to form, and denser clumps of gas within them were squeezed together even more dramatically by gravity until they heated up sufficiently for the process of fusion to begin once again. Stars ignited, and the thermonuclear reactions taking place inside them produced new elements: carbon, oxygen, nitrogen, along with many of the other elements we find on Earth.

Most of this first generation of stars in the universe no longer exist, since they would have exploded as supernovae long ago, spewing much of their elemental contents out into space, leaving behind compacted matter in the form of neutron stars or black holes. Heavier elements—that is, anything beyond iron in the periodic table—are only created during violent events such as novae, supernovae, and neutron star mergers. The hotter and the more extreme the conditions in a star, the further the nucleosynthesis process is able to go, and the heavier the elements that can be formed, such as silver, gold, lead, and uranium. This is because the interiors of stars only reach the required temperature and density to make heavier elements during these final intense moments of their lives, when they are densely compressed, while at the same time violently shedding their outer layers.

The matter ejected from exploding stars blends with interstellar gas, which can clump together again to form a new generation of stars. The fact that we find such heavy elements on Earth tells us that our Sun is such a second-generation star (at least). It is why you might have heard it said that we are all quite literally made of stardust, for indeed it is within stars that many of the atoms in our bodies were made.

Now that I hope I have given you a sense of how matter was formed in the universe and the intimate relationship between matter and energy, space and time, we are ready to plunge down into the microcosm, a world of the very small that cannot be described by the general theory of relativity. It's time to explore the second pillar of physics: quantum mechanics.

CHAPTER 5

THE QUANTUM WORLD

In 1799, Joseph Banks, president of the august Royal Society of London, founded a new establishment: the Royal Institution of Great Britain, with the aim of introducing 'useful mechanical inventions and improvements' and 'teaching [the general public] courses of philosophical lectures and experiments'. Ever since then, the Ri, as it is commonly known today, has continued to put on public lectures and events, including its Friday Evening Discourses—public lectures delivered in its Faraday lecture theatre—which have been an integral part of its programme since they were set up by Michael Faraday himself in 1826. I have had the honour of giving two of these, the last one in 2013, when I talked about the subject of this chapter: quantum mechanics.

Quantum mechanics is seen, quite rightly, as the most fascinating, yet at the same time most mind-boggling and frustrating scientific theory ever devised by humankind. In a particular segment of my lecture at the Ri, I discuss the famous 'two-slit experiment', which describes what the American physicist Richard Feynman called the 'central mystery of quantum mechanics'. After outlining just how astonishing the results of the two-slit experiment are—subatomic particles, fired one by one through a screen with two narrow slits in it, behaving as though they each travel through *both* slits at once, and giving rise to an interference pattern on a second screen— I issued a challenge to my audience. If anyone were able to come up with a 'commonsense' account of how this is possible, they should get in touch with me, as they will no doubt be up for a Nobel Prize.

I said this as a lighthearted joke—safe in the knowledge that no one has ever found a simple explanation of this classic result despite many decades of debate and hundreds of ingenious tests, leading physicists to reluctantly conclude that whatever is going on really does *not* have a commonsense explanation. This really is the way matter behaves in the quantum world, and we just have to accept it. I also assumed, when I cast down the proverbial gauntlet, that I was addressing just the few hundred members of the Ri audience that Friday evening. But the Ri posts much of its educational material online, which included my lecture; and since then I have received hundreds of emails from amateur scientists claiming to have solved this central quantum mystery and suggesting that maybe physicists have forgotten to consider this or that mechanism or detail.

I used to respond, but I confess that I don't any more. So, let me make amends for my lack of correspondence with those folks who continue to puzzle over the mysteries of quantum mechanics, and describe some of its most important, and non-intuitive, features. In this chapter we will take a brief look at what this second pillar of modern physics tells us about the microcosm. Having devoted my own research career, now careering into its fourth decade, to its study and application, first in nuclear physics and more recently in molecular biology, you won't be surprised to hear that I regard quantum mechanics as the most powerful and important theory in all of science. After all, it is the foundation on which much of physics and chemistry is built, and it has revolutionised our understanding of how the world is built from the tiniest of building blocks.

A QUANTUM MECHANICS PRIMER

The status of physics towards the end of the nineteenth century appeared to be complete. It had produced Newtonian mechanics, electromagnetism, and thermodynamics (which I will talk about in chapter 6) and showed that together these three areas of physics successfully described the motion and behaviour of all everyday-size objects and pretty much all phenomena we encounter around us, from cannonballs to clocks, storms to steam trains, magnets to motors, and pendulums to planets. Collectively, the study of all these things is referred to as Classical Physics, and it is still predominantly what we are taught in school.

However, classical physics, while still pretty good, is not the whole story. When physicists turned their attention to the microscopic constituents of matter—atoms and molecules—they discovered new phenomena they couldn't explain with the physics they knew. It seemed that the laws and equations they were using no longer applied. Physics was about to undergo a seismic paradigm shift.

The first major theoretical breakthrough—the concept of the 'quantum'—was made by the German physicist Max Planck. In a lecture in December 1900, he proposed the revolutionary idea that the heat energy radiated by a warm body is linked to the frequency at which its atoms vibrated, and consequently that this radiated heat is 'lumpy' rather than continuous, emitted as discrete packets of energy, which became known as quanta. Within a few years, Einstein had proposed that it wasn't just Planck's radiation that was emitted in lumps, but that all electromagnetic radiation, including light, came in discrete quanta. We now refer to a single quantum of light—a particle of light energy—as a photon.

Einstein's proposal, that light is quantum in nature, was more than just a hunch. It explained one of the biggest outstanding scientific mysteries of the time, called the photoelectric effect—a phenomenon in which light, when shone on a metal surface, can knock electrons out of the metal's atoms. This effect could not be explained if light were a wave because if so, then increasing the intensity (the brightness) of the light would mean increasing its energy, and we would expect the electrons knocked out from the metal to fly off faster. But, they don't. There are just more of them. But if the energy of the light is proportional to its frequency rather than its intensity, as Einstein proposed, then increasing its frequency (for example, from visible to ultraviolet) would cause the electrons to be knocked out with more energy. And, conversely, keeping the frequency (colour) of the light the same but increasing its brightness would just mean that *more* photons would be produced, and more electrons knocked out. This is exactly what is seen in experiments, and Einstein's explanation fitted beautifully.

And yet there was, and still is, plenty of contrary evidence suggesting that light is made up of waves rather than a stream of particles. So which is it? Is light a wave or a particle? The answer, frustratingly, flying in the face of intuition and common sense, is that it can behave like either, depending on how we look at it and the sort of experiment we devise to probe it.

And it is not just light that has this schizophrenic nature. Particles of matter, such as electrons, can exhibit a wavelike nature, too. This general notion, tested and confirmed for almost a century now, is known as wave-particle duality and is one of the central ideas of quantum mechanics. This does not mean that an electron is both a particle and a wave at the same time—but rather that, if we set up an experiment to test the particle-like nature of electrons, we find that they do indeed behave like particles. But if we then set up another experiment to test if electrons have wavelike properties (such as diffraction or refraction or wave interference), we see them behaving like waves. It's just that we cannot carry out an experiment that would show both the wave and particle nature of electrons *at the same time.* It is absolutely vital to stress here that, while quantum mechanics correctly predicts the outcomes of such experiments, what it does *not* tell us is *what an electron is*—only what we see when we carry out certain experiments to probe it. The only reason this no longer drives physicists crazy with exasperation is that we have learnt to accept it. This balance between how much we can simultaneously know about an electron's particle nature (its position in space) and its wave nature (how fast it is travelling) is governed by Heisenberg's uncertainty principle, which is regarded as one of the most important ideas in the whole of science and a foundation stone of quantum mechanics.

The uncertainty principle puts a limit on what we can measure and observe, but many people, even physicists, are prone to misunderstanding what this means. Despite what you will find in physics textbooks, the formalism of quantum mechanics does not state that an electron cannot *have* a definite position and a definite speed at the same time, only that we cannot *know* both quantities at the same time. A related common misunderstanding is that humans must play some kind of crucial role in quantum mechanics: that our consciousness can influence the quantum world, or even bring it into existence when we measure it. This is nonsense. Our universe, all the way down to its elementary building blocks at the quantum scale, existed long before life began on Earth—it wasn't sitting in some fuzzy limbo state waiting for us to come along, measure it, and make it real.

By the mid-1920s, physicists were beginning to realise that the concept of quantisation is more general than just the 'lumpiness' of light or the 'waviness' of matter. Many physical properties, familiar to us as continuous, are, in fact, discrete (digital rather than analog) once you zoom down to the subatomic scale. For example, the electrons bound within atoms are 'quantised' in the sense that they can only have certain specific energies and never energies in between these discrete values. Without this property, electrons would continuously leak energy while orbiting the nucleus,[1] meaning that atoms would not be stable and complex matter, including life, could not exist. According to nineteenth-century (pre-quantum) electromagnetic theory, negatively charged electrons should spiral inwards towards the atom's positively charged nucleus. But their quantised energy states prevents this from happening. Certain quantum rules also define which energy states the electrons occupy and how they arrange themselves within atoms. As such, the rules of quantum mechanics dictate how atoms can bind together to make molecules, making quantum mechanics the foundation of the whole of chemistry.

Electrons are able to jump between energy states by emitting or absorbing the correct amount of energy. They can drop to a lower state by emitting a quantum of electromagnetic energy (a photon) of exactly the same value as the difference in energies between the two states

---

1 The term 'orbit' here is in fact wrong, since atoms are not miniature solar systems and electrons are not localised particles like tiny planets going round the sun.

involved. Likewise, they can jump to a higher state by absorbing a photon of the appropriate energy.

The sub-microscopic world, down at the scale of atoms and smaller, therefore behaves very differently from our familiar everyday world. When we describe the dynamics of something like a pendulum or tennis ball, or a bicycle or a planet, we are dealing with systems comprising many trillions of atoms, which are far removed from the fuzziness of the quantum realm. This allows us to study the way these objects behave using classical mechanics and Newton's equations of motion, the solutions of which are an object's precise location, energy or state of motion, all knowable simultaneously at any given moment in time.

But if we wish to study matter on the quantum scale, we must forgo the mechanics of Newton and use the very different mathematics of quantum mechanics. Typically, we would solve Schrödinger's equation to calculate a quantity called the wave function, which describes not the way an individual particle move along definite path, but the way its 'quantum state' evolves in time. The wave function can describe the state of a single particle or group of particles and has a value that provides us with the *probability* of, say, finding an electron with any given set of properties or location in space *if we were to measure that property*.

The fact that the wave function has value at more than one point in space is often wrongly taken to mean that the electron itself is physically smeared out across space when we are not measuring it. But quantum mechanics does not tell us what the electron is doing when we are not looking—only what we should expect to see when we *do* look. If you are not reassured by this statement, you are not alone. It is not meant to reassure you (or to discourage you, for that matter); it is simply stating what all physicists agree on when it comes to the meaning of quantum mechanics.

Beyond this, there is a whole host of different ways of explaining the nature of the quantum world. These are known as the 'interpretations' of quantum mechanics, and the arguments between advocates of these different views have raged for as long as quantum mechanics has been around and show no sign of abating.

WHAT DOES IT ALL MEAN?

Despite its tremendous success, if we dig a little deeper into what quantum mechanics tells us about the microcosm, we could easily lose our minds. We ask ourselves, 'But how can it be so? What am I not 'getting'?' The truth is, no one really knows for sure. We do not even know if there is any more to 'get'. Physicists have tended to use terms like 'strange', 'weird', or 'counter-intuitive' to describe the quantum world. For, despite the theory being powerfully accurate and mathematically logical, its numbers, symbols and predictive power are a façade hiding a reality we find difficult to reconcile with our mundane, commonsense view of the everyday world.

There is, however, a way out of this predicament. Since quantum mechanics describes the subatomic world so remarkably well, and since it is built on such a complete and powerful mathematical framework, it turns out we can manage just fine by learning how to use its rules in order to make predictions about the world and to harness it to develop technologies that rely on those rules, leaving the hand-wringing and head-shaking to the philosophers. After all, this laptop I am typing on would not exist were it not for the development of quantum mechanics that allowed us to create modern electronics. But if we take this pragmatic attitude, we must accept that we become no more than quantum *mechanics* ourselves—practitioners and technicians who do not care *how* or *why* the quantum world behaves the way it does, but who simply accept it, and move on. Every fibre of my being tells me that this should not be enough for a physicist. Is it not the job of physics to *describe* the world? Quantum mechanics, without an interpretation of its equations and symbols, is just a mathematical framework that allows us to calculate and predict the results of experiments. That should not be enough. Physics should be about *explaining what our results tell us about how the world really is*.

The fact that many physicists will not agree with this statement is a failing that can be traced back to one of the greatest thinkers in the history of science: the father of quantum mechanics, Niels Bohr. So influential was he that even as I write this I feel a sense of guilt—that I am betraying one of my great heroes. And yet I must stand true to my convictions. Without doubt, Bohr's philosophical views have shaped the way generations of physicists think about quantum mechanics, but they have also, in the eyes of an increasing number, discouraged and stifled progress. Bohr argued that it is wrong to think that the task of physics is to find out how nature *is*—or to know the 'real essence of the phenomena'—but rather to concern itself only with what we can *say* about nature: the 'aspects of our experience'. These two opposing views, the first ontological and the second epistemological, can in fact *both* be correct: what a physicist should be able to say about nature, even at the quantum scale, should be the same as how nature is, or as close to it as we can get, but always trying to edge closer. This 'realist' view is one that I have always found myself siding with in the end, despite having serious doubts now and again.

On the other end of the scale, there is a danger lurking in the shadows should we overstress the weirdness of quantum mechanics rather than focussing on its power and success as a scientific theory. For doing so attracts the attention of charlatans just as a bright light attracts moths. The undeniably inexplicable predictions of quantum mechanics—such as entanglement, i.e., separated particles being instantaneously linked across space—have over the years provided fertile ground for all manner of pseudo-scientific nonsense, from telepathy to homeopathy. Generations of physicists have been trained to follow Bohr's pragmatic dogma—known as the Copenhagen interpretation of quantum mechanics, named after the city of Bohr's famous Institute for Theoretical Physics where so much of the earlier mathematical foundations of the theory were laid out in the mid-1920s—in part to avoid the sort of philosophical musings that can spill over into new-age baloney.

Like all physics students for generations, I was taught quantum mechanics by first being introduced to its historical origins and the work of Planck, Einstein, Bohr, and others. But my education quickly moved on to the mathematical techniques (the toolkit) I needed to make use of the theory. And along with the maths, I learnt a pile of concepts named after the theory's founding fathers: Born's rule, Schrödinger's equation, Heisenberg's uncertainty principle, Pauli's exclusion principle, Dirac notation, Feynman diagrams . . . the list goes on. But while all of this is important to know if we are to make sense of the quantum world, what I was not taught were the arguments and philosophical debates that took place between all these great physicists, which lasted throughout their lives and which, to a large extent, remain unresolved.

Much of the interpretational difficulty with quantum mechanics revolves around the so-called 'measurement problem': How does the ephemeral quantum world come into sharp focus when we carry out a measurement? Where is the boundary between the quantum and the classical worlds—between things that do not have well-defined properties when left to their own devices, and the reassuring solidity of what we measure and see? Many of the founding fathers—men such as Niels Bohr, Werner Heisenberg, and Wolfgang Pauli—believed it was pointless to worry about such matters and advocated following the Copenhagen philosophy I described earlier. They were happy to split the world in two, quantum behaviour and classical behaviour, without tying down how one transitioned into the other upon measurement. To them, quantum mechanics worked and that was enough. But this positivist attitude can hinder the advance of science. While it may well help lead us to a better understanding of some phenomena and even to developing new technologies, it does not help us to truly *understand*.[2]

The history of science is littered with examples of this sort of attitude. One of the most

---

2 Of course, my Copenhagenist colleagues would vehemently disagree with me here. They would argue that they do understand all there is to be understood about what quantum mechanics can and cannot tell us and that it is the realists who refuse to accept or understand this.

obvious comes from ancient cosmology. For two millennia, from antiquity until the birth of modern science, there was an almost universal hegemony and acceptance of the geocentric model of the universe: that the Earth is at the centre of the cosmos and that the Sun, along with all the planets and stars, orbits around us. A positivist back then would have argued that since this model works so well in predicting the motion of heavenly bodies, it was unnecessary to look for alternative explanations for how or why they moved across the sky in the way we see. Indeed, there was a time when the geocentric model was more accurate at matching astronomical observations than the correct, and much simpler, Copernican heliocentric model. But interpreting a theory in a particular way 'just because it works' is intellectual laziness, and certainly not in the true spirit of what physics should be about. The same should be true of quantum mechanics. The renowned quantum physicist John Bell once famously said that the aim of physics is to *understand* the world, and 'to restrict quantum mechanics to be exclusively about piddling laboratory operations is to betray the great enterprise'.

Sadly, too many physicists, even today, do not grasp this—yet another argument for why philosophy is not just pointless navel gazing, but can contribute to the advancement of science. If you were to conduct a poll among quantum physicists (at least those who care about such matters), you would find that a significant, though decreasing, fraction will still adopt the pragmatic Copenhagen view. But a growing number see it as an abdication of the role of physics and instead subscribe to one of a number of alternative interpretations—a list that includes such exotic-sounding ideas as the many worlds interpretation, the hidden variables interpretation, the dynamical collapse interpretation, the consistent histories interpretation and the relational interpretation—and I have left out a number of others. No one knows which, if any, of these different ways of describing reality at the quantum scale is the correct one. They all work; they all make, so far, the same predictions of the results of experiments and observations,[3] and all emerge from the same mathematics. Sometimes, advocates of these different interpretations can defend them dogmatically, treating their favourite version almost like religions, which is not how science is going to progress.

And yet, slow progress *is* being made in trying to understand the quantum world. Experimental techniques are becoming ever more subtle, and certain explanations are being ruled out. The hope is that one day we will indeed find out how Nature really does perform her quantum trickery. If this sounds sensible to you, there are plenty of physicists who will disagree. The positivists argue that science is nothing more than a tool for predicting the outcome of experiments and that those who worry about what quantum mechanics tells us about reality by reading more than they should into its mathematics are indeed better suited to doing philosophy instead. In fair-

---

3 Although some realist interpretations, such as spontaneous collapse models, do make predictions that others do not, and so are in principle testable.

ness, not all advocates of this positivist, Copenhagenist view of reality have been dismissive of attempts to dig deeper. In the early 2000s a new anti-realist interpretation called Quantum Bayesianism (or Qbism) appeared, whose proponents see reality as being entirely subjective and down to personal experience. Critics have even likened it to solipsism.

Choosing an interpretation of quantum mechanics should be more than just a matter of philosophical taste. The fact that they all make the same predictions about the world does not mean that all these interpretations are equivalent or that we are free to choose the one we like the best on a whim. Explaining some aspect of reality through physics is a two-step process. First, we find the mathematical theory, which of course may or may not be correct. But if we believe it is right—like Einstein's field equations of general relativity or Schrödinger's equation in quantum mechanics—then we next need ways of interpreting, or explaining, what the mathematics means. These are the stories we attach to the maths. Without them, we cannot connect our symbols and equations, however aesthetically pleasing we find them, to the physical universe we observe. And we need to find the right story just as much as the right mathematical theory.

The different interpretations of quantum mechanics paint very different pictures of reality: either there are parallel universes (the many worlds interpretation) or there are not; either there is a physical nonlocal quantum field (the pilot wave hidden variables interpretation) or there isn't. Nature does not care about our petty squabbles regarding the correct interpretation of quantum mechanics—it gets on with doing things the way it does, and exists independently of our perceptions. If we have a problem with agreeing on how the quantum world behaves, then that is our problem. Einstein believed this. He was a realist, too. He believed that physics should be about describing how the world really is, and if there is more than one description that fits the mathematics of quantum mechanics, then we should not be satisfied. I feel I am in good company in this regard.

ENTANGLEMENT, MEASUREMENT, AND DECOHERENCE

That said, even Einstein could get things wrong on occasion. One of the most profound and inexplicable predictions of quantum mechanics is the idea of entanglement. In the quantum world, two or more particles can be linked across space instantaneously in a way that almost defies logic. Technically, this is known as nonlocality, and it can be encapsulated in the idea that what happens 'over here' can instantaneously affect, and be affected by, what happens 'over there'. We say that the two particles are described by the same 'quantum state': the same wave function. Einstein always felt uncomfortable about nonlocality and entanglement, deriding it as 'spooky action at a distance', and refused to accept that any communication between subatomic particles could travel across space faster than light, as that would violate special relativity. But in principle, particles located at opposite ends of the universe can still be connected in this way. Entanglement was shown by the quantum pioneers to follow naturally from their equations, and experiments carried out in the 1970s and '80s confirmed that Einstein was wrong on this: we now know empirically that quantum particles really can have an instantaneous long-range connection. Our universe really is nonlocal.

Today, many researchers working in fields such as quantum optics, quantum information theory, and even quantum gravity see a profound link between entanglement and the central problem of measurement in quantum mechanics. We must first acknowledge that a quantum system—say, an atom—is in reality part of its surrounding world, and so treating it as isolated is not strictly correct. Instead, we must include in our calculations the influence of its surrounding environment. Such an 'open quantum system' presents us with a much more complex problem to solve, but at the same time, it allows us to make some headway in understanding what it means to carry out a measurement on a quantum system beyond what Niels Bohr referred to simply as 'an irreversible act of amplification' as the way to describe how quantum fuzziness is crystallized into reality when we carry out an observation.

In fact, it is now clear that the environment surrounding a quantum system, such as an atom, can itself do the 'measuring'. We don't require a conscious observer. We can think of the atom as becoming ever more entangled with its surroundings, such that its quantum nature leaks out into the environment like heat dissipating from a warm body. This leaking out of the ephemeral quantum behaviour is known as decoherence and is part of an active area of study at the moment. The stronger the coupling between the quantum system and its environment, the more entangled it becomes, and the faster its quantum behaviour disappears.

Whether or not this process fully explains the measurement problem is still a matter of debate in some quarters. The thorny issue of how to solve the measurement problem and the boundary between the quantum world and the large classical world was first made famous by Erwin Schrödinger in the mid-1930s, when he came up with his famous thought experiment.

Despite being one of the pioneers and founders of the field, Schrödinger tried to highlight his own misgivings about the meaning of quantum mechanics. He asked what would happen if we were to shut a cat in a box with a radioactive substance and a container with lethal poison. All the while the box is closed, we cannot say whether or not a particle has been emitted by the radioactive material, triggering a mechanism that releases the poison, killing the cat. All we can do is ascribe probabilities to the two likely outcomes: when we open the box, either a particle has been emitted and the cat is dead, or it hasn't, and the cat is still alive. But according to the rules of quantum mechanics, and as long as the box is closed, the subatomic particle obeys the laws of the quantum world, and we must regard it as being in a quantum superposition of having been both emitted and not emitted at the same time.

But now, within the closed box, the fate of the cat rests on this quantum event. Schrödinger argued that since the cat is itself made of atoms, albeit trillions of them, each a quantum entity, it too should exist in quantum superposition: a state of being both dead and alive simultaneously. However, we only ever see one definite outcome when we open the box to look. That is, the cat is either dead or alive, never in this limbo state.

A sensible way of resolving the issue is to assume that such quantum superpositions decohere away into their surroundings and therefore do not survive for long when we consider complex macroscopic objects like cats, which are never in two states at once, even before we open the box to check. In fact, while an isolated radioactive atom must be described as being in a superposition of having both decayed and not decayed until observed, it is surrounded by a complex environment of air, Geiger counter, and cat, all of which it rapidly becomes entangled with, so that the both-at-once option doesn't survive.

So, has the problem been solved? And do the two options of dead *or* alive cat now reflect nothing more than our own ignorance of its fate, until we open the box? If not, then we are still left with the mystery of what physical process is taking place when we open the box. What has happened to the option we don't see? Subscribers to the many worlds interpretation of quantum mechanics believe there is a neat and simple explanation for this. They argue that there are now two parallel realities in which each option is realised. What we find when we open the box reflects which reality we exist in.

Other physicists, not prepared to accept the idea of a potentially infinite number of parallel realities, have come up with a range of alternative interpretations that still demand the existence of an objective reality in the absence of measurement, but all of which contain some strange aspect of reality hidden somewhere. For example, another way of interpreting quantum theory was first developed by the French physicist Louis de Broglie in the 1920s and then improved several decades later by David Bohm. According to this interpretation, the quantum world is made up of particles guided by waves. Their properties are hidden from us—and are called hidden variables—but describe a quantum world without any of the fuzziness of the standard Copenhagen picture of reality. Rather than an electron itself exhibiting both wavelike or particle-like properties depending on how we measure it, there are both waves *and* particles, but it is only the particles that we ever detect. A small but dedicated community of physicists around the world feel that this so-called de Broglie–Bohm theory has much to offer, but it remains a largely unexplored option among the corpus of quantum interpretations.

Fascinating though it is, I will leave this discussion here, since many other books cover it in greater depth than I have space for. In any case, I leave the issue of the interpretation of quantum mechanics unresolved, since that is where we stand at the moment.

Having focussed thus far on the basic building blocks of matter and energy, the spacetime in which they exist, and the quantum nature of reality underpinning it all, I have ignored some equally fundamental concepts in physics that emerge when large numbers of particles come together to make up complex systems. So, let us leave the world of the very small behind for now and zoom out again to investigate what happens with the emergence of complexity, and explore such profound ideas as order, chaos, entropy, and the arrow of time.

CHAPTER 6

THERMODYNAMICS AND THE ARROW OF TIME

As we leave behind the quantum world, with its randomness and uncertainty, our familiar Newtonian world comes back into sharp focus. The steaming, swirling cup of coffee on the table, the ball that just bounced into the back garden from next door, or the jet flying high overhead are all, if you think about it, made of matter and energy assembled into systems of varying levels of complexity. So, if we want to understand the physics of the world we see around us, we need to understand how particles interact and behave in large collections. The area of physics that helps us to understand the behaviours of large numbers of interacting bodies is statistical mechanics.

You might also recall that, while familiarizing ourselves with matter and energy in chapter 4, we touched on the fact that energy can transform from one form into another while the total amount of energy in a system remains the same. The energy of a bouncing ball flips constantly between its potential energy, due to its height above the ground, and its kinetic energy of motion. At the very top of its bounce, it is entirely in the form of potential energy, and just before it hits the ground, when the ball is moving at its fastest, this potential energy will have been transformed to kinetic energy. This all sounds fairly straightforward—but we also know that a ball will not keep bouncing forever: it loses energy in the form of heat, from friction with the air and from collision with the ground. This change from kinetic energy to heat is fundamentally different from the transformation between kinetic and potential energy because it is a one-way process. We would be astonished if we saw the ball suddenly regain its bounce, without any external help.

So why should this be so? Where does this 'one-way-ness' come from?

The answer is that a ball loses its bounce for the same reason that heat always flows from a warm cup of coffee to the colder surrounding air and never back again, and why the sugar and cream in the coffee never un-dissolve and un-mix. Welcome to the field of thermodynamics—the third major pillar of physics (along with general relativity and quantum mechanics). While statistical mechanics describes how a large number of particles interact and behave in a system, thermodynamics describes the heat and energy of the system and the way these change over time. As you will see, these areas of study are highly interconnected, and so physicists often learn about them together. We will look at them together, too.

STATISTICAL MECHANICS AND THERMODYNAMICS

Consider a box full of air in which all the molecules are bouncing around randomly. Some are moving quickly, while others are slower. But if the box is maintained at a fixed temperature and pressure, then the total amount of energy it contains remains constant. This energy is distributed among its molecules in a very particular way: the total available energy is spread out according to a simple statistical rule. Suppose you inject some hotter air (faster-moving molecules) into the box and then leave it alone: the random collisions of these new molecules with the original cooler ones will cause their energy to be distributed. The hot molecules will slow down while simultaneously causing others to speed up. Eventually, the air will settle back down into a new equilibrium. This time, the most likely energy of any molecule will be slightly higher than it was before, and the overall temperature in the box will have been raised a little.

The way the energy in the box is spread among the molecules is called a Maxwell-Boltzmann distribution—after two of the greatest scientists of the nineteenth century, who developed the field of statistical mechanics. 'Distribution' refers to the shape of the curve on a graph linking the varying speeds of the molecules to the number having each speed. Or, put another way, it is the line that links points corresponding to the probability than any molecule will have a given speed. There will be a particular speed that it is most likely for molecules to have, corresponding to the highest point on the curve, with speeds faster or slower being less likely; and the shape of the distribution changes as the temperature of the box increases, with the peak in the probability distribution moving towards higher speeds. When the molecules have settled down to a Maxwell-Boltzmann distribution, we say that the air in the box has reached thermodynamic equilibrium.

The tendency towards a statistical state of equilibrium is associated with a very important concept in physics, known as entropy. The entropy of a system, if left alone, will always increase: that is, a system will always relax from a 'special' (ordered) state to a less special (mixed-up) one. Physical systems unwind, cool down, and wear out. This is referred to as the second law of thermodynamics, and at its heart it is no more than a statement of statistical inevitability: if left

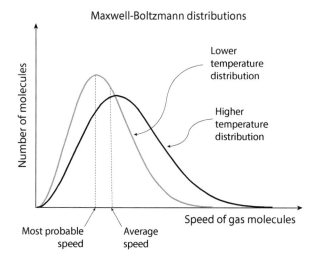

Maxwell-Boltzmann distributions

FIGURE 2. Maxwell-Boltzmann distribution—molecules of gas in a box will distribute themselves evenly and share their energy until they reach thermal equilibrium. The curve of number of molecules versus their speed is known as a Maxwell-Boltzmann distribution and has a peak at the most probable speed. This peak moves to higher speeds as the overall temperature of the gas increases. Note that the most probable speed is not the same as the average speed, since there are more particles with speeds greater than the peak value.

alone, everything always eventually returns to a state of equilibrium.

Imagine that all the molecules of air in our box start off clustered in one corner. The entropy of the box in this initial state is low, since its contents are in a special, more ordered state. If left alone, the random motion of these molecules will cause them to spread out quickly to fill the whole box until their distribution reaches equilibrium. Just as the speeds of the hot molecules eventually settle into a state of thermodynamic equilibrium, the air in the box goes from a state of low entropy to a state of high entropy as it spreads out. When the air molecules are evenly distributed throughout the box, entropy will be at a maximum.

Here is an even simpler example. An ordered pack of cards in which each suit is separated and arranged in ascending order is said to have low entropy. It is in a highly ordered state, which is ruined if we shuffle the pack—we say that its entropy increases. By shuffling further, it is overwhelmingly more likely that the cards will get even more mixed up than it is for them to return to their original ordered arrangement. This is because the unshuffled pack is a unique arrangement of the cards, whereas there are very many ways for the cards to be mixed up. So it is much more likely that shuffling will go in one direction—from unshuffled to shuffled, from low entropy to high entropy.

A more interesting definition of entropy is as a measure of something's ability to expend energy in order to carry out a task. When a system reaches equilibrium, it becomes useless. A fully charged battery has low entropy, which increases as the battery is used. A discharged battery is in equilibrium and has high entropy. This is where the distinction between useful energy and waste energy comes in. When a system is ordered and in a special (low-entropy) state, it can be used to carry out useful work—like a charged battery, a wound-up clock, sunlight, or the chemical bonds between carbon atoms in a lump of coal. But when the system reaches equilibrium, its entropy is maximised, and the energy it contains is useless. So, in a sense, it is not energy that is needed to make the world go around, it is low entropy. If everything were in a state of equilibrium, nothing would happen. We need a system to be in a state of low entropy, far from equilibrium, to force energy to change from one form to another—in other words, to do work.

We consume energy just by being alive, but we can see now that it has to be of the useful, low-entropy kind. Life is an example of a system that can maintain itself in a state of low entropy, away from thermal equilibrium. At its heart, a living cell is a complex system that feeds (via thousands of biochemical processes) on useful, low-entropy energy locked up in the molecular structure of the food we consume. This chemical energy is used to keep the processes of life going. Ultimately, life on earth is only possible because it 'feeds' off the Sun's low-entropy energy.

The second law of thermodynamics and the relentless march of entropy applies to the entire universe, too. Imagine that our box of air is now a cloud of cold gas expanded to the size of a galaxy. If a group of molecules in the gas randomly drift closer together than average, then the mutual, very weak gravitational attraction between them might be enough to pull them closer together so that they form a denser clump of gas than average.[1] The more gas molecules clump

---

1 Of course, if we are dealing with small numbers of molecules, then gravity is never going to play a role in controlling their behaviour. Only when vast numbers of them are involved can their cumulative mass have a gravitational influence.

together, the more effective gravity becomes at attracting more molecules. This gravitational clumping process was the reason stars formed: vast clouds of gas collapsed together until these regions were dense enough for thermonuclear fusion (of hydrogen into helium) to begin, and stars ignited. This can appear puzzling when you first think about it, because the process of clumping together seems like it is resulting in a tidier, more ordered, and more 'special' state, and hence the end state should have lower entropy than when all molecules are spread out evenly. So, has gravity caused the entropy of the gas to decrease and the second law of thermodynamics to be violated?

The answer is no. Whenever matter clumps together gravitationally its entropy increases, for the same reason that the entropy of a ball increases as it rolls down a hill due to the pull of the Earth's gravity. Think of this clumping like a stretched spring being released, or a clock unwinding, their entropy increasing as they lose the ability to do useful work. Thus when the molecules of gas in a certain part of the cloud

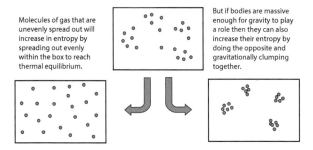

Molecules of gas that are unevenly spread out will increase in entropy by spreading out evenly within the box to reach thermal equilibrium.

But if bodies are massive enough for gravity to play a role then they can also increase their entropy by doing the opposite and gravitationally clumping together.

FIGURE 3. Increasing entropy—particles in a box that are slightly out of equilibrium (low entropy) can increase their entropy either by redistributing themselves back to equilibrium or clumping together under gravity. Either way, they increase their entropy and satisfy the second law of thermodynamics.

find themselves, by chance, temporarily closer together than when evenly spread out, this represents a temporary departure from maximum entropy. For entropy to increase again, to satisfy the second law, these molecules can do one of two things. They can either drift apart again, back to their original state of thermal equilibrium, or they can go the other way and clump together due to their mutual gravitational attraction. Either way, their entropy increases.

You should now be asking: What would cause such a drift away from maximum entropy to start with? Wouldn't that drift itself violate the second law? The answer is that the matter and energy in our universe did not start in a state of thermal equilibrium, but rather in a very special, low-entropy state set by the conditions at the Big Bang itself. These initial conditions, down at the quantum level, seeded spacetime with irregularities, which became writ large on the fabric of the cosmos as the universe expanded, so that a certain amount of lumpiness was automatically built into the distribution of matter. As the universe continued to 'unwind', matter that was close enough together to feel the pull of gravity eventually clumped together to form stars and galaxies. The molecules of hydrogen and helium gas in space fell together into the gravitational wells of the stars, causing an increase in entropy as they did so. But, crucially, this entropy did not reach a maximum—stars are not systems in thermal equilibrium, but remain reservoirs of low entropy, with the thermonuclear fusion reactions within them releasing excess energy in the form of light and heat. It is this low-entropy energy from our own star, the Sun, that makes life on Earth possible. Plants make use of it during photosynthesis to create biomass, locking useful low-entropy energy in the molecular bonds of their organic compounds, which can then be accessed by other living creatures, including eventually humans, that consume the plants as food.

The Earth itself also has a store of useful energy that, together with the Sun's energy, drives its climate, while the gravitational energy of the Moon and Sun control the tides of the oceans—all of which can provide us with other useful reservoirs of low entropy that we can tap into. For example, water at the top of a waterfall drops under the pull of gravity so that its potential energy is converted into kinetic energy, which we can make use of to drive hydroelectric power plants generating electricity for our use. There will of course always be some loss in efficiency—the second law needs to see some overall increase in entropy in the form of waste heat.

But there is something far more profound going on here than simply the transformation of energy from one form to another.

A DIRECTION TO TIME

If a physical system—including the entire universe—must always move from an ordered state of low entropy to a disordered state of high entropy, then this gives us a direction to the flow of time itself: the second law of thermodynamics allows us to distinguish between past and future. This might sound a little strange; after all, you don't need the second law to tell you that yesterday was in the past. You have a memory of the events of that day stored in your brain, though the events themselves are gone forever. Whereas tomorrow is unknown to you—it has yet to happen. This arrow of time pointing from past to future is, we feel, an intuitively more fundamental property of reality on which the second law of thermodynamics sits. In fact, it is the other way around: think of the second law of thermodynamics as the *origin* of time's arrow. Without the second law there would be no future or past.

Imagine watching a movie of our box of air (and let us imagine that the molecules of air are big enough for us to see). They will be bouncing around, colliding with each other and with the walls of the box, some of them moving faster and others slower. But if the air is in thermal equilibrium, then we would not be able to tell whether the movie is being run forwards or backwards. Down at the scale of molecular collisions, we cannot see any directionality to time. Without an increase in entropy and a drive to equilibrium, all physical processes in the universe could happen equally well in reverse. However, as we saw, this tendency of the universe and everything in it to unwind towards thermal equilibrium is entirely down to the statistical probability of events at the molecular level progressing from something less likely to happen to something more likely, according to the laws of thermodynamics. The directionality of time pointing from past to future is not mysterious; it's just a matter of statistical inevitability.

With that in mind, even the fact that I know the past but not the future is no longer so strange. As I perceive the world around me, I increase the amount of information stored in my brain, a process which, as my brain is doing work, produces waste heat and increases my body's entropy. Even our very ability to distinguish between the past and the future is, from a thermodynamical perspective, no more than our brains obeying the second law.

DETERMINISM AND RANDOMNESS

The above ideas may leave you feeling uneasy— and justifiably so. Surely, the difference between the past and future is more than just the statistical drive of randomly colliding molecules toward equilibrium, or the difference between an unshuffled and shuffled pack of cards. After all, the past is fixed—we remember only one course of events: one history. In contrast, the future is open to us with its infinite possibilities.[2] Most of the events that will happen tomorrow will be unexpected, and my day could unfold in myriad dif-

---

2 Of course, some things are more likely than others. . . . I am almost entirely certain that the Sun will rise tomorrow, and that I will be a day older; and I am pretty sure I won't wake up with the sudden ability to speak fluent Japanese or to run 100 metres in under ten seconds.

ferent ways, depending on the coming together of millions of different factors. So, is there in fact a difference between past and future, at a level deeper than simple statistics, which is based on the notion that we have one past but many possible futures? Put another way, is our fate sealed or is our future governed by chance? Is the future fixed or yet to be determined? These are age-old philosophical questions, touching on the nature of free will itself.

When physicists talk about a process as being 'deterministic', they are usually referring to the concept of 'causal' determinism: the idea that past events cause future events. But if this is the case, then nothing is left to chance, and everything that happens does so for a reason, because of what happened just before it: cause and effect. In principle, therefore, the state of the entire universe at the present moment can be traced back in time step by step, all the way to the Big Bang. And if this is true, then surely events in the present fix events in the future so that, *in principle*, we should be able to predict that future. And the term 'events' here also includes the firing of neurons in our brains that define our thought processes and hence our decision making. After all, our brains are also made of atoms. There is no extra magical ingredient that exempts them from the laws of physics.

In a universe in which everything is predetermined, we would have no free choice with regard to our actions and decisions, since there is only one version of the future, just as there was one version of the past. (Remember I discussed Einstein's block universe idea in chapter 3.) But the order of events, the past causing the future and not the other way around, is driven by the second law of thermodynamics, without which the events we have labelled 'future' ones could just as likely have caused the 'past' ones.

But if this is the case, how is it that we are unable to predict the future with any degree of confidence? After all, even our most powerful supercomputers cannot tell us for sure if it is going to rain next week. In the case of the weather, the reason is straightforward. If you think about the sheer complexity of what we are trying to model and the number of variables we would need to know very precisely—from temperature variations in the atmosphere and the oceans to air pressure, wind direction and speed, solar activity, and so on—in order to make an accurate prediction, you will see that the task becomes increasingly difficult the further into the future we want to make a forecast. So, while meteorologists can confidently predict whether it will be sunny or overcast tomorrow, predicting if it is going to rain on this date next year is impossible. Crucially, this does not mean that such knowledge couldn't *in principle* be known—since in a deterministic universe the future is already preordained—it is just that, *in practice*, we would need to know the current conditions of the Earth's climate to astonishing accuracy and have stupendous computational power to feed in all the data to make a precise simulation that could then be evolved mathematically to give a reliable prediction.

It is this chaotic *unpredictability* that give rise to the famous 'butterfly effect': the idea that the tiny, seemingly inconsequential disturbance of the air caused by the flapping of a butterfly's wings on one side of the world could gradually develop and grow until it dramatically affected the course of a hurricane on the other side of the world. This does not mean that there is a specific butterfly to which we can trace the cause of a hurricane, but rather that *any* tiny changes to the initial conditions can give rise to widely varying outcomes if we continue to evolve the system in time.

The equations of physics describe a deterministically evolving world. Knowing the precise initial conditions of a system (where each constituent particle is and how it is moving at a given moment in time, and fully understanding the forces between all the particles) would allow us to compute how that system evolves in a *perfectly deterministic way*. Cause and effect. The future could (in principle) be laid bare for us.

The problem, of course, is that we can never do this in practice. This inability to know or control the initial conditions of a system, as well as all other continuing influences, to infinite accuracy can be seen even in systems much simpler than the weather. The toss of a coin cannot be exactly repeated in order to achieve the same outcome time and again. If I toss a coin and get 'heads', it's too difficult for me to repeat the toss and make it spin the same number of times so as to definitely land 'heads' again. In a deterministic universe such as ours, our destiny is entirely mapped out, yet we are unable to predict it with any confidence.

But what about quantum mechanics? Isn't that where true randomness and indeterminism enter at a fundamental level? Does quantum mechanics not rescue us from the bleak determinism of a preordained, fixed future in which we feel we are no longer making free choices but are just cogs in an orderly clockwork universe? The truth is, we have no clear answer to this question yet. We must also take care to distinguish unpredictability from indeterminism. It is quite true that the probabilistic nature of the quantum world means that events are *unpredictable*: that we cannot know in advance exactly where an electron will be, or in which direction it is spinning, or precisely when a radioactive atom will decay. All we can do with quantum mechanics is assign probabilities to the outcomes of different measurements. However, while this unpredictability *might* be down to true indeterminism, the mathematics of quantum theory does not require this. Indeterminism is an interpretation we impose on the mathematics to describe what we measure. For example, most cosmologists favour the many worlds interpretation of quantum mechanics in which everything is fully deterministic.

There is another way in which unpredictability and the appearance of randomness come into physics, and that is through the phenomenon of chaotic behaviour. Chaos appears in nature when there is an instability within a system, such that tiny changes to the way the system evolves over time can quickly grow. There's that butterfly effect again. Sometimes even simple systems following simple, deterministic physical laws can behave in highly unpredictable and complex ways that seem to be truly random. But unlike in the quantum domain, where we don't know whether unpredictability is due to true indeterminism or not,[3] the unpredictability of a chaotic system is not—despite initial appearances—due to true randomness.

There is also a fascinating flip side to chaos theory: that simple rules, applied repeatedly, can lead to seemingly random behaviour, but then sometimes go on to produce beautiful structures and complex patterns of behaviour that look highly ordered. Unexpected complexity emerges where there was none before, while never violating the second law of thermodynamics. The field of science dealing with this sort of emergent behaviour is known as complex systems, and it is beginning to play a major role in many exciting areas of research, such as biology, economics, and artificial intelligence.

In summary, then, it may well be that our universe is indeed completely deterministic, and any unpredictability about its future evolution is entirely due to the shortcomings in our own ability to know with certainty what will happen next.

---

3 Since it depends on which interpretation of quantum mechanics we choose.

This could either be because, at the quantum level, we cannot observe the state of a system without disturbing it and altering the outcome, or because we cannot, in practice, ever have *complete* knowledge of a system, and the build-up of uncertainties means we can never be sure what the future holds.

WHAT THEN IS TIME?

Having taken a brief look at determinism and randomness in physics, let us return once more to the central theme of this chapter, namely the direction of time emerging from thermodynamics. Note that we have now been confronted with three *different* perspectives on what time is, each arising from one of the three pillars of physics.

Firstly, according to special relativity, time is not absolute; it does not tick by independently of events taking place in three-dimensional space but must instead be combined with space into four-dimensional spacetime. This is not just a mathematical trick. It is forced upon us by the properties of the real world, tested again and again in experiments and shown to be just the way the universe is. Einstein's theory of gravity (general relativity) then tells us that spacetime *is* the gravitational field itself—the stronger the field, the more curved spacetime is. So, the lesson from relativity is this: time is part of the physical fabric of the universe, a dimension that can be stretched and warped by gravity.

This is very different from the almost trivial role played by time in quantum mechanics, where it is nothing more than a parameter: a number that you plug into an equation. Knowing the state of a system at some time t_1 allows us to compute the state of the system at any other time, t_2, and so on. And it works in reverse too: knowing the state of a system at a later time t_2 allows us to compute it at an earlier time, t_1. The arrow of time in quantum mechanics is reversible.

In thermodynamics, time has yet another meaning. Here, it is neither a parameter nor a dimension, but an irreversible arrow pointing from past to future, in the direction of increasing entropy.

Many physicists believe that we will one day combine all these three different notions of time. For example, we have not yet heard the last word on quantum mechanics, since we still do not fully understand how the deterministic equations that describe the dynamics of a quantum state—and in which time can flow in either direction—tie in with the irreversible, one-way process of measurement. There are strong hints from the rapidly developing field of quantum information theory that the way a quantum system interacts and becomes entangled with its surrounding environment is similar to the way a hot object leaks heat to its colder surroundings. This would see a coming together of quantum mechanics and thermodynamics.

A neat experiment at the University of Queensland in Australia in 2018 showed just how puzzling this all is by demonstrating that at the quantum level, events occur with no definite causal order. Basically, in physics, causality means that if an event A takes place before an event B (in some frame of reference) then A may or may not have influenced or even caused B. But the later event B could not have influenced or caused event A. At the quantum level, this sensible causality was shown to break down. This has led some physicists to argue that the arrow of time really does not exist at the quantum level but is only an emergent property when we zoom out to the macroscale.

However, it has been the quest to bring together the first two pillars of physics that has occupied the minds of so many physicists for a century. Entire careers have been dedicated to trying to understand how to combine quantum mechanics and general relativity into one all-encompassing theory of quantum gravity. This unification of the two most important ideas in twentieth-century physics is the subject of the next chapter.

CHAPTER 7

UNIFICATION

Physicists' relentless drive to unify their theories—to bring together the laws of the universe and encapsulate them in a single neat mathematical equation—a 'theory of everything'—often appears to be no more than an obsession with simplicity and compactness, an effort to package up the complexity of all natural phenomena using the minimum number of underlying principles. In fact, it's subtler than that. Throughout the history of physics, the more we've discovered about the workings of nature, the more connections we've found between seemingly unconnected forces and particles, and the fewer rules and principles we've needed to explain an ever-wider range of phenomena. Unification is not something we deliberately set out to achieve; it has emerged as a result of our deeper understanding of the physical world. But this success undeniably comes with a certain aesthetic appeal that drives us to keep going along the same lines. And we have been astonishingly successful at it.

Mathematically, the quest to unify the laws of physics has often involved a search for abstract symmetries, patterns that hide deep truths about nature. We saw in chapter 2 just how central symmetry has proven to be in physics, and the way it leads to laws like the conservation of energy and momentum. But I'm afraid that to truly appreciate its importance and the role that different symmetries have played in theoretical physics over the past century is somewhat beyond the remit of this short book.

The hunt for a unified theory is sometimes described as an attempt to gather all the forces of nature into one framework, suggesting that there exists just one 'superforce' and that the different interactions we know of in nature—electromagnetism, gravitation and the two short-range forces within the confines of atomic nuclei—are all different aspects of this single force. Physicists have so far had a good deal of success with this broad project of unification. I have already described how Newton understood that what causes the apple to fall from the tree is the same universal force (gravity) that controls the motion of the heavenly bodies across the sky. This was not at all obvious at the time, even though it might seem so to us today. Before Newton, it was believed that objects fell to the ground because everything had a 'tendency' to move to its 'natural' place—towards the centre of the world—and that the motion of the Sun, Moon, planets, and stars was subject to very different principles. Newton's law of universal gravitation brings these phenomena together by stating that all masses are attracted towards each other, with a force proportional to the product of their mass and inversely proportional to the square of the distance between them. It doesn't matter whether it is an apple or the Moon; the same formula governs the way both are attracted by the Earth.

Another huge leap forward along the path to unification took place almost two centuries after Newton, when James Clerk Maxwell showed that electricity and magnetism are in fact different facets of the same electromagnetic force. So, the electrostatic attraction between a scrap of paper and a balloon that has been rubbed on your clothing has its origin in the same electromagnetic force that attracts a paper clip towards a magnet. Almost all phenomena we see in nature are due ultimately to one or other of these two forces: gravity and electromagnetism. It was therefore natural to ask whether we can go further and bring them together in a combined theory.

We have already seen that, at a fundamental level, the gravitational field is nothing more than the shape of spacetime itself, a revelation that was also due to a unifying idea. By combining space with time, Einstein revealed a profound truth: that only in four-dimensional spacetime can all observers (however fast they are moving relative to each other) agree on the separation between two events. A decade later, his general theory of relativity gave the world a new and more accurate picture of how mass and energy cause this spacetime to curve. But that wasn't enough for Einstein, who spent the most part of the next four decades of his life searching unsuccessfully for a unified theory that would combine his theory of gravity with Maxwell's electromagnetic theory.

We now know that there are, in addition to gravity and electromagnetism, two other forces—the strong and weak nuclear forces—that only act over very tiny distances, but which are just as important as far as the fundamental laws of nature are concerned. And it was the unification of the electromagnetic force with one of these nuclear forces that would be the next step forward in twentieth-century physics.

But this important advance in our understanding of the nature of the fundamental forces only came about with the evolution of quantum mechanics from a theory describing the microcosm in terms of particles and waves to one involving fields. I touched very briefly on the meaning of fields in chapter 3 in the context of gravity and electromagnetism. We are now ready to tackle the meaning of a quantum field.

QUANTUM FIELD THEORY

I may have given you the impression that once quantum mechanics was completed almost a hundred years ago, most physicists busied themselves with applying it to real problems in physics and chemistry, leaving just a few of the more philosophically minded to carry on arguing about what it all meant. To a large extent, this version of history is true. But it is also true that quantum mechanics continued to develop in sophistication throughout the first half of the last century. The basic mathematical formalism—the equations and the rules—was certainly in place by the late 1920s, but Paul Dirac soon managed to combine quantum theory with Einstein's special theory of relativity. He also brought together quantum mechanics and Maxwell's electromagnetic field theory to produce the very first quantum field theory. This developed into a powerful and very precise way of describing the electromagnetic interaction of matter with light at the quantum level.

Dirac's quantum field theory describes how electrons emit and absorb photons, and how two electrons will repel each other, not by some invisible force that links them across space, but by the exchange of photons. By the 1930s, the distinction, at the quantum level, between the physics of particles and the physics of fields was swept away. So, in the same way that photons are the particle-like manifestations of the electromagnetic field—lumps of pure energy at the quantum scale—so too are the localised particles of matter, such as electrons and quarks, just manifestations of their more fundamental associated quantum fields. However, unlike photons and the electromagnetic field, this is not so obvious when it comes to the matter particles. The reason for this is that photons can bunch together in unlimited numbers, giving rise to what we perceive as an electromagnetic field on the macroscale, whereas matter particles like electrons and quarks are less sociable, thanks to one of the rules of quantum mechanics called the Pauli exclusion principle, which states that no two identical matter particles can occupy the same quantum state. This means we do not perceive their quantum fields so easily.

By the late 1940s, mathematical problems with the description of quantum fields were finally resolved, and the theory known as quantum electrodynamics (QED) was completed. To this day, it is regarded as the most accurate theory in all of science. It is also the physical theory that explains at a fundamental level almost everything in the world around us, since it underpins all of chemistry and the nature of matter—from the way the electronic circuitry and microchips in my laptop work to the neurons firing in my brain, commanding my fingers to move across the keyboard. This is because QED is at the heart of all interactions between atoms.

And yet, for all its power, QED still describes only *one* of the four forces of nature: electromagnetism.

During the late 1950s and '60s, physicists used beautiful but complicated mathematical reasoning to combine QED with a field theory of the weak nuclear force. They showed that the weak force was, at a fundamental level, also generated by exchanged particles equivalent to the role played by exchanged photons in describing the electromagnetic force. Today, we have a unified theory describing a single 'electroweak' interaction that, through a process called symmetry breaking, splits into two distinct physical forces: electromagnetism (manifested by the exchange of photons) and the weak force, carried by the exchange of the W and Z bosons, which were subsequently discovered at CERN in 1983 and have since been extensively studied. The split between the two forces (the symmetry breaking) is due to another field, called the Higgs field, which gives the W and Z particles mass while leaving the photon massless. This unification means that, at a fundamental level, the four forces of nature are reduced to just three: the electroweak force, the strong nuclear force, and gravity (which in any case is not actually a force at all, according to general relativity). You may disagree with me as to whether this has helped simplify matters.

In parallel with this advance, another quantum field theory was developed to describe the strong nuclear force that holds the quarks together inside protons and neutrons. A subtlety

of the strong force is that the way it acts between quarks involves a property called 'colour
charge', which deserves a brief mention. Just as
particles that feel the electromagnetic force
come in two types of electric charge, which we
refer to simply as positive and negative,[1] the particles that feel the strong force (quarks) come
in three types of 'charge', named colour charge
to distinguish them from electric charge. Note
that the word 'colour' here is not to be taken
in any way literally. The reason three types of
colour charge were needed, rather than just two
(as with electric charge), was to explain why
protons and neutrons must each contain three
quarks; and the reason the analogy with colour
was chosen was because of the connection with
the way the three different colours of light (red,
blue and green) combine to produce white light.
Thus, the three quarks in a proton or a neutron
each carry a different colour charge: red, blue or

---

1 And which could equally well have been called 'left' and
'right', 'black' and 'white', or 'yin' and 'yang', to indicate that
they are opposite to each other.

green, which combine to produce a particle that
has to be 'colourless'.

The rule was that quarks could not exist
by themselves because they carried colour;
they could only exist in nature by sticking together to make up colourless combinations.[2]
For this reason, the field theory of the strong
nuclear force that binds quarks together became known as quantum chromodynamics, or
QCD. The exchange particles between quarks
are the gluons, a rather more evocative and appropriate name, I think you'll agree, than that
of those weak force–carrier particles, the W
and Z bosons.

Let us then take stock. Of the four known
forces of nature, three are described by quan-

---

2 The other type of particles made of quarks, called mesons, contain a quark and an antiquark, which must both have
the same colour charge because antiparticles always carry the
opposite properties. So, you could have a meson made up of
a red quark (of some flavour, such as up, down, or strange)
together with an anti-red quark of some other flavour. The
flavours of the quark and antiquark define the type of meson,
while their colour and anti-colour cancel out to ensure a colourless particle. Complicated? You betcha!

tum field theories. The electromagnetic and the weak nuclear force are linked together by the electroweak theory, while the strong force is described by quantum chromodynamics. A yet-to-be fully developed theory that connects these three forces together is known as a grand unified theory (or GUT). But until we find one, we must make do with a loose alliance of the electroweak theory and QCD, known as the Standard Model of particle physics.

Even its most ardent defender will admit that the Standard Model is probably not the last word on the matter. It has survived this long in part because we have nothing better to replace it with and in part because its predictions have so far been validated by experiments, such as the discovery of the Higgs boson in 2012 (more of which later). And yet despite this being the best description we have of three of the four forces of nature, physicists would like nothing better than make some new discovery that conflicts with the Standard Model, in the hope of discovering a deeper and more accurate description of reality. But as long as the predictions of the Standard Model continue to be confirmed by experiments, it lives to fight another day.

Of course, this whole discussion of quantum field theories omits a very important ingredient: gravity.

THE QUEST FOR QUANTUM GRAVITY

We have discovered that the description of our everyday world at the length, time, and energy scales appropriate for Newtonian physics is only an approximation, and that beneath it are more-fundamental physical theories that come into their own at the extreme scales. At one end, we have quantum field theory, which has led us to the Standard Model of particle physics and which accounts for three of the four known forces in the universe. At the other extreme, we have the general theory of relativity, which gives us the Standard Model of cosmology that encompasses the other force, gravity. This standard model of the very large is called a variety of different names, such as the concordance model,

or the Lambda–cold dark matter model, or the
Big Bang cosmology model. I will discuss it more
fully in the next chapter.

Therefore, a question that physicists are often
asked is *why* we feel it is so important, indeed
whether it should even be possible, to keep
going with our obsession with unification, to
try to combine these two models describing entirely different scales: the quantum realm and the
cosmic realm. Surely each works well in its own
domain, and that should be enough for us. But
again, I must stress that the purpose of physics is
not simply to account for what we observe or to
find some useful application based on it; physics
is about gaining the deepest and most complete
understanding of reality.

So, this is where we are at the moment: stuck
with two successful frameworks—quantum
field theory and general relativity—which just
don't seem to want to fit together. Indeed,
they appear to have very little in common:
their mathematical structures are incompatible. And yet this cannot be the whole story.
We know that spacetime reacts to the matter

within it. We also know that matter at the sub-atomic scale behaves according to the rules of quantum mechanics, which must surely in turn affect the behaviour of spacetime. If an unobserved electron is in a quantum superposition of being in two or more states at once, as we know electrons can be—for example, if their quantum state is spread out over some volume of space or in a superposition of different energies at once—then surely the spacetime around this electron must reflect this fuzziness too. The problem is that general relativity just *isn't* 'quantum-y', and it is far from straightforward how we can make it so. One of the problems with this is that subatomic particles have such tiny masses that their effect on spacetime is nigh impossible to measure.

Still, the issue remains: How do we quantise the gravitational field? What do we need to do to bring quantum field theory and general relativity together? And if they are truly as incompatible as they seem to be, then which one of these two incredibly successful theories needs to 'give way' to get us to quantum gravity?

STRING THEORY

In the mid-1980s, a candidate theory of quantum gravity was developed. It was based on a mathematical idea called supersymmetry, which I mentioned briefly in chapter 2. This candidate theory became known as superstring theory, and it captured the imagination of many mathematical physicists of my generation. Supersymmetry suggests a relationship between the two general types of elementary particles in the Standard Model: the matter particles, or fermions (quarks and electrons and their cousins), and the force carrier particles, or bosons (the photon, gluons, and W and Z bosons).

String theory had originally been proposed in the late 1960s as a theory of the strong nuclear force, but when quantum chromodynamics was developed in the '70s and found to be so successful, string theory fell out of favour and was seen as no longer necessary. But it was soon realised that by incorporating into string theory the idea of supersymmetry, it could be reborn as a candidate for a much grander undertaking

than a theory of the strong force: a theory of
everything.

The basic premise of supersymmetric string
(or superstring) theory is that one way to unify
all the forces is to add more dimensions to space
beyond the three we are aware of. This idea goes
back to work by the German theoretical physicist
Theodor Kaluza, who noticed, just after the
end of the First World War, that if he solved
Einstein's field equations of general relativity in five-dimensional spacetime instead of
four, then electromagnetism emerged out of
the mathematics as vibrations in this fifth, un-
seen, dimension. Kaluza showed his work to
Einstein, who initially liked it. It seemed to
do for electromagnetism what Einstein had
achieved for gravitation: changing its fundamental description from a physical force to pure
geometry.

Yet, despite this elegant way of unifying light
(electromagnetism) and gravity (general relativity), most physicists—including Einstein
himself—soon became sceptical of Kaluza's
work, as there was no experimental evidence

to suggest that this extra dimension of space existed.

A few years after Kaluza's original idea, the Swedish physicist Oskar Klein suggested that the reason the fifth dimension is hidden is because it is curled up on itself, and therefore too tiny to be detected. There is a standard analogy that helps to explain what this means. From a distance, a hose looks like a one-dimensional line, but zoom in and you see that it is in fact a two-dimensional surface wrapped around into a cylinder. The second spatial dimension (the circular direction around the hose) was too small to be seen from a distance. Klein suggested the same thing applied to Kaluza's fifth spatial dimension, which was curled up into a circle a billionth of a trillionth of the size of an atom. Despite Kaluza-Klein theory not leading to a unification of gravity and electromagnetism, it did help researchers understand the relevance of the higher dimensions in superstring theory. However, now, instead of just one hidden spatial dimension, there needed to be six, all rolled up into an impossible-to-visualise six-dimensional ball. Superstring theory thus states that there are ten dimensions: four of spacetime that we experience plus the six hidden dimensions.

To this day, many researchers looking to unify the forces of nature still work on string theory. They argue that we have come so far, using successful ideas like quantum field theory and supersymmetry to understand three of the four forces; therefore surely gravity can also be tamed. They may well be right.

String theory begins with the quantum mechanical properties of matter within spacetime. Its central idea is that all elementary point-like particles are in fact tiny strings, vibrating in the hidden dimensions. These strings would be far smaller than the scales currently probed by particle physics and so we can only experience them as point particles. The problem that emerged by the 1990s was that it appeared there were five *different* versions of string theory, and no one knew which one was the correct one. So a new, even grander framework was proposed which unified all five versions under one umbrella. This all-encompassing framework is now called

M-theory, which is a supersymmetric theory with eleven, rather than ten, dimensions. Yet again, it seemed, another hidden dimension was needed to help with the grand unification programme.

So, is that it? Is M-theory our ultimate 'theory of everything'? Sadly, we cannot yet say. While the mathematics is elegant and powerful, we still don't know if string theory or M-theory are the right descriptions of reality. In the next chapter, I will discuss some of the outstanding issues and controversies surrounding this subject. In any case, M-theory has a worthy adversary in the race for unification. This rival theory is just as speculative, but a number of theoretical physicists see it as a purer and more sensible way of tackling unification. It is called loop quantum gravity, and it came to the fore in the last decade of the twentieth century.

LOOP QUANTUM GRAVITY

Loop quantum gravity does not start from quantum field theory, but from the other direction—from general relativity. It assumes that spacetime itself, rather than the matter it contains, is the more fundamental concept. Aesthetically, it would seem sensible to try to quantise the gravitational field—which, according to general relativity, *is* spacetime itself. Thus, if we shrink down to small enough length scales, we should see space become grainy and discrete. In the same way that Max Planck proposed, in 1900, that heat radiation ultimately comes in quantum lumps, quantizing space suggests there should be a smallest length that cannot be further divided. However, the quanta of gravitational energy are the quanta of space itself, which means that they don't exist as lumps *within* space . . . they *are* lumps *of* space.

It is thought that the tiniest unit of space—a quantum of volume—is one Planck length, or 10^{-35} m, across. I have always enjoyed trying to find ways of describing how tiny this volume is. For example, an atomic nucleus contains as many Planck volumes inside it as there are cubic metres in the Milky Way galaxy.

This discretisation of space seems inevitable if we want to quantise the gravitational field. And it therefore follows that time must also be 'lumpy'. So the smooth space and time that we experience is nothing more than a large-scale approximation of the lumpy quanta of gravity, smeared out because the individual pixels of spacetime are too small for us to perceive.

Loop quantum gravity contrasts dramatically with string theory, which predicts that, just as the three forces covered by the Standard Model (electromagnetism and the strong and weak nuclear forces) are in fact quantum fields manifested as force-carrying particles, so too is the gravitational field mediated by a quantum particle of gravity: the graviton, a massless state of a string. In string theory, this quantum of the gravitational field exists *within* spacetime, whereas in loop quantum gravity, it is spacetime itself that is quantised.

Loop quantum gravity refers to the closed paths that take you from a quantum of space, via its links to adjacent quanta, around in a loop and back to the starting point. The nature of these loops determines the curvature of spacetime. They are not physical entities like strings.

The roads to Unification

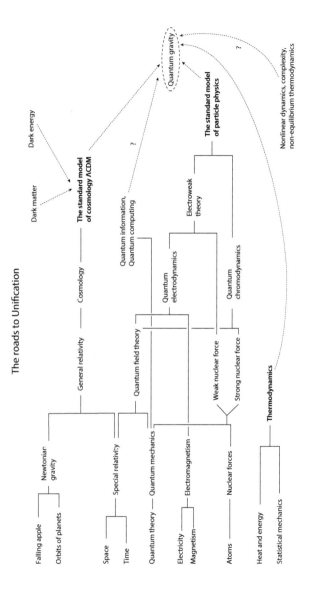

All that is real is the relationship between the loops.

In a sense, loop quantum gravity is modest in its scope. But when you consider it more carefully you begin to realise that, if it is indeed the correct description of reality, then it is not so much that events take place within space and for a duration of time, but rather that the universe, and everything in it—all matter and energy—is nothing more than quantum fields coexisting and superimposed onto each other. And these fields do not require space and time to exist in, since spacetime is itself *one* of these quantum fields.

In summary, we cannot yet claim to have a genuine theory of everything, nor do we understand yet how to bring quantum mechanics and general relativity together. Rather, we have

FIGURE 4. (OPPOSITE) Unification—A (simplified) chart showing how concepts in physics (theories, phenomena, forces) have come together over the years. Note that while the chronology is correct (running from left to right), you should not read too much into it. For example, special relativity appears directly below Newtonian gravity even though it came centuries later.

candidate theories that show some promise, but which still leave many questions unanswered. Brilliant physicists have built their careers on one or the other such theory, but just as with different interpretations of quantum mechanics, there is a lot of sociology of science involved, and views on which theory shows the most promise really do depend on who you speak to. Broadly then, in the red corner we have string theory, which is our current best stab at unifying the four forces of nature, but which despite three and a half decades of research is still speculative. Some physicists claim that despite all the progress it has made, it is now reaching something of a crisis because it hasn't delivered on its early promise. Indeed, it can be argued that it is not yet even a proper scientific theory, since it has not made any testable predictions. Then, in the blue corner, we have loop quantum gravity, which seems to be the most sensible way of quantising spacetime, but which does not tell us how to then combine gravity with the other three forces. Whether one or the other of these two approaches is correct, or whether we need to somehow merge the two, or even look for an entirely new theory, we still do not know.

This leads us nicely on to where the current outstanding problems and controversies are in fundamental physics, and what advances are likely in the coming decades.

CHAPTER 8

THE FUTURE
OF PHYSICS

The remarkable success of twentieth-century physics might suggest that all we have left to do is iron out a few creases, refine our experimental measurements, and put the finishing touches to our mathematical theories—that most of what there is to know is already known and we are just dotting a few 'i's and crossing the final 't's. You may have got the impression that there is no need for another Newton or Einstein (or indeed a Maxwell, Rutherford, Bohr, Dirac, Feynman, Witten, or Hawking) to come along and bring about a new revolution in physics, because we are already within touching distance of a theory of everything that explains the workings of the entire universe.

Unfortunately, or fortunately if you're a research physicist just starting out in your career and looking for big problems to tackle, the truth is far from this. In fact, I would say we are further away from the end of physics today than we thought we were twenty or thirty years ago. We speak of the Standard Model as describing all the elementary building blocks of matter and energy, but we are now pretty sure that everything we have found only makes up 5 percent of the universe. The other 95 percent, known as dark matter and dark energy, is still to some extent mysterious. We are confident it's out there, but we don't know what it is made of or how it fits into our current theories. In this chapter, I will explore this mystery along with other outstanding challenges in fundamental physics.

DARK MATTER

The rotational speed of galaxies, the motion of entire galaxies within galaxy clusters, as well as the large-scale structure of the entire universe, all point towards a significant component of the universe consisting of a near-invisible matter component. We call it 'dark,' not because it is hidden behind other, visible matter, or even because it is actually dark, but because, as far as we can tell, it doesn't feel the electromagnetic force and so does not give off light or interact with normal matter, other than gravitationally,[1] and so a better name for it would have been invisible matter. Think for a moment about why, if you slam your hand down on a solid table, it doesn't pass straight through. You might regard this as trivial: surely it is because both your hand and the table are made of solid stuff. But don't forget that down at the level of atoms, matter is mostly empty space—diffuse clouds of electrons surrounding a tiny nucleus—and so there should be plenty of room for the atoms that make up

---

1 Of course, there are matter particles, such as neutrinos, that also do not feel the electromagnetic force. However, they interact instead with other matter via the weak nuclear force, and so are not what is referred to as dark matter. Even dark matter itself may yet be found to interact via one or more of the other three forces, but it would have to be very weakly indeed (or we would have measured it by now). Physicists haven't entirely given up hope of such a small non-gravitational interaction, as that would increase the chances of dark matter particles being detected or created in an accelerator.

your hand to easily pass through the atoms of the table without any physical matter coming into contact. The reason they don't is because of the electromagnetic force between the electrons in the atoms of your hand and the electrons in the atoms of the table, repelling each other and providing the resistance we experience as solidity. However, if your hand were made of dark matter, then it would pass straight through as though the table weren't there—the gravitational force between them being too weak to have much effect.

It has long been known that galaxies have much more mass than can be accounted for if one measures all the normal matter they contain in the form of stars, planets, and interstellar dust and gas. At one point it was thought that dark matter might be made up of long-dead stars and black holes—objects made of normal matter, but which do not emit light. However, overwhelming evidence now suggests that this invisible stuff must be made up of a new form of matter, most likely a new type of particle yet to be discovered.

Originally, dark matter was proposed to explain the large-scale dynamics of entire clusters of galaxies. Further evidence then came from the way stars moved within spiral galaxies, circulating like undissolved coffee granules on the surface of a mug of instant coffee after it has been stirred. Most of the stars—and hence, you would think, most of the mass—in a galaxy are concentrated at its core, which would require those in the outer rim to be moving around the centre more slowly. The observed higher-than-expected orbital speeds of these outer stars suggest that there must be some additional invisible stuff present, extending out beyond the visible matter we can see and providing the extra gravitational glue to stop the outer stars from flying off.

Dark matter can also be seen from the way it curves space around it. This phenomenon manifests itself in the way light bends while on its path from very distant objects to our telescopes. The amount of bending can only be explained by the extra gravitational curvature of space provided by the dark matter of galaxies that the light passes on its way to us.

So, what do we know about dark matter other than that it provides this necessary extra gravitational attraction? Might this not be accounted for by something less exotic than a new form of matter? Indeed, some astrophysicists suggest that there may be no need for dark matter at all—if we are allowed to modify the properties of the gravitational force at large distances. An idea known as MOND (modified Newtonian dynamics) is one such suggestion and, on the face of it, this idea can sound quite appealing. However, while MOND, or other related hypotheses that modify general relativity, can explain away some of the observed effects, there is plenty that they do *not* explain. None of these models have been able to match the observational data for galaxy clusters, particularly colliding galaxy clusters (such as the famous Bullet Cluster), the detailed structure of the cosmic microwave background radiation, globular star clusters, or, more recently, tiny dwarf galaxies.

The existence of dark matter also seems necessary to explain the structure of the early universe. In contrast with normal matter, which through its interaction with the electromagnetic field kept its energy high, dark matter cooled down more quickly as the universe expanded and therefore started to clump together gravitationally earlier. One of the most important results in astrophysics in recent years has been the confirmation from sophisticated computer simulations of galaxy formation that we can only explain the real universe if it does indeed contain large quantities of dark matter. Without it, we would not get the rich cosmic structures we see today. Put more bluntly, without dark matter, most galaxies, and hence stars and planets, could never have formed in the first place. This remarkable conclusion is supported beautifully by data showing subtle fluctuations in the temperature of deep space, the imprint of the very young universe on the cosmic microwave background radiation. It was recognised back in the late 1970s that these fluctuations in the cosmic microwave background, while helpful in providing the seeding for the present-day distribution of matter in the universe, were too tiny to explain how galaxies could form. Dark matter helped provide the extra clumping that was needed. It was one of the great scientific triumphs of the end of the twentieth century when the COBE satellite[2] measured these fluctuations to be just what had been predicted. Since then, further space missions have mapped these wrinkles in the cosmic microwave background with ever-increasing resolution: NASA's WMAP mission in the first decade of this century, then the European Space Agency's Planck satellite, which launched in 2009.

While we are left in little doubt that dark matter is real, we are still in the dark as to what it is made of. It is a growing source of frustration in astrophysics that, in parallel with the accumulation of evidence in support of dark matter, we have failed to find out what it actually is. The consensus now is that it consists of a new type of heavy particle (heavy by the standards of elementary particles, that is), and most of the experimental effort thus far has been

---

2 The Cosmic Background Explorer, also referred to as Explorer 66, was a satellite dedicated to cosmology, which operated from 1989 to 1993. Its goals were to investigate the cosmic microwave background radiation of the universe.

focused on building sophisticated underground detectors that can capture extremely rare events when such a dark matter particle streaming in from space collides head-on with an atom in the detector. To date, no signal from these increasingly sophisticated and sensitive experiments has been picked up.

And yet, physicists looking for dark matter remain optimistic. Most likely, they say, it will be in the form of slow-moving particles, making up what is known as 'cold dark matter'. And there is no shortage of suggestions for what these particles might be, with such wonderful-sounding names as axions, sterile neutrinos, WIMPs,[3] and GIMPs[4]. Many feel confident that experimental evidence will emerge soon. But then, we've been saying that for some time now.

I should at this point say just a little about neutrinos, which for a while were the leading candidates for dark matter. These are elusive yet abundant particles that we know exist, which have a

---

3 Weakly interacting massive particles
4 Gravitationally interacting massive particles

tiny mass and are almost invisible. You would need a light-year's thickness of lead shielding to have even a fifty-fifty chance of blocking them. You could say that they are, to all intents and purposes, 'dark matter'. However, they cannot be *the* dark matter that we are searching for because, being so light, they travel at near light speed—too fast to remain bound within galaxies and thus to explain galaxies' anomalous properties. We refer to neutrinos as hot dark matter, because they move so fast.

And as if the unresolved problem of dark matter weren't big enough for physicists, we now know of another mysterious substance filling the universe, which plays a vital role in shaping it.

DARK ENERGY

In 1998, astronomers studying the faint light of supernovae in distant galaxies used it to calculate the speeds at which those galaxies were receding from us due to the expansion of the universe. They found that they were moving away more slowly than their distance from us suggested they should be. Since the light now reaching us from these galaxies left them when the universe was very young, their slower-than-expected recession speeds meant that the universe must have been expanding more slowly in the past. So, rather than the cumulative gravitational attraction of all the matter in the universe—both normal and dark matter—slowing down the expansion of the universe, something else was at work, making it expand more quickly now than it did in the past.

This mysterious repulsive substance acting against gravity and stretching space ever more quickly became known as dark energy. According to our present understanding, dark energy may ultimately result in what is called the 'heat death' of the universe many billions of years from now as space continues to expand ever more rapidly and to cool as it settles towards a state of thermodynamic equilibrium. But until we truly understand the nature of dark energy, and indeed the properties of the very early universe (see the next section), we should not be too quick to conjecture about its final fate. It's a long way off, and anything could happen between now and then!

Until a few years ago, I would have said we know even less about dark energy than we do about dark matter, but that is now changing. There is a quantity in Einstein's equations of general relativity, known as the cosmological constant (and denoted by the Greek letter Λ, or lambda), that fits the bill. What we call dark energy is most likely the energy of empty space itself—what is referred to as the quantum vacuum. We have seen how everything ultimately comes down to quantum fields in the end. All the different particles that make up matter and energy, whether quarks, electrons, photons, or Higgs bosons, can be regarded merely as localised *excitations* of these quantum fields—like waves on the surface of an ocean. However, if you were to remove all the particles from a volume of space, this does not get rid of the field. Instead, we say it is left in its ground, or vacuum, state, but there will still be virtual particles popping in and out of existence within this vacuum all the time, borrowing the energy from their surroundings in order to exist, but paying it back just as quickly when they disappear again. So to say that the quantum vacuum of empty space has zero energy would be the same as claiming a calm ocean has no depth. The equivalent of water beneath the ocean surface is this dark energy—it is the cosmological constant.

However, having a mathematical symbol for dark energy does *not* mean we entirely understand its nature yet. Astronomical measurements suggest that the cosmological constant has a certain numerical value, but, like the mass of the Higgs boson in the Standard Model, we do not know why it has this value. This long-standing problem in physics is known as fine-tuning and is very unsatisfying. In fact things are even worse than this. The discrepancy between this calculated vacuum energy from quantum field theory and the observed vacuum energy from cosmological measurements is so huge that it's one of the most embarrassing and unresolved problems in physics. You see, the calculated value is a ridiculous 120 orders of magnitude bigger than the observed value.

Our 'best guess' cosmological model—the equivalent of the Standard Model in particle physics—which contains under its umbrella what we currently know about dark matter and dark energy, is called the ΛCDM model (or Lambda–cold dark matter model). And similar to the way deeper quantum field theories underpin the loose alliance of the Standard Model of particle physics, so too does general relativity underpin the ΛCDM cosmological model.

There is one more important ingredient of the ΛCDM model, which most, but by no means all, cosmologists claim is needed to explain the properties of the universe we see. It is called cosmic inflation, and it provides a possible answer to that perennial question: How did the universe and all the matter and energy it contains come into being in the first place?

INFLATION AND THE MULTIVERSE

As we touched on at the very beginning of this book, since the dawn of human history we've created many myths about the origins of the universe. Today, physics has given us a demystified explanation of how the universe began, with overwhelming observational evidence to back it up. But did the Big Bang itself have a cause? Was there something that triggered the birth of our universe in the first place?

The simplest answer is that there was no 'before' the Big Bang, for it marked the birth of both space and time. An idea put forward by Stephen Hawking and James Hartle, called the 'no boundary' proposal, states that, as we wind back the clock closer and closer to the Big Bang, time begins to lose its meaning and becomes more like a dimension of space. We therefore end up with smooth four-dimensional space at a point of the universe's origin. So it is meaningless to ask what happened before the Big Bang, in the same way that it is meaningless to ask what point on the surface of the Earth lies south of the South Pole.

But the Big Bang model is not enough on its own to explain the universe we see today. In particular, two problems puzzled cosmologists half a century ago. The first is called the flatness problem. This is yet another fine-tuning issue and relates to the density of matter and energy in the universe, which appears to have a just the right value to make space almost perfectly flat.[5] The second problem is called the horizon problem. The furthest we can see out into space is probably only a tiny fraction of the entire universe, and there exists a horizon beyond which we can never see. This horizon marks the edge of what is known as the visible universe. It exists because the universe hasn't been around forever, and light takes a certain time to reach us. An added complication is that the universe is expanding, and at some distance space is stretching faster than light can travel through it (like trying to walk up a rapidly descending escalator).

Consider a galaxy near the edge of the visible universe in one direction and another galaxy near the edge in the opposite direction. Due to the expansion of the universe, any intelligent

---

5 It is hard to visualise what we mean by 'flat' 3-D space. The easiest way is to imagine restricting our space to just two dimensions. Now, it is clear that a page in a book is flat, whereas the surface of a ball is not.

beings living in one of these distant galaxies would be completely unaware of the existence of the other galaxy, since light from it won't have reached them yet, nor will it ever. In fact, the regions of space containing the two galaxies could never have been in contact and cannot ever have shared information. Why is this a problem? Because in every direction we look and as far out as we can see, the universe looks the same. Both of those distant galaxies look very much the same (to us in between them) in terms of their physical properties, composition, and the structure of matter within them. How can this be if they were never in contact in the past?

To solve these two issues—the flatness problem and the horizon problem—a concept known as cosmic inflation was proposed forty years ago. It went like this: when the universe was just a fraction of a second old, it underwent a short period of exponential expansion due to yet another quantum field, called the inflaton field, during which it grew stupendously rapidly to a trillion trillion trillion trillion times the size it was before. This solves the problem of the finely tuned density giving rise to the flat spacetime we see today, because any tiny amount of curvature got stretched out by inflation.

The way inflation solves the horizon problem is more interesting. The usual explanation is that distant parts of the universe that do not appear to ever have had the chance to be in contact, and thus to synchronise their physical properties, were in fact in contact at the beginning, but that inflation caused space to expand so rapidly they appear now to be too far apart to have ever been causally connected.

I said this is the 'usual explanation', but if you think about it, there are two things not quite right with referring to inflation as being 'rapid' expansion. First, for distant parts of the universe to be able to communicate with each other when they were close together surely required them to stay closer together for longer, not zoom apart too quickly. Secondly, when we refer in mathematics to something being exponential, we mean that it varies slowly to begin with and then speeds up (the slope becoming steeper). This is a better way of thinking about the inflationary early universe. It started expanding slowly, then sped up. Then, at some point, this exponential expansion changed to what is called a 'power law' expansion, where instead of the expansion speeding up, it started to slow down again—until, that is, dark energy kicked in halfway through the universe's life and started to speed the expansion up again.

Of course, this tells you nothing about why the idea is so attractive, or why or how it works. So, let us spend a little time unpacking its meaning.

To appreciate how inflation works, you must first understand the difference between positive and negative pressure. Imagine you are holding an inflated balloon. The air inside it exerts a pressure on its inner surface, pushing outwards. If you were to now squeeze the balloon between your hands you would be expending energy to compress its air to a smaller volume, increasing its density, and this energy gets stored in the balloon's air molecules. Now, consider the reverse process: relax your hands so that the balloon expands back to its original size and the air inside becomes less dense again. The energy stored in its molecules must now also drop back to what it was originally.[6] So, allowing the volume inside the balloon to expand means its energy decreases. This is the situation with 'normal', positive pressure: it loses energy as it expands.

But what if the balloon were filled with an unusual substance that did the opposite? What if, when it expanded in volume, its density didn't drop, but remained constant, and the energy per unit volume stayed the same, too, so its total energy *increased*? This is what we mean by something with 'negative pressure'—instead of the energy of the balloon's contents increasing when compressed, it increases when it *expands*. The closest example to this in our everyday world is a rubber band, since stretching it puts more energy into it.

And this is exactly what we have with the inflaton field filling space: it's like a rubber band, and has the property that every time the

---

6 Of course, this energy does not return to the muscles in your arms, but is lost instead as waste heat to the balloon's surroundings.

volume of space doubles, its total energy also doubles in order to maintain a constant field density. So, the inflaton field gives the universe energy, just as you would give a rubber band energy by stretching it.

You should be asking two questions here. Firstly, why does the inflaton field cause the expansion of space? After all, a rubber band does not spontaneously expand of its own accord. And secondly, given that the inflaton field generates energy, where does that energy originate from? Both questions have crafty but logical answers that can be found, you won't be surprised to hear, in the equations of general relativity.

Einstein's field equations tell us that gravity can be caused by pressure as well as by mass and energy. So, while something with positive pressure, like the molecules of air in a balloon, gives rise to normal attractive gravity, a substance with negative pressure will cause the opposite: antigravity—pushing everything apart rather than pulling it together. The inflaton field has the property that the repulsive effect of its negative pressure (or antigravity) is bigger than the normal attractive gravity caused by its energy, and so it causes space to expand at an accelerating pace.

As for where the energy of the inflaton field came from in the first place, the answer is that it is borrowed from its own gravitational field. Think of a ball on top of a hill: it has a store of positive potential energy that it can convert into kinetic energy if it rolls down. But a ball at the bottom of the hill has no potential energy, while a ball down in a hole has negative potential energy (since it needs energy put into to lift it back up to ground level). It is as though our universe began with no space and no energy, but a quantum fluctuation caused it to start rolling down a gravitational energy slope. As it rolled down it gained positive energy, paid for as it descended deeper into the gravitational valley by its increasing negative gravitational potential energy (see figure 5). Cosmologist refer to this as the ultimate free lunch—something from nothing. It is a very neat answer to the question: where did all the matter and energy in the universe come from in the first place?

Another way of understanding why gravitational energy is negative is to consider the following example: Start with two masses far enough apart that they can hardly feel each other. As they drift together they will gradually gain in gravitational attraction, but this gravitational energy is negative in the sense that you would need to put positive energy in to pull them apart again and get them back to the zero energy they started with.

When inflation ended, the energy of the inflaton field decayed into normal energy, which condensed out into all the matter we have today. The stuff of the universe was created from energy borrowed from its own gravitational field—the ultimate in creative accounting.

But just because inflation theory solves these problems in cosmology does not mean that it is correct. While most cosmologists subscribe to this theory, there are others who disagree, and there are indeed some subtle issues that have not yet been resolved. One critic is Stephen Hawking's long-term collaborator Roger Penrose. Instead of inflation, Penrose has proposed his

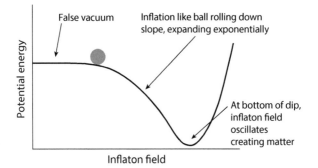

FIGURE 5. Inflation—The universe gained its positive energy (from which it created all matter) by 'rolling down' a gravitational potential energy slope, expanding as it did so.

own model, called conformal cyclic cosmology, in which the universe goes through an infinite series of epochs, each of which starts with a phase resembling a Big Bang. At the end of each cycle, all that remains, after even the black holes have evaporated, is thermal radiation. This, Penrose conjectures, is similar to the smooth high-energy radiation that would fill the universe just after the Big Bang, and with a clever connection between the low entropy of the early universe and the high entropy at the end (nothing can escape the second law of thermodynamics), he can attach the end of one aeon to the beginning of another and see everything start again with a new Big Bang. Suffice it to say that this proposal is even more controversial than inflation theory.

And since we are deeply in the realm of speculation, why stop now? A fashionable idea in cosmology at the moment is known as eternal inflation. In this scenario, our universe is just a small bubble within an infinite, higher-dimensional space known as the multiverse, which has been undergoing inflation forever. In this scenario, the Big Bang that created our universe was but a quantum fluctuation 13.82 billion years ago, which created a bubble in this eternally inflating space. The space within this bubble—our universe—stopped inflating and slowed down to expand at a more sedate rate, while the multiverse outside continued its runaway inflation. And so, rather than a very brief period of inflation taking place *after* the Big Bang, now we have things the other way around with *our* Big Bang marking the *end* of inflation in our part of the multiverse.

What's more, eternal inflation predicts there will be other bubble universes within the multiverse, possibly an infinite number of them, all forever separated from each other and all being driven apart rapidly by the ever-expanding inflaton field.

This idea has an added benefit that many cosmologists find appealing. I have mentioned before that physicists do not like fine-tuning—that is, for there to be no underlying reason for why certain physical quantities have the values they do. This comes to a head when we consider that our most fundamental constants have just the right values for a universe such as ours to exist. If gravity were ever so slightly weaker, galaxies and stars might never have formed, and if the charge on the electron were very slightly stronger, atoms would collapse, and complex matter could not exist. So, the eternal inflation multiverse theory answers the question: Why is our universe so finely tuned as to be suitable for stars and planets, and life, to exist? The answer is that all possible bubble universes can exist, all obeying the same laws of physics, but each with its own set of fundamental physical constants. We just happen to be in one that is just right for life to emerge and contemplate how lucky it is.

I should also just add here, to avoid any confusion: these bubble universes are *not* the same thing as the parallel realities of the multiverse (or many-worlds) interpretation of quantum mechanics, which are due to the different possible outcomes of measurement of the quantum world. The bubble universes in the eternal inflation theory are not parallel, overlapping realities, but completely independent of each other.

And before I move on, I want to add one more important point. We might wonder whether our universe is infinite in extent (even though we cannot see beyond our visible horizon), and it could well be. So how can infinite space fit inside a finite bubble floating in the multiverse alongside other bubble universes? The answer is rather strange: to us, on the inside, the universe could be infinite in extent, but finite in time. However, this is because we have a warped view of space and time from within our bubble. Viewed from 'the outside', our universe would appear finite in size but existing in endless time (see figure 6). It's

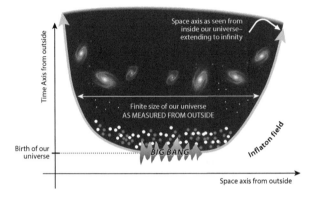

FIGURE 6. How can an infinite space fit into a finite volume?—
Two views of our universe: from 'outside' it always has a finite volume, but for us, within our spacetime, the space axis
is curved around so that it is pointing along the time axis to
infinity. For us it looks as though all times coincide to give an
infinite spatial extent.

a neat (but really conceptually tough—sorry!)
way of understanding how infinite space can fit
inside a finite volume.

INFORMATION

One topic I have not said much about that
brings together all three pillars of fundamental
physics—quantum mechanics, general relativity,

and thermodynamics—involves the role that information plays in physics. It is now understood that information is more than just an abstract notion and can in fact be quantified precisely. A long-standing puzzle, first highlighted by Stephen Hawking, was what happens to information, say this book you are reading, if you were to throw it into a black hole. The book will of course be lost forever, but what about the information it contained? By that, I mean the physical information that is encoded in the words of the book and that would be required to reconstruct them. You see, quantum mechanics tells us that information cannot be destroyed and must always be conserved.[7] Hawking described how black holes slowly evaporate, losing their energy in what is known as Hawking radiation, and quantum mechanics tells us that, in principle,

---

7 This comes about because, according to quantum mechanics, time is reversible. Therefore, just as a quantum state now uniquely determines a future state, so should a future quantum state uniquely determine a past one. But this wouldn't be possible if the information contained in this state is destroyed.

this radiation carries within it all the information that has been swallowed by the black hole, including the information needed to reconstruct this book. Do we know this for sure? Again, only a final theory of quantum gravity is going to lay this issue to rest.

The study of the mathematics of black holes has also led to the discovery that the maximum amount of information that can be stored in a volume of space is proportional, not to the volume of space, as might be expected, but to the surface area surrounding that volume. This idea became known as the holographic principle and is proving to be a powerful tool in theoretical physics. At its heart, it comes about because of a profound connection between information and energy. By storing more and more information in a volume of space, you increase its energy. And since energy is equivalent to mass, this means strengthening its gravitational field, to the point when the volume of space will collapse into a black hole. The holographic principle states that all the information will now be encoded on the black hole's event horizon. It is thought that this idea even applies to the information needed to describe the entire universe. The role of information is likely to become increasingly important in connecting up the three pillars of physics.

ER = EPR

In 2013, two leading physicists, Juan Maldacena and Leonard Susskind, proposed an idea that might yet provide a new route toward unifying gravity and quantum mechanics. While it is far too early to judge if they might be right, it's also too fascinating for me not to mention it in passing. Known simply as ER = EPR, it suggests that there may be a deep and profound link between quantum entanglement (two particles connect across space) and wormholes in spacetime. But note that 'ER = EPR' is not an algebraic equation, despite the 'equals' sign (otherwise you might wish to cancel the E and the R from both sides, leaving just P = 1, which is meaningless). Instead, it refers to the initials of the authors (Einstein, Podolsky, and Rosen) of two classic papers published just a few weeks apart in 1935.

These two papers had hitherto been thought to be completely unrelated. 'ER' refers to Einstein and Nathan Rosen, who proposed that two black holes might be linked by a tunnel outside our dimensions, an idea that emerges from the mathematics of general relativity. 'EPR' refers to the second paper the two published with Boris Podolsky, in which they outlined their misgivings about the idea of entanglement in quantum mechanics—what Einstein referred to as 'spooky connections'. The novel suggestion of Maldacena and Susskind is that both these profound ideas, wormholes and entanglement, might in fact be one and same phenomenon. Time will tell if they are on the right track.

A CRISIS IN PHYSICS?

Will we then ever reach a complete understanding of reality, or will we be forever peeling back layers of the onion to reveal deeper truths underneath? This has certainly been true so far. First, we discovered that everything is made of atoms, then that these atoms are themselves made of smaller parts—electrons orbiting around a dense nucleus. Later, we peered into the nucleus itself to discover that it is made up of smaller building blocks: protons and neutrons, which in turn are composed of even tinier quarks, which are themselves manifestations of energy fields—or, possibly, even far smaller vibrating strings in higher dimensions. Will it ever come to an end?

Some theoretical physicists, dazzled by the beauty of their equations, have ploughed on, postulating ever-more-exotic notions that have become increasingly difficult to test experimentally, judging them only on their explanatory power and mathematical elegance—important criteria, I agree, but not the traditional benchmarks for validating scientific theories. So, instead of patting ourselves on the back for how far we've come, should we consider the possibility that we might be straying too far from the path of physics?

Many physicists will no doubt argue that these past few years have been tremendously exciting for fundamental physics, considering the widely reported discoveries of the Higgs boson at the Large Hadron Collider in 2012, followed by gravitational waves at the LIGO (Laser Interferometer Gravitational-Wave Observatory) facilities in the United States in 2016. But the truth is that both these observational discoveries, vital though they are, 'merely' confirm predictions made by theorists a long time ago—fifty years in the case of the Higgs, and a full century for gravitational waves. I know this sounds more than a little dismissive, and I do not want to downplay the extraordinary achievements of the thousands of experimental physicists and engineers who played a part in these two remarkable discoveries. But, when I say 'merely,' I mean that there weren't many physicists who *didn't* expect these experimental confirmations to be made one day. In the case of the Higgs, even though the discovery led to the award of the physics Nobel Prize the following year, it went to the theorists who predicted it back in the 1960s, not to the experimentalists who made the confirming observation.

I guess I should make a more careful distinction here between the discovery of the Higgs boson and detection of gravitational waves. The former was by no means a foregone conclusion; many physicists, including Stephen Hawking, had doubted its existence before 2012. Gravitational waves, in contrast, were entirely expected, since they had not only been predicted by general relativity, but had been indirectly observed many years ago in the behaviour of binary pulsars (pairs of neutron stars in orbit around each other).

In fact, if I look back over the past three decades and consider some of the exciting breakthroughs and discoveries in fundamental physics, such as the top quark, Bose-Einstein condensates, quantum entanglement, neutron star mergers, and exoplanets, I could argue that none of these was completely unexpected. In fact, only one discovery in physics during this period was truly revolutionary and surprising (to the astronomers who first saw it, if not all cosmologists)—that of dark energy in 1998. Otherwise, when it comes to testing our theories and models at the furthest extremes of fundamental physics—the quantum and the cosmic scales—there has been experimental silence. Many of the ideas and speculative theories I have discussed in this chapter might well turn out to be correct. But it's worth pointing out that the traditional types of experiments that have served to verify or falsify scientific theories in the past are unlikely to be able to help us in the future to reach a sufficient level of confidence in their veracity.

When the Large Hadron Collider first started running in 2010, it was only the latest in a long line of particle accelerators around the world, going back almost a century, that have been smashing subatomic matter together at increasingly higher energies. Physicists had waited a long time for the LHC and had high hopes that it would help them answer a number of the outstanding questions and remove uncertainties from the Standard Model. But, above all else, it was billed as the accelerator that would find the Higgs boson, and it duly did—surely, a resounding success and a justification for the huge cost of the project. But since then, there has been mounting frustration that nothing more has been discovered—both from scientists in other disciplines envious of the funding that

CERN receives, and from theoretical physicists impatient for confirmation of their latest predictions.

And what of the Higgs discovery itself? What new insights has it given us about the nature of matter? It's worth noting that the Higgs boson is merely the particle manifestation (excitation) of the more fundamental Higgs field—yet another quantum field that pervades all space and an important ingredient of the Standard Model, because the way other particles move through the Higgs field is what gives them their mass. For instance, the W and Z bosons, the carriers of the weak force, would have no mass without it, and would be more like their cousin, the massless photon. But the W and Z do have mass, and it is the Higgs mechanism that explains how they acquire it—through their interaction with the Higgs field in a way that the photon does not. Final proof of the Higgs field's existence was found not by detecting it directly, but indirectly, through the creation of the evanescent quantum of the field: the Higgs boson.

Finding the Higgs was a remarkable achievement. But, in truth, it was a box to be ticked. The Higgs field was bolted onto the Standard Model, which lived to fight another day. The discovery of the Higgs hasn't opened up many new avenues in fundamental physics research, because it didn't progress our understanding beyond what physicists already knew and expected. The Standard Model remains a consistent framework for our understanding of the building blocks of matter, but it is not a fully coherent or predictive unified theory.

Of course, there are still plenty of data to sift through at the LHC from the most recent run, which came to an end in December 2018, so we might still find something new once all the data have been analysed. But the fact remains that there are still a number of outstanding questions to answer, and we may have to look beyond the LHC to do so. These questions include: Why is gravity so much weaker than the other forces? Why are there just three generations of quarks and leptons? And where does the Higgs's own mass come from? Probably most pressing of all, and therefore most frustrating because it has not been found, is whether we will find any evidence of supersymmetry.

Just because we *want* supersymmetry to be true does not make it so. Sure, it solves many problems and provides useful insights. It is also neat and logical and aesthetically pleasing. But the longer we go without finding any experimental proof of supersymmetry, the more frustrated we become. At the same time, critics of superstring theory grumble that the field continues to be attractive to the brightest minds because it offers jobs. Young researchers feel safer following in the footsteps of their professors and fear that if they don't, they will lose out on funding and career progression. Meanwhile, university physics departments, competing for scarce resources, see research in string theory as a cheap way of working at the forefront of physics. But as long as progress remains slow, with no new experimental evidence emerging to bolster the efforts of those in the field, dissenting voices will grow louder.

Some might argue that if supersymmetry is correct, then we should probably have found evidence of it by now at the LHC. The simplest class of supersymmetry models (what is called constrained minimal supersymmetry) is already looking unlikely. But this does not mean that we give up on it entirely just yet—we may just be looking for it in the wrong place. After all, it is not only on string theorists' wish lists. More 'down-to-earth' particle physicists also want to know if nature is supersymmetric. Supersymmetry allows us to understand a connection between the electroweak force and the strong nuclear force described by QCD. It also links together the matter particles and the force carrier particles. It would even explain why the Higgs boson has the mass that it does. But solving all these problems comes at a price: supersymmetry predicts the existence of a whole host of new particles that have yet to be discovered.

I should of course say that there is a nice added bonus if supersymmetry is true: the lightest of these yet-to-be-observed supersymmetric particles fit the bill as the constituents of dark matter.

REASONS TO BE OPTIMISTIC

Theoretical physicists have not just been sitting around waiting on news from their experimental colleagues. Enthralled by the splendour of their mathematics, they have forged ahead without them. No sooner had the latest version of string theory (M-theory) been proposed in the mid-1990s by Edward Witten than a powerful new idea was developed by Juan Maldacena in 1997. It is known as gauge/gravity duality (or, to give it its technical name, AdS/CFT[8]), and it describes how the strings in string theory relate to the field theories describing the three quantum forces. This mathematical idea has since been developed more generally to tackle problems in other areas of theoretical physics, such as hydrodynamics, quark-gluon plasma, and condensed matter, and Maldacena's paper has become one of the most important pieces of work in modern theoretical physics, having been cited over

---

8 Which stands for anti–de Sitter/conformal field theory correspondence

17,000 times in other peer-reviewed papers to date.

Powerful ideas like gauge/gravity duality convince many physicists that string theory is the right path to pursue. But even if it turns out not to be the correct theory of quantum gravity, what it has done is provide physicists with a useful and precise mathematical toolbox that has at least shown us there *is* a way of combining quantum mechanics and general relativity consistently, and so it gives us hope that the project of unification is in principle possible. But the fact remains that just because string theory or gauge/gravity duality are mathematically beautiful, this does not make them true.

Where will the final answer come from, then? Maybe from string theory, maybe from the study of black holes, maybe from those working on quantum information theory trying to build quantum computers, or maybe even from condensed matter theory. It is becoming clearer that similar forms of mathematics apply across all these areas. In the search for a correct theory of quantum gravity, we may not even need to quantise gravity, after all. Maybe trying to *force* quantum field theory and general relativity towards each other is the wrong approach. There is some evidence that quantum field theories may already contain within them the essence of curved spacetime, and that general relativity may be closer to quantum mechanics than we thought.

It would be fascinating to know which of the many ideas and theories in this chapter turn out to be correct and which will be consigned to the rubbish heap of wrong science. For me personally, the biggest unanswered question in physics is one that has vexed me all my professional life: What is the correct interpretation of quantum mechanics? In chapter 5, I touched on a few of the candidate ideas and mentioned that for many physicists this really is a problem for the philosophers to address, since it has not stopped the application of quantum mechanics or slowed the progress of physics. But a growing number of physicists, including yours truly, see the foundations of quantum mechanics as a vitally important field, and suspect that a resolution of the longstanding issue of its interpretation will ultimately lead to new physics. It may even be linked to one or more of the other outstanding problems in fundamental physics, such as the nature of time or the ultimate theory of quantum gravity.

These problems sometimes seem so difficult to overcome that it wouldn't surprise me if we ended up needing an advanced artificial intelligence to help us. Maybe an AI of our invention will emerge as the next Newton or Einstein, and we may have to accept that our puny human brains are just not smart enough to figure out the ultimate nature of reality on our own.[9]

I have focussed in this chapter on the future of physics, mainly with regard to mathematical physics and physics at the extremes of the very smallest and largest scales. But is this fair? Are these justifiably the true frontiers of physics? Advances in physics are not all about striving to see smaller or further—and the everyday scales, in terms of size and energy, are no less fascinating. In fact, in terms of how physics will transform our lives in the twenty-first century, the real

---

9 Maybe it will inform us that answer is, indeed, 42.

excitement is in areas like condensed matter physics and quantum optics, and in areas in which physics overlaps and merges with chemistry, biology, and engineering. So, rather than delve into some of those topics here, I will use them as examples of how the technological applications of physics are shaping our world and I will explore these, some might say, more 'useful' aspects of the physics enterprise in the next chapter.

CHAPTER 9

THE USEFULNESS
OF PHYSICS

Wherever you are right now as you're reading this book, look around you. So much of what we humans have created and built has only been possible thanks to our understanding of the laws of nature: the forces that shape our world and the properties of the matter that these forces act on. It would therefore be impossible to list all of the applications of physics—all the trappings of our modern world that have emerged from the discoveries made by physicists over the centuries[1]—so I will instead focus on two topics. The first is the way physics has underpinned,

---

1 Of course, I am not claiming that this knowledge and understanding has come about exclusively because of the work of physicists, since I could make a similar claim if I were writing about chemistry, or engineering, or mathematics.

overlapped with, and even merged with other disciplines, both pure and applied, and the role it continues to play in a number of exciting new interdisciplinary research fields. The second is a brief look at a selection of new applications that will undoubtedly arise from current physics research, with a particular focus on the exciting prospect of new quantum technologies.

After getting this far in the book you will be forgiven for thinking that physicists' obsession with unifying the mathematical principles that govern the workings of nature is all very well—a testament to humankind's tenacious drive to understand the universe—but so what? Surely, you might think, the discovery of the Higgs boson won't have any sort of direct impact on our daily lives; nor will the hoped-for theory of quantum gravity help to eradicate poverty and disease. But this is not the right way to look at things. Fundamental, curiosity-driven science has, time and again, led to technological advances that have revolutionised our world. Most physics researchers, particularly those working in academia, are not typically motivated by the potential applications of their work, and if you look back at the great discoveries in science which later proved to have practical benefit, you will find that many of them were made out of a burning desire simply to understand the world and to satisfy scientists' curiosity.

Consider a superficial comparison between physics and engineering. A mechanical or electrical engineering student will study many of the same topics as a physics student, such as Newtonian mechanics, electromagnetism, computing, and the mathematical techniques required for solving certain types of equations that crop up on a regular basis. Indeed, many applied physicists end up working in engineering industries, further blurring the boundaries between the two disciplines. But, typically, a physicist will ask the 'Why?' and the 'How?' questions in order to expose the underlying principles that govern the workings of nature, whereas an engineer is not normally motivated by these deeper principles and will rather put his or her understanding to work, using it to build a better world. Both physicists and engineers are problem solvers, but they tend to have different motivations for seeking solutions.

Just to offer a particular example, the brilliant engineering success of satellite navigation systems (the US GPS being the most important one over the past few decades) clearly demonstrates the value of pure physics research that underpins the engineering. GPS systems are now such an integral part of our lives that we could not live without them. Not only do we take for granted the fact that we no longer get lost in unfamiliar parts of the world, but GPS has allowed us to see our planet from above and map it with remarkable detail, enabling us to study the way the Earth's climate is changing, or to predict natural phenomena and help with disaster relief. In the future, global positioning satellites will link with AI systems to transform transport, agriculture, and many other industries. And yet without the knowledge that came from fundamental physics research, GPS would not have been possible. For example, the atomic clocks onboard satellites, which are needed to ensure that we can locate them precisely in order to pinpoint our position on the ground, only work because engineers had to take the quantum nature of atomic vibrations into account, along with the relativistic corrections to the rate of flow of time that Einstein's theories explained.

There are countless other technological examples of physics and engineering overlapping in ways that have changed the world as we know it. And engineers aren't the only people physicists have long had a close working relationship with. Today, many physicists work alongside scientists from a wide range of disciplines, such as medicine, neuroscience, computer science, bioengineering, geology, environmental science, and space science. You will also find physicists applying their logical, numerate, and problem-solving skills outside of science in professions ranging from politics to finance.

WHERE PHYSICS, CHEMISTRY, AND BIOLOGY MEET

Throughout the history of science, there has always been a strong overlap between physics and its sister discipline, chemistry. Indeed, some of the greatest scientists of all time, most notably Michael Faraday, have been claimed by both subjects. And it isn't just chemistry; the role of physics in biology, in particular, has a fascinating history. The community of physicists interested in biological problems is incredibly diverse, and their work has led to a very vibrant field of research called biophysics. But is biophysics a branch of physics, or is it no more than the application of methods from physics to the problems of biology? Does this distinction even matter? If physics ultimately underpins chemistry and chemical processes, and the phenomena within living organisms are themselves nothing more than complex chemistry, then surely it follows that physics must lie at the heart of biology. After all, everything, living or inanimate, is ultimately made of atoms and is subject to the laws of physics.

In an effort to dig down and identify the fundamental principles that govern the workings of biology, as is their wont, physicists ask, 'What distinguishes life from non-life *made up of the same ingredients*?' The answer is rooted in physics:

life has the ability to maintain itself in a state of low entropy, far from thermal equilibrium, and is able to store and process information. Therefore, one has the feeling that a full understanding of what makes life special has to come from fundamental physics. In writing this, I can imagine my colleagues in chemistry and biology rolling their eyes with exasperation at this typical physicist's sense of self-importance. On the other hand, it is true that many of the early advances in molecular biology and genetics in the twentieth century were made by physicists, such as Leo Szilard, Max Delbrück, and Francis Crick. Crick, in particular, who discovered (with James Watson and Rosalind Franklin) the double helix structure of DNA, was hugely influenced by yet another physicist, Erwin Schrödinger, whose remarkable 1944 book, *What is Life?*, is still relevant today.

On the applied side, physicists have been key to the development of many of the techniques that are used to probe living matter, from X-ray diffraction to MRI scanners. Even the humble microscope, without which no biology lab could function, was invented by physicists, thanks to hundreds of years of research into the nature of light and the way lenses refract and focus it, culminating in the work of Antonie van Leeuwenhoek and Robert Hooke, who both used the microscope in the seventeenth century to study living organisms. Indeed, if you consider the many contributions to science made by Hooke, you will find that, by today's definition, he is most definitely a physicist rather than a biologist.

One particular new area of research that I have personally become interested in over the past twenty years is called quantum biology. This subject should not be confused with the comments I made earlier about all life being ultimately made of atoms and hence at some basic level subject to the rules of the quantum world like everything else in the universe. That is, of course, taken as a given. Rather, quantum biology refers to recent research in theoretical physics, experimental biology, and biochemistry which suggests that some of the more counterintuitive ideas in quantum mechanics, such as tunneling, superposition, and entanglement, might be playing an important role inside living cells. Key experimental observations regarding the way enzymes work, or in the process of photosynthesis, seem to require a quantum explanation. This has come as a huge surprise to many scientists who refuse to believe that such delicate and strange behaviour could impact on the machinery of life, and the jury is still out on some of these ideas. But don't forget that life has had almost four billion years of evolution to find any shortcuts that would give it an advantage. If quantum mechanics can make a particular biochemical process or mechanism more efficient, then evolutionary biology will make use of it. It isn't magic, it's just . . . well . . . physics.

THE QUANTUM REVOLUTION CONTINUES

In the twentieth century (and the beginning of the twenty-first), there is no doubt that quantum mechanics has had a profound impact on our lives, despite operating at length scales far smaller than our senses can detect. In describing the subatomic world so successfully, it under-pins not only physics and chemistry, but modern electronics, too. For example, an understanding of the quantum rules that explain how electrons behave in semiconductor materials like silicon has laid the foundation of our technological world. Without an understanding of semicon-ductors, we would not have developed the tran-sistor and, later, the microchip and the com-puter. That handheld supercomputer we all carry around with us today (our smartphone), without which many of us would now feel utterly lost, is packed full of electronic magic, none of which would have been possible without quantum mechanics. The same goes for many familiar de-vices in our homes, from televisions and games consoles to modern LED lighting and smoke detectors, and, of course, the internet. Indeed, the entire telecommunications industry relies on technological applications of quantum mechan-ics, such as lasers and optical amplifiers. And no modern-day hospital could get by without the applications of quantum mechanics, from MRI, PET, and CT scanners to laser surgery.

And the quantum revolution is only just getting started. We are about to witness many new technological marvels in the coming decades, emerging from current research in quantum physics, such as smart materials and topological materials. Take graphene, for example: single layers of carbon atoms arranged in a hexagonal crystal lattice. Depending on how it is shaped and manipulated, graphene acts as an insulator, a conductor, or even as a semiconductor.

What's more, recent research suggests that two layers of graphene twisted at a particular angle to each other can, under certain conditions of low temperature and an applied weak electric field, behave as a superconductor, through which current can flow with no electrical resistance whatsoever—yet another quantum phenomenon. This technique, known as twistronics, will, it is predicted, have applications in a wide range of electronic devices that have yet to be invented.

And there's so much more. A new generation of devices and technologies are currently being developed that will become ubiquitous within our lifetimes—devices that can create and manipulate exotic states of matter by utilising the tricks of the quantum world in new ways. Advances in areas such as quantum information theory, quantum optics, and nanotechnology will allow us to develop a range of such devices. For example, highly accurate quantum gravimeters will be able to map tiny changes in the Earth's gravitational field, so that geologists can locate new mineral deposits or locate pipes under roads to minimise disruption when workers need to access them. Quantum cameras will have sensors that let us see *behind* obstacles; quantum imaging will allow non-intrusive mapping of brain activity with the potential to tackle conditions like dementia. Quantum key distribution (QKD) will enable us to exchange information securely from one place to another. Quantum technologies will also help us build artificial molecular machines that can carry out a multitude of tasks.

Medicine in particular is a good example of where the quantum world is likely to have a big impact in the coming years. Down at length scales even smaller than living cells, we are going to see a range of spectacular new technologies emerging, such as nanoparticles with unique quantum properties that allow them to attach to antibodies to help tackle infections, or to be 'programmed' to replicate only inside tumor cells, and even to take images of cells from the inside. Then, quantum sensors will allow us to make far more precise measurements and help with imaging of individual biomolecules. And with the help of quantum computers, which I will discuss in the next section, we should be able to sequence DNA far more quickly than ever before, as well as solve certain tasks that involve searching through all that 'big data' on every aspect of our health, all the way down to the molecular level.

I am deliberately being very selective in my examples here, as there are thousands of technological and engineering advances in communications, medicine, energy, transport, imaging, and sensing that will come about thanks to physics. But one area does deserve further expansion.

QUANTUM COMPUTERS AND
21ST-CENTURY SCIENCE

If you thought the quantum revolution of the last century was impressive, just wait and see what the rest of the twenty-first century has in store. These advances are not only going to give us smarter toys that some might argue just make our lives more complicated; they will help us address some of the biggest challenges facing humanity and transform our world in as yet unimaginable ways. One of the most exciting future applications of physics, without doubt, is the quantum computer. Such a device would be very different from conventional computers and will be used for a wide range of tasks that are impossible today even with the most powerful supercomputers. Quantum computers are expected to help humanity solve many of the most difficult problems in science, especially if combined with advances in artificial intelligence.

Quantum computers rely in a very direct way on the more counterintuitive features of the quantum world. In classical computing, information is stored and processed in the form of 'bits' (which stands for binary digits). A single bit of information can have one of two values: zero or one. Combinations of electronic switches, each one a physical manifestation of a bit of information that is either on or off, are used to make logic gates, the building blocks that make up a logic circuit. In contrast, quantum computers operate on what are called quantum bits, or 'qubits', which are not restricted to holding just one or the other of these binary states. Instead, a qubit can exist in quantum superposition of both zero and one simultaneously, and, as such, can store much more information.

The simplest example of a qubit would be an electron whose quantum spin can point either parallel (call this spin 'up') or antiparallel (spin 'down') to an applied magnetic field. If an additional electromagnetic pulse is then applied, it can flip the electron's spin over from parallel (0) to antiparallel (1). But because an electron is a quantum particle, the electromagnetic pulse can also put it in a superposition of spin up (0) and down (1) at the same time. Two entangled electrons, can be put into a superposition of four possible quantum states—00, 01, 10 and 11—simultaneously. With many more qubits, complicated quantum logic circuits can be developed.

When multiple qubits are entangled together, they can act coherently and therefore process multiple options simultaneously, which makes them far more powerful and efficient than their classical counterparts. But there are problems with realising such a device. Quantum entangled states are extremely delicate and can only be maintained under special conditions for short periods of time. The challenge is not only to isolate and protect these states from their surrounding environment, which destroys quantum coherence, but to be able to control the input and output of the information that the qubits process. And this gets progressively more difficult the larger the number of entangled qubits. Once the computation has been completed, one of the possible final states in the superposition of the qubits is selected and has to be amplified so as to be readable using a macroscopic (classical) device, which is just one of the many outstanding problems of implementation that have yet to be solved.

Despite these difficult challenges, many research labs around the world are today in a race to build the first true quantum computer. Not that many years ago, it wasn't even clear if such a device would be possible, but now researchers talk about their dream being realised in the next decade or two, and rudimentary prototypes already exist. There are currently a number of different approaches to building a quantum computer, and it is not yet clear which will be the most practical. Typically, qubits can be created from any subatomic particles that exhibit quantum behaviour and which can be entangled together, such as electrons and photons, or ions suspended in electromagnetic fields, or atoms trapped by laser beams, or special liquids and solids in which the quantum spin of their atomic nuclei can be probed using nuclear magnetic resonance.

Computing giants IBM and Google are currently involved in the race to build the first true quantum computer, but neither has so far been able to build a stable multi-qubit system that can last long enough to make quantum computing practically viable yet. There are also many smaller start-up companies working on the problem. Some focus on the issue of stability, while others are working on increasing the number of entangled qubits. But progress is being made, and I have no doubt that ubiquitous quantum computing will become a reality in my lifetime.

It is important to point out that it is not just designing the hardware that poses a challenge. Quantum computers will also need their own special software to run on them, and quantum algorithms are still in short supply. The best-known examples are Shor's factorization algorithm and Grover's search algorithm. What has already been demonstrated is that such algorithms would allow quantum computers to outperform their classical counterparts in some surprising ways. They will by no means replace current computers at all tasks but will instead be very well suited to solving particular mathematical problems. We will continue to use the ever-increasing power and processing speed of classical computers to run our daily lives, especially as we advance on a number of fronts with AI, Cloud technologies, and the Internet of Things (the idea that many devices in our homes and workplaces will be connected and talking to each other). And classical computers will also continue to process the ever-increasing mountains of data we have.

There are problems, however, that even the most powerful classical computers of tomorrow will not be able to solve. The beauty of quantum computers is that their processing speed scales exponentially with the number of qubits. Consider the information content of three non-quantum switches. Each can be either 0 or 1, and so there are eight different combinations: 000, 001, 010, 100, 011, 101, 110, 111. But three entangled qubits allow us to store all eight combinations at once. Each of the three digits is both a 1 and a 0 at the same time. On a classical computer, the amount of information increases exponentially with the number of bits. So N bits means 2^N different states. A quantum computer with N

qubits can make use of all 2^N states at once. The hard part is designing algorithms able to make use of this large information space.

Quantum computers will one day be used to solve problems across a wide range of disciplines, in mathematics, chemistry, medicine, and artificial intelligence. Chemists are eagerly looking forward to the prospect of using quantum computers to model highly complex chemical reactions. In 2016, Google developed a rudimentary quantum device that was able to simulate a hydrogen molecule for the first time, and since then, IBM has succeeded in modelling the behaviour of more-complex molecules. It stands to reason that to understand the nature of the quantum world, you need a quantum simulation. After all, it takes one to know one. Eventually, researchers hope they will be able to use quantum simulations to design synthetic molecules and develop new drugs. In agriculture, chemists could use quantum computers to discover new catalysts for fertiliser that would help reduce greenhouse emissions and improve food production.

In AI, quantum computers will dramatically speed up complex optimisation problems in machine learning. This is vital across a range of industries where increasing productivity and efficiency to maximise output is key. Quantum computers are here likely to revolutionise the field of systems engineering by helping to deliver optimisation insights to streamline output and reduce waste. In the not-so-distant future, quantum engineers will be proficient in a wide range of subjects—from quantum mechanics and electronic engineering to systems engineering, AI, and computer science.

Most exciting of all, for me personally (assuming I am still around to witness it), is that by the mid-twenty-first century, we may well see quantum computers running AI programs that will finally answer some of the most important questions of fundamental physics. They, rather than humans, might be making the big breakthroughs.

There's another reason why I have chosen quantum computing as my example of future technology. A number of theoretical physicists are pinning their hopes on quantum computing to help them out. This is because a quantum computer by its very nature should be in a position to accurately simulate the quantum world and maybe even help them find the right theory of quantum gravity.

My hope, in the subject matter I have covered in this book, is that I have given you a flavor of what physics has enabled us to understand about our world and how we as a species continue to make use of that knowledge. In the final chapter, I want to zoom out and describe how a physicist, or indeed anyone with scientific training, thinks about the world, and how we come to know what we do about it. In other words, how does this great edifice of science—not just the scientific knowledge itself, but the process of gaining it—work, and why do we trust it?

CHAPTER 10

THINKING LIKE A PHYSICIST

ON HONESTY AND DOUBT

I want to share with you what I think is an interesting story. In 2017, I presented a documentary for BBC television called *Gravity and Me*, in which I explored how our understanding of this fundamental concept that shapes our world has evolved throughout the history of science, from an invisible Newtonian force to the structure of spacetime itself. What made the project even more fun was that we developed a smartphone app that monitors its user's location by recording their GPS coordinates (latitude, longitude, and altitude above sea level) at regular intervals. It then uses this information to calculate the rate at which time is passing for the user. According to general relativity, time flows at different rates depending on the strength of the gravitational field at that location. Someone on a mountaintop is further away from the centre of the Earth than someone at sea level, and so the mountain dweller feels a very slightly weaker gravitational pull by the Earth. This means that time up on the mountaintop runs ever so slightly faster than at sea level. It's a tiny effect: less than a trillionth of a second faster for each second that passes down at sea level. So, even if someone spent all their life at the top of the mountain, all other factors being equal (impossible, I know), they would live for about a millisecond less than they would have if they'd spent their life at sea level—as measured by a very accurate, but otherwise useless hypothetical clock floating out in space. Compared with the far greater benefits of breathing clean mountain air or a healthy diet and regular exercise, this advantage is somewhat pointless. Still, the physical effect is real, and the app was a bit of fun.

To create the app, we had to take another factor into consideration. As I discussed in chapter 3, moving clocks run more slowly than stationary ones. So you can slow your time down, relative to someone standing still, by moving. This is an even smaller effect than the one due to gravity, as we do not tend to move about at anywhere near the speed of light, where the effect becomes appreciable. Nevertheless, the app took motion into consideration by checking the user's position at regular intervals, and if he or she had changed location significantly, it could work out how fast they had travelled.

Now, here's the crucial bit. Our planet is not a perfect sphere; it bulges out at the equator. So, someone standing at the equator is further from the centre of the Earth than someone at the North Pole (by about twenty-two kilometres), and so, like the mountain dweller, they should feel a slightly weaker gravitational pull. Therefore, clocks at the Pole, where gravity is stronger, should be ticking ever so slightly slower than those at the equator (this is called general relativistic time dilation). However, the Earth is also spinning, and clocks at the equator are moving faster than clocks at the Pole (as measured by the adjudicating clock floating out in space) so equator clocks should tick more slowly than pole clocks (special relativistic time dilation). These two effects, due to special and general relativity, work against each other, so which one wins? Which clock is ticking more slowly? I calculated these two effects separately and found that a clock at the pole ticks, overall, more slowly because it feels stronger gravity, despite the clock on the equator moving faster.

All of this cool mathematical information was incorporated into the app, which implemented my formulae. An enthusiastic social media campaign meant that we persuaded thousands of people to download the app and use it before the programme aired. We even received video diaries from a number of people, such as a pilot and a mountaineer, who provided a record of their app's results.

Then we hit a snag.

My very smart producer, Paul Sen, called me one evening, a week before the editing of the programme was scheduled to finish and just before I was due to record the voice-over—for an anticipated transmission on the BBC soon after that. He said he'd been reading some material on an online physics forum which suggested that I might have screwed up. I immediately dropped what I was working on and went back to consult my calculations. I also quickly emailed half a dozen colleagues to check what I had done.

I had indeed made a very basic mistake. The two effects—the slowdown of time at the Pole because it feels stronger gravity and the slowdown of time at the equator because it is moving faster—*cancel out exactly*! In fact, all clocks at sea level tick at the same rate, everywhere on Earth, and the time they measure is called International Atomic Time (IAT). The surface of the Earth is a geoid, an equipotential gravitational surface on which the cancellation between the two effects due to special and general relativity is not a coincidence. When our planet first formed billions of years ago, hot and malleable, its spin forced it into a more stable, bulged-out (oblate) shape, thus *ensuring* that all points on its surface are sitting in the same gravitational potential. So time flows at the same rate everywhere, provided it is measured at sea level—climb higher and your time speeds up, go down below Earth's surface and it slows down.

The numbers that were being produced by my app were wrong, and the formulae had to be corrected. But the problem was more serious than that. I had explained how the app worked in the programme, and my mistake was there for all to see. The documentary couldn't be broadcast in its current form.

I told my producer, who immediately asked the BBC to delay transmission. The easiest solution would of course have been to reshoot the scenes in which I had made the mistake. No one would be any the wiser. But I quickly realised that this gave me a wonderful opportunity to show how real science works. Instead of covering up my blunder, I should come clean about it, to show that in science it's OK to make mistakes. So, we shot some new scenes in which I confessed my error in all its glory and explained why I had been wrong. This admission did not require any particular courage or strength of character on my part, since making mistakes is normally the way science progresses: they are inevitable, and we learn from them. After all, if we didn't make mistakes, how would we ever discover anything new about the world? This is where science differs from, say, politics. I mean, how often do you hear politicians admitting unequivocally that they are wrong?

The history of science is full of examples of learning from the mistakes of the past, with new hypotheses and theories replacing older ones as our understanding of the workings of nature grows or new empirical evidence becomes available. But how do we explain to wider society the value of this approach: forming a hypothesis, testing it, then rejecting it if it doesn't fit the data? This is all a far cry from so much of public discourse taking place today, particularly on social media, where the loudest voices tend to be from those who value personal opinion and preconceived prejudice over evidence, reproducibility, and rigour.

Is there then a lesson that scientists can teach society, or would we just be accused of arrogance and 'elitism'?

Another trait closely related to our obsession with honesty, and almost unique to scientific research, is the importance of doubt. This trait can sometimes be our own worst enemy when it comes to explaining to wider society how science works. We state that we can never be completely certain about something, that a scientific theory is only our current best guess at an explanation, and that as soon as this theory conflicts with new observations or data, we must be prepared to revise or discard it for something better. But some people then say, 'If you are not sure of anything, how can we trust or believe anything you tell us? Without certainty, what can we cling to?' This response is understandable. It is in our nature to want to *know for sure*, not just to have some temporary 'best guess'.

But to think in this way is to misunderstand how science progresses. The trustworthiness of science comes not from certainty, but from its very openness about its uncertainty, always calling into question what we currently understand and being prepared to replace that knowledge with a deeper understanding if something better comes along. In other walks of life, this attitude might be regarded as fickle. But not in science. Scientific progress depends on scientists' unwavering commitment to the qualities of honesty and doubt.

Here is another example of the way scientists think that might come as a surprise to you. People are often shocked to hear that many physicists—other than those who had dedicated years of their lives to building the Large Hadron Collider—were hoping that the Higgs boson would *not* be found. You see, not finding the Higgs would have meant that there really was something wrong with the Standard Model, opening the door to exciting new physics. Merely ticking a box to confirm something we already suspect to be true is just not as exciting as finding out that one needs to pursue hitherto unexplored paths of research.

On the other hand, we physicists are sometimes accused by well-meaning but amateur scientists of not being open-minded *enough* to entertain their new theories, such as claims that they have found some flaw in Einstein's relativity. The truth is: I would love for Einstein to be proven wrong, for that would mean we would need a new and better theory to replace his, just as general relativity improved upon Newtonian gravity. But physicists have been relentlessly checking, prodding, and poking Einstein's ideas for a century now, and still relativity theory keeps coming through with flying colours. A better theory may one day be discovered, of course, explaining everything that relativity does and more. But we have yet to discover it.

And so, as part of our ongoing, centuries-long effort to find ever-more-fundamental explanations of physical phenomena, we keep trying to tear down our existing theories, to test them to destruction. If they survive, then we trust them . . . until something better comes along.

ON THEORY AND KNOWLEDGE

When, in general conversation, someone says they have a theory, what they tend to mean is that they have an opinion on something—a view that may be based on some form of evidence or observation, but equally well one that is no more than a guess, or a hunch, based on ideology or prejudice or some other belief system. Such a 'theory', which may or may not turn out to be correct, is very different from what we mean by a scientific theory[1]—which also, of course, may or may not be correct, but which, in contrast to a mere opinion, must satisfy a number of important criteria. Firstly, it must put forward an explanation of what we observe, either in nature or in an experiment, and provide evidence for that explanation. Secondly, a scientific theory must be verifiable in accordance with the scientific method: it must be testable, and those tests or observations have to be repeatable. Finally, a good scientific theory makes new predictions about aspects of the world that it explains, which can then also be tested by further observations or experiments.

Our most successful scientific theories, such as relativity, quantum mechanics, the Big Bang

---

1 I am thinking here of theories in the natural sciences rather than in, say, economics or psychology.

theory, Darwinian evolution, plate tectonics, or the germ theory of disease, have all undergone rigorous scrutiny and have all emerged as the best explanations we have. None of these can be dismissed, as one often hears (particularly regarding Darwinian evolution), as 'just a theory'. Such a statement ignores what it means for a scientific theory to be successful—that it has explanatory power, that it is backed up by evidence, and that it makes predictions that can be tested, and yet it remains falsifiable, in the sense that if observations or experimental results contradict its predictions then it cannot be a correct theory, or at best cannot be the whole story.

How then should we counter those who wish to undermine science and the scientific method—those who claim that their opinion should be valued above evidence and that their 'theory' should be given as much credence as the scientific theory it purports to challenge or dispute, without the need to be held to the same standards? While we might find it amusing that some people believe the Earth to be flat, or that the Apollo Moon landings were a hoax, or that the world was created just a few thousand years ago, what about the people who hold views that not only go against established science, but which are genuinely harmful to society, such as those who deny anthropogenic climate change, those who refuse to vaccinate their children because they believe in a baseless link between MMR and autism, or those who prefer magic and superstition to modern medicine?

I find it frustrating that I do not have a clear answer to these questions. I have devoted half my academic career in physics to my research, trying to understand for myself how the universe works. The other half I have spent teaching, communicating, and explaining what I have learnt. So, I cannot simply absolve myself of any responsibilities to engage and debate scientific issues with the wider public; many of these issues are too important *not* to address. But I also know how hard it is to shift someone's strongly held views on a matter, however misguided I believe they are.

In a very real sense, conspiracy theories are the polar opposite of scientific theories in that they seek to assimilate whatever evidence there is against them and interpret it in a way that supports rather than repudiates their core idea, thus making them *unfalsifiable*. Many who hold such views will always try to interpret and favour evidence in a way that confirms their pre-existing hypotheses. This is known as confirmation bias. Often, in the case of ideological beliefs, we also hear the term 'cognitive dissonance', whereby someone will feel genuine mental discomfort when confronted with evidence supporting a view contrary to their own. This potent combination of confirmation bias and the avoidance of cognitive dissonance works to reinforce pre-existing beliefs. So, trying to persuade someone in this frame of mind with scientific evidence can often prove to be a waste of time.

Many people, facing an avalanche of widely different views through both the mainstream and social media, understandably find it difficult to know what to believe. How can they tell accurate evidence-based information from fake news? One thing scientists can do is to tackle the issue of false balance. Thus, when almost every climatologist in the world acknowledges that the Earth's climate is changing rapidly due to humankind's activities and that something needs to be done urgently if we are to prevent its catastrophic consequences, the news media does not need to have a climate change denier provide 'the other side of the argument'. Because when this happens, the public is left with the impression that both points of view are equally valid. Apart from the weight of scientific evidence in their favour, the difference between someone arguing that anthropogenic climate change is real and another denying it is that the former really hopes that he or she is wrong.

A scientist will always admit that *maybe* climate change is not happening; maybe evolution theory is wrong, or relativity is wrong. Maybe gravity won't always pull me down to the ground, and through meditation I should be able to levitate. But these 'maybes' do not mean we don't know. We do know that we will continue to test our theories, and if they hold up we trust them and talk about them with non-scientists. But, as scientists, we are prone to expressing ourselves in terms of honesty and doubt. Just as the word 'theory' has a different meaning in science compared with everyday conversation, so too does the word 'certain' mean something particular to scientists. Deep down, of course, I *am* actually quite certain that it is impossible to overcome the force of gravity through meditation in order to float off the ground. I am also certain that the Earth is round, that it is billions of years old, and that life evolves.

Am I certain that dark matter exists? Almost.

ON TRUTH

I have often heard it said that there are different ways of getting to 'the truth', or indeed that there are different sorts of truth. No doubt a philosopher or a theologian reading this will regard my simplistic physicist views on the matter as hopelessly naïve, but, for me, absolute truth refers to what is real and what exists independently of human subjectivity. So, when I talk about science as being the quest for truth, I mean that scientists are constantly trying to get as close as possible to the ultimate nature of things, to an objective reality out there waiting to be discovered and understood. It can sometimes feel as though this objective reality is nothing more than a collection of facts about the world that we discover slowly until we know them all. But remember that in science we can never claim to know something for certain. There is always the chance that, at some later time, we will arrive at an even deeper understanding, taking us closer to that ultimate truth we seek.

In practice, there are many ideas and concepts in science about which we have reached such a level of confidence that we can safely regard them as facts. If I jump off a roof, the Earth will pull me downwards (and I pull it upwards ever-so slightly) according to a simple mathematical relation that is as close as we will ever get to a statement of fact. We do not yet know everything there is to know about gravity, but we do know its effect on objects in our world. If I drop a ball from a height of five metres, I know without having to check with a stopwatch that it will be in the air for one second before it hits the ground—not two seconds, or half a second, but one second. One day we may find a new theory of quantum gravity, but it will never predict that my ball will take twice or half as long as Newton's equation of motion predicts. That is an absolute truth about the world. There is no philosophical argument, no amount of meditation, no spiritual awakening or religious experience, or gut instinct or political ideology that could ever have told me that a ball dropped from a height of five metres would take one second to hit the ground. But science can tell me.

In a sense, then, the remaining gaps in our understanding of the laws of the universe—the nature of dark matter and dark energy, whether inflation theory is correct, the right interpretation of quantum mechanics, the true nature of time, and so on—are not going to change our understanding of the forces, matter, and energy that make up our everyday world. Future advances in physics are not going to render what we already know obsolete. They will just refine it and give us a deeper understanding.

PHYSICS IS HUMAN

In the end, physicists are like everyone else. We want our ideas and theories to be correct, and we will often defend them in the face of emerging evidence to the contrary. Even the most brilliant physicists have been known to downplay problems with their theories and to amplify their criticisms of a rival idea. Confirmation bias exists in science just as it does in all walks of life, and scientists are not immune to it. We strive for tenure and promotion, to compete for funding, meet project deadlines, 'publish or perish', and work hard to gain the respect of our peers and the approbation of our superiors.

And yet, part of our training in the scientific method is to develop humility and honesty in research to enable us to act against our baser instincts. We learn not to be blinded by our desires or misled by our biases and vested interests. It is sometimes hard to see this if you focus on individuals—and there have been a number of well-documented examples of fraud and corruption in scientific research. But, as research communities, we have built-in corrective procedures, such as the peer review of scientific papers (and yes, I know this is not an ideal way to evaluate research), and we rigorously train young scientists in the ethical and responsible conduct of research. This means that the scientific method is, by its very nature, self-correcting. It demands repeatability and the continued honest and critical assessment of ideas. Weak theories die out eventually, however hard their advocates try to keep them alive, and even if it sometimes takes a generation or two to free ourselves from the hegemonic shackles of a particularly dominant theory that has passed its 'sell by' date.

The best physicists are often those who have been able to zoom out and free themselves from the prejudices of consensus, fashion, or reputation—even their own. But this is more likely to happen when a theory is already known not to be the final word on a subject, or if there are rival theories, each with its own staunch advocates. And remember that physics, just like all science, is not a democracy. All it takes is one new experimental observation to bring down a widely accepted theory and replace it with a new one. Thereafter, it is the new theory that must constantly justify itself by being held up against the bright light of observational data.

Many of the more speculative ideas in fundamental physics today—some of which I described in chapter 8—might be considered as failing to meet the requirements of what constitutes a proper scientific theory, because they cannot be checked against experiment. Among these, I would include (for now at least) string theory, loop quantum gravity, black hole entropy, and multiverse theories. And yet, thousands of theoretical physicists around the world are carrying out intensive research in these subjects. Should they stop working in these areas because their theories can't yet be tested? Are they wasting public funds that could be better poured into more 'useful' areas of research? And what drives these physicists on if they have no way of testing their theories? Are they being blinded by the beauty of their equations? It is certainly true that a few physicists have even gone so far as to claim that they do not *need* to test their theories against data, but only against each other, for mathematical consistency and elegance, which strikes me as a dangerous road to go down.

However, being too harsh on these 'searchers in the dark' can also show a lack of imagination and appreciation of the history of ideas in science. When Maxwell wrote down his electric and magnetic field equations and derived from them the wave equation for light, no one knew, not even Maxwell himself, how this knowledge would be used by Heinrich Hertz, Oliver Lodge, Guglielmo Marconi, and others to develop radio. Nor did Einstein anticipate, when developing his theories of relativity, that they would one day be used to give us accurate satellite navigation, which you access using the technological wonders crammed into that supercomputer in your pocket that would have been impossible without the abstract speculations of the early quantum pioneers.

So, the inflationary cosmologists and the string theorists and the loop quantum gravity researchers continue on their quests, and rightly so. Their ideas may turn out to be wrong—or they may change the course of human history. Or we may have to wait for another Einstein, perhaps even an AI, to help us out of our current confusion. We cannot yet say. But what we *can* say is that, if we ever stop being curious about the universe and investigating how it—and we—came to be, then that is when we stop being human.

The human condition is bountiful beyond measure. We have invented art and poetry and music; we have created religions and political systems; we have built societies, cultures, and empires so rich and complex that no mere mathematical formula could ever encapsulate them. But, if we want to know where we come from, where the atoms in our bodies were formed—the 'why' and 'how' of the world and universe we inhabit—then physics is the path to a true understanding of reality. And with this understanding, we can shape our world and our destiny.

ACKNOWLEDGMENTS

It's not an easy balancing act to try to cover the vast expanse of fundamental physics in a short book such as this, aimed at a lay audience, while still having the space to allow for a level of detail that takes into account the very latest thinking in many topics, and to weave them together. I leave you to be the judge of whether I have succeeded or not. I also wanted to avoid regurgitating some of the overused metaphors and analogies that one so often reads in popular science books. Many of these eventually go out of date, or even turn out to be wrong, given our advancing understanding.

And even if all of this can be achieved, there is another problem.

The island of our physics knowledge is surrounded by an ocean of the yet-to-be-explained, but this island is growing in size all the time. This book is meant to be an exploration of its shoreline—the very limits of our current understanding. But describing this shoreline concisely and accurately is not an easy undertaking for any one person. Although I can call upon over three decades of research in theoretical physics, a quarter of a century of university teaching and almost as long as a science communicator and author, honing my skills in finding the right language to use to unpack complex concepts, I am nevertheless very aware of my limitations when it comes to fully understanding those areas of physics outside my expertise. I am therefore enormously indebted to colleagues and collaborators for all the many fruitful discussions I have had with them over the years. I am also very grateful to all those who gave up their precious time to read through this manuscript and, in doing so, offered me advice and suggestions that have helped fill in the gaps in my understanding. Often, they suggested subtle changes to the wording to make an explanation more precise while never sacrificing clarity and simplicity.

I have enjoyed being (just a little) polemical here and there in expressing my views on unresolved problems in physics. I have tried as much as possible to highlight where there is still debate and speculation, particularly where I have been critical of the consensus view, whether in the foundations of quantum mechanics, or in the choice of preferred approaches to quantum gravity or inflation theory. My excuse is that these are not necessarily my personal views alone (even though I stand by them), but rather, the views of physicists whom I respect and who work at the very forefront of research in their fields.

I would, in particular, like to thank my colleagues in the Physics Department at Surrey University, Justin Read, Paul Stevenson, and Andrea Rocco, for their many useful comments. I am also grateful to Michael Strauss at Princeton for clarifications on a number of aspects of astronomy, and to Andrew Pontzen at UCL, with whom I have had several fruitful recent discussions on the nature of dark matter and the meaning of inflation theory. Thanks also go to two of my favourite science writers, Philip Ball and John Gribbin, for their insights, which have been invaluable.

I have tried as best I can to take into account all the comments and suggestions made by those named above. No doubt there will still be details that some might not entirely agree with, but hopefully there aren't too many of these. One thing I know for sure is that they have made this book far better than I could have hoped for had I not sought their help.

I have for many years now had the pleasure of presenting the BBC Radio 4 series *The Life Scientific*, in which I interview many of the world's leading scientists. This has given me the opportunity to dig a little deeper into the latest ideas in fundamental physics, in particular in esoteric areas such as particle physics and cosmology. As such, I am indebted to Sean Carroll, Frank Close, Paul Davies, Fay Dowker, Carlos Frenk, Peter Higgs, Lawrence Krauss, Roger Penrose, and Carlo Rovelli, all of whom have been wonderful guests on my programme. If there is anything in this book they don't wholeheartedly endorse (and I am sure there will be), then I hope they forgive me. They didn't read the manuscript, but their insights have certainly helped clarify my thinking.

Finally, I owe a huge debt of gratitude to my editor at Princeton University Press, Ingrid Gnerlich, for her enthusiastic support, advice, and suggestions on the book's structure and format that have helped me mould it into its final version, with much appreciated additional help from my copyeditor Annie Gottlieb.

It goes without saying that the biggest 'thank you's go to my lovely wife, Julie, for her patience and support, and to my almost-as-lovely agent, Patrick Walsh—we make a good team.

FURTHER READING

Here is a list of popular science books that expand on the subject matter of this book

GENERAL

Peter Atkins, *Conjuring the Universe: The Origins of the Laws of Nature* (Oxford and New York: Oxford University Press, 2018).

Richard P. Feynman et al., *The Feynman Lectures on Physics*, 3 vols. (Reading, MA: Addison-Wesley, 1963; rev. and ext. ed., 2006; New Millennium ed., New York: Basic Books, 2011); available in full online for free, http://www.feynmanlectures.caltech.edu.

Roger Penrose, *The Emperor's New Mind: Concerning Computers, Minds, and the Laws of Physics* (Oxford and New York: Oxford University Press, 1989).

Lisa Randall, *Warped Passages: Unraveling the Mysteries of the Universe's Hidden Dimensions*

(London: Allen Lane; New York: HarperCollins, 2005).

Carl Sagan, *The Demon-Haunted World: Science as a Candle in the Dark* (New York: Random House, 1996).

Steven Weinberg, *To Explain the World: The Discovery of Modern Science* (London: Allen Lane; New York, HarperCollins, 2015).

Frank Wilczek, *A Beautiful Question: Finding Nature's Deep Design* (London: Allen Lane; New York: Viking, 2015).

QUANTUM PHYSICS

Jim Al-Khalili, *Quantum: A Guide for the Perplexed* (London: Weidenfeld and Nicolson, 2003).

Philip Ball, *Beyond Weird: Why Everything You Thought You Knew about Quantum Physics Is . . . Different* (London: The Bodley Head; Chicago: University of Chicago Press, 2018).

Adam Becker, *What Is Real? The Unfinished Quest for the Meaning of Quantum Physics* (London: John Murray; New York, Basic Books, 2018).

Sean Carroll, *Something Deeply Hidden: Quantum Worlds and the Emergence of Spacetime* (London: OneWorld; New York: Dutton, 2019).

James T. Cushing, *Quantum Mechanics: Historical Contingency and the Copenhagen Hegemony* (Chicago and London: University of Chicago Press, 1994).

David Deutsch, *The Fabric of Reality: Towards a Theory of Everything* (London: Allen Lane; New York: Penguin, 1997).

Richard P. Feynman, *QED: The Strange Theory of Light and Matter* (Princeton and Oxford: Princeton University Press, 1985).

John Gribbin, *Six Impossible Things: The 'Quanta of Solace' and the Mysteries of the Subatomic World* (London: Icon Books, 2019).

Tom Lancaster and Stephen J. Blundell, *Quantum Field Theory for the Gifted Amateur* (Oxford and New York: Oxford University Press, 2014).

David Lindley, *Where Does the Weirdness Go? Why Quantum Mechanics is Strange, but Not as Strange as You Think* (New York: Basic Books, 1996).

N. David Mermin, *Boojums All the Way Through: Communicating Science in a Prosaic Age* (Cambridge, UK, and New York: Cambridge University Press, 1990).

Simon Saunders, Jonathan Barrett, Adrian Kent, and David Wallace, eds., *Many Worlds? Everett, Quantum Theory, & Reality* (Oxford and New York: Oxford University Press, 2010).

PARTICLE PHYSICS

Jim Baggott, *Higgs: The Invention and Discovery of the 'God Particle'* (Oxford and New York: Oxford University Press, 2017).

Jon Butterworth, *A Map of the Invisible: Journeys into Particle Physics* (London: William Heinemann, 2017).

Frank Close, *The New Cosmic Onion: Quarks and the Nature of the Universe* (Boca Raton, FL: CRC Press / Taylor and Francis, 2007).

Gerard 't Hooft, *In Search of the Ultimate Building Blocks* (Cambridge, UK, and New York: Cambridge University Press, 1997).

COSMOLOGY AND RELATIVITY

Sean Carroll, *The Big Picture: On the Origins of Life, Meaning, and the Universe Itself* (New York: Dutton, 2016; London: OneWorld, 2017).

Albert Einstein, *Relativity: The Special and the General Theory,* 100th Anniversary Edition (Princeton, NJ: Princeton University Press, 2015).

Brian Greene, *The Hidden Reality: Parallel Universes and the Deep Laws of the Cosmos* (London; Allen Lane; New York: Alfred A. Knopf, 2011).

Michio Kaku, *Hyperspace: A Scientific Odyssey through Parallel Universes, Time Warps, and the 10th Dimension* (Oxford and New York: Oxford University Press, 1994).

Abraham Pais, *'Subtle is the Lord . . .': The Science and the Life of Albert Einstein* (Oxford and New York: Oxford University Press, 1982).

Christopher Ray, *Time, Space and Philosophy* (London and New York: Routledge, 1991).

Wolfgang Rindler, *Introduction to Special Relativity*, Oxford Science Publications (Oxford and New York: Clarendon Press, 1982).

Edwin F. Taylor and John Archibald Wheeler, *Spacetime Physics* (New York: W. H. Freeman, 1992); free download, http://www.eftaylor.com/spacetimephysics/.

Max Tegmark, *Our Mathematical Universe: My Quest for the Ultimate Nature of Reality* (London: Allen Lane; New York: Alfred A. Knopf, 2014).

Kip S. Thorne, *Black Holes and Time Warps: Einstein's Outrageous Legacy* (New York and London: W. W. Norton, 1994).

THERMODYNAMICS AND INFORMATION

Brian Clegg, *Professor Maxwell's Duplicitous Demon: The Life and Science of James Clerk Maxwell* (London: Icon Books, 2019).

Paul Davies, *The Demon in the Machine: How Hidden Webs of Information Are Finally Solving the Mystery of Life* (London: Allen Lane; New York: Penguin, 2019).

Harvey S. Leff and Andrew F. Rex, eds., *Maxwell's Demon: Entropy, Information, Computing*

(Princeton, NJ: Princeton University Press, 1990).

THE NATURE OF TIME

Julian Barbour, *The End of Time: The Next Revolution in Physics* (Oxford and New York: Oxford University Press, 1999).

Peter Coveney and Roger Highfield, *The Arrow of Time: A Voyage through Science to Solve Time's Greatest Mystery* (London: W. H. Allen; Harper Collins, 1990).

P.C.W. Davies, *The Physics of Time Asymmetry* (Guildford, UK: Surrey University Press; Berkeley, CA: University of California Press, 1974).

James Gleick, *Time Travel: A History* (London: 4th Estate; New York: Pantheon, 2016).

Carlo Rovelli, *The Order of Time, trans. Simon Carnell and Erica Segre* (London: Allen Lane; New York: Riverhead, 2018).

Lee Smolin, *Time Reborn: From the Crisis in Physics to the Future of the Universe* (London: Allen Lane; Boston and New York: Houghton Mifflin Harcourt, 2013).

UNIFICATION

Marcus Chown, *The Ascent of Gravity: The Quest to Understand the Force that Explains Everything* (New York: Pegasus, 2017; London: Weidenfeld and Nicolson, 2018).

Frank Close, *The Infinity Puzzle: The Personalities, Politics, and Extraordinary Science behind the Higgs Boson* (Oxford: Oxford University Press; New York: Basic Books, 2011).

Brian Greene, *The Elegant Universe: Superstrings, Hidden Dimensions, and the Quest for the Ultimate Theory* (London: Jonathan Cape; New York: W. W. Norton, 1999).

Lisa Randall, *Knocking on Heaven's Door: How Physics and Scientific Thinking Illuminate the Universe and the Modern World* (London: Bodley Head; New York: Ecco, 2011).

Carlo Rovelli, *Reality Is Not What It Seems: The Journey to Quantum Gravity*, trans. Simon Carnell and Erica Segre (London: Allen Lane, 2016; New York: Riverhead, 2017).

Lee Smolin, *Three Roads to Quantum Gravity* (London: Weidenfeld and Nicolson, 2000; New York: Basic Books, 2001).

Lee Smolin, *Einstein's Unfinished Revolution: The Search for What Lies Beyond the Quantum* (London: Allen Lane; New York: Penguin, 2019).

Leonard Susskind, *The Cosmic Landscape: String Theory and the Illusion of Intelligent Design* (New York: Little, Brown, 2005).

Frank Wilczek, *The Lightness of Being: Mass, Ether, and the Unification of Forces* (Basic Books, 2008).

INDEX

A NOTE ON THE TYPE

This book has been composed in
Adobe Text and Futura PT

ADOBE TEXT, designed by Robert Slimbach
in 2010 for Adobe Originals, is a Transitional
serif typeface between calligraphic
Renaissance and high-contrast Modern styles.

FUTURA PT, designed by Vladimir Yefimov
and Isabella Chaeva for ParaType (ParaGraph),
is a geometric sans-serif typeface based on
Paul Renner's original design developed by the
Bauer Type Foundry in 1927.